zhōng guó dāo fǎ yì shù zhī tài jí dāo

中國刀法藝術之太極刀

THE
COMPLETE
TAIJI DAO

Yin Cheng Gong Fa
Traditional Chinese Martial Arts Training System

THE COMPLETE TAIJI DAO

太極刀

The Art of the Chinese Saber

張雲

Zhang Yun

Blue Snake Books
Berkeley, California

Published by Blue Snake Books, an imprint of North Atlantic Books
Huichin, unceded Ohlone land
aka Berkeley, California

Cover and book design by Jan Camp
Photographs by Chris Young

Printed in the United States of America

The Complete Taiji Dao: The Art of the Chinese Saber is sponsored and published by North Atlantic Books,
an educational nonprofit based in the unceded Ohlone land Huichin (*aka* Berkeley, CA) that collaborates
with partners to develop cross-cultural perspectives; nurture holistic views of art, science, the humanities,
and healing; and seed personal and global transformation by publishing work on the relationship of body,
spirit, and nature.

North Atlantic Books' publications are distributed to the US trade and internationally by Penguin Random
House Publisher Services. For further information, visit our website at www.northatlanticbooks.com.

Library of Congress Cataloging-in-Publication Data
Zhang, Yun.
 The complete Taiji Dao : the art of the Chinese saber / Zhang Yun.
 p. cm.
 Summary: "Introduces the principles and practice of Taiji Dao and provides illustrated discussions of the
history of Chinese swords, with special emphasis on the history and features of the dao; the Taiji principles
from which Taiji Dao practice derives; the basic skills and techniques of Taiji Dao; detailed descriptions
and photographs of the traditional Taiji Dao form, including applications"—Provided by publisher.
 ISBN 978-1-58394-227-7
 1. Swordplay—China. I. Title.
 GV1149.5.C6Y86 2009
 796.860951—dc22   2009002092

                    3 4 5 6 7 8 9 SHERIDAN 25 24 23 22

僅以本書獻給我的師爺武學大師王培生先生

This book is dedicated to my grandmaster, great martial artist Wang Peisheng.

Grandmaster Wang Peisheng practicing Taiji Dao

ACKNOWLEDGMENTS

Here, I want to give my special thanks to Susan Darley first. She edited the entire book and even wrote first drafts for some sections of the text. Her hard work, comparable in some ways to that of a co-author, added polish and precision to my words and made it possible for this book to be produced quickly.

Susan Darley practicing Taiji Dao

I also want to express deep gratitude for the assistance of others who made this book possible as well: Chris Young and Josh Hehr for taking all the photographs; Marko Cekic for processing some old photographs; and Tom Kimmerle for assisting me in demonstrating the applications. David Ho, Rich Parke, and Taotao Zhang were of great help in editing and translation efforts. Peter Capell proofread the entire book and gave me many useful suggestions. Strider Clark, Patrick Ingram, Clayton Shiu, and Josh Hehr appear in and helped take the many photographs showing movements using a variety of swords and sword skills. I would also like to extend special thanks to Thomas Chen, who offered valuable historical information and photographs. Finally and always, I deeply appreciate the longstanding support for my martial arts life offered to me by my wife, Mrs. Haihui Zhang.

CONTENTS

FOREWORD BY STRIDER CLARK

It has been almost twenty years since I was introduced to the arts of Yin Cheng Gong Fa. Since that summer in 1989 when I first met Master Zhang Yun, I have had some extraordinary experiences in training. I have lived in Beijing and met many talented masters through the family of Yin Cheng Gong Fa. One of the greatest of these many experiences was being able to train with my late great grandmaster, founder of Yin Cheng Gong Fa, Wang Peisheng. It is from this invaluable opportunity that I can relate my experience of witnessing the highest-level weapons skills I have ever encountered in my life.

I have written many times about my time in Beijing and my training with the various members of the Yin Cheng Gong Fa family. I learned many different skills and styles from Master Wang as well as several different weapons. These included Yin Style Bagua Dao (broadsword), Bagua Jian (straight double-edged sword), Pan Long Gun (coiling dragon short staff), Taiji Qiang (spear), and Taiji Dao. Many students from abroad can attest to Master Wang's high-level, empty-hand skills but not so many were fortunate enough to see, let alone study, his incredible skills with various weapons. When he taught me Yin Style Bagua Dao, he stated that he had not taught this skill to anyone completely since he was sixteen years old; yet here he was, at age seventy-four, performing the entire set as perfectly as if he were a young man in his prime.

When Master Wang began teaching weapons, we students had to prepare mentally for the toughest eight hours of training we had ever been put through. At that time, I was twenty-one and in great shape as I had been living there and training for a minimum of six hours everyday. When Master Wang taught, he also participated in his own class, performing each movement over and over to help us learn. We simply could not keep up with him or even execute many of the moves with the balance and speed that he achieved. I was often exhausted and could hardly stand while Master Wang was still balancing on one leg with a sword in hand and teaching with fiery enthusiasm. There were many times when we suggested he take a break and have some tea. This break was actually for us to recover from trying to follow him, rather than for Master Wang who could very easily have continued on without it.

Aside from the astonishing physical ability and stamina that Master Wang displayed at age seventy-four, there was something else very special about the experience of holding a weapon and facing him: it was an absolutely terrifying experience! Even when, with a smile on his face, he was casually explaining a technique, he instilled great fear. No matter where you moved, how you moved, he was there in perfect form ready to kill you. There was nothing you could do; you felt helpless and at his mercy. It didn't matter if you had a spear and he a sword or vice versa. Whatever he held, he had complete control.

I think back to the skills he demonstrated, especially now that I am older and understand more about weapons skills in general. I have had many great opportunities to study weaponry with many great masters. This training includes the Filipino arts of Arnis and Escrima, Kosho Shorei Kempo, and Shaolin Kung Fu, all of which have many useful skills. What was so different about Master Wang's training was his ability to utilize the internal martial arts principles in his weapons skills. The major gem in his skills was his ability to gain and maintain complete control over his opponent and his opponent's weapon. This aspect is easy to talk about but rarely executed to such a high level.

With a single step and gentle stroke of his weapon, Master Wang could take your balance, control your weapon, distract your mind, and make you tight and unable to move. This experience results in an entirely different feeling from what you get when working with most external martial arts weapons skills. I had felt beaten or outmaneuvered in many weapon-training exercises. The individuals I practiced with were much better than I and their timing and movement faster and more precise. However, I never felt the level of sensitivity and control that Master Wang could so perfectly inflict with every confrontation. I have, since that training, had many opportunities to practice and learn more about weapons. As a prison guard in a maximum-security facility, I survived two shank (knife) attacks. Still after that and many more experiences, nothing can compare to my time with Master Wang and his lessons on how to use a weapon.

This high-level weapons skill was developed under many special conditions over hundreds, if not thousands of years in China. Today when we learn Chinese martial arts, we first usually learn stances, forms, and empty-hand techniques. Later, as we become proficient in these skills, we go on to learn weapons. It is important to note that in ancient times this process was reversed. Weapons skill was of the greatest importance and was taught and practiced intensively because without it, one could be killed. Weapons such as the sword and spear reigned as essential tools of life from self-defense to military operations. From this constant use and refinement, students were able to transfer these weapon skills to their hands and then use their hands in much the same fashion as their sword or spear. This kind of transfer was famously illustrated by the great spear master Ji Longfeng, who created new empty-hand techniques from many of his spear skills. It is widely believed that it was this achievement that led him to create the style of Xingyi Quan.

One major difference between empty-hand technique and weapons technique is the level of skill involved. In empty-hand fighting, there are many things that can enhance your technique. Physical strength and size can be very helpful in adding to your blocking and striking and in your ability to grab and throw your opponent; in empty-hand fighting, you can still win after taking one or more blows or making a mistake. In weapons fighting, however, these factors do not help much. In high-level or highly refined weapons dueling, it comes down to pure skill. If any mistake is made—for example, your timing is off, or you slip—you are dead. There is usually no second chance because you will have already either lost a limb or your life.

This is where Taiji Quan, and its weapons skills, becomes a very powerful tool in successful weapons combat. Taiji sensitivity and sticking ability, or *jin,* become very useful when facing an opponent in a weapons fight. The broadsword is known for its chopping and powerful slicing techniques. It is easy to forget internal principles when wielding such a powerful weapon. The Wu Style Taiji Dao as taught by Grandmaster Wang Peisheng, however, adheres to the internal martial arts principles and has a fluid tenacity that utilizes control and listening to the opponent's movement.

The Taiji *dao* is a devastating weapon as it has more length than a normal broadsword and can deal better with the long reach of the deadly spear. It also has a characteristic ring at the pommel that allows the wielder to exercise precise control over the blade. This control is achieved by the delicate hold of the index finger, the middle finger, and the thumb, and the slight pulls on the ring that can quickly change the angle of the blade. The blade is characteristically sharp on one side like the typical broadsword but has the added edge on the other side at the tip as well. This allows for upward cuts to the underside of the opponent's wrist.

The Taiji *dao,* in itself, is a very ingenious and remarkable weapon, having been refined by great masters and their vast knowledge in true combat. It beautifully illustrates the subtle and sophisticated principles and theory of Taiji Quan and the graceful skills they generate.

This book, like the ones before it, has set out to preserve and share the incredible skills of Wu Style Taiji Quan. We could not appreciate the phenomenal skills of this system without its greatest representative, Wang Peisheng, who, with great love and dedication, passed it to others like Master Zhang Yun, the author of this book.

Master Zhang learned internal martial arts from Grandmaster Wang Peisheng and, starting when he was sixteen, from Master Luo Shuhuan. He has studied and practiced Taiji Dao for almost thirty years. Master Wang told me that Master

Zhang is a diligent student. He thinks hard and can remember details clearly and accurately. He can understand and explain Taiji principles and summarize them into lessons that students can understand. My fellow martial arts colleagues and I feel that Master Zhang has a remarkable ability to teach the principles of internal martial arts with great clarity. He has been hailed by Master Wang as innovative and skilled in grasping the deepest and most subtle of details. He has opened our minds to understand many high-level martial arts principles.

The information provided in this book includes not only the exact skills and knowledge that were passed down to Master Zhang but also a summary of the insights and abilities he gained from systematic and hard practice and study. I feel truly blessed to have been able to learn from him and to be a part of the Yin Cheng Gong Fa family. I owe my life to my Master Zhang Yun, as he has taught me and nurtured my skills and my spirit for over twenty years. He also gave me the precious gift of being able to meet and study with his brothers and his grandmaster, Wang Peisheng.

I am very confident that this book provides a detailed study of an amazing weapon that is part of an equally amazing heritage. This heritage has been preserved and passed along by a wonderful group of men and women, those of the Yin Cheng Gong Fa family and my beloved Master Zhang Yun.

Strider Clark
New York, NY
May 10, 2008

Strider Clark practicing sword technique

FOREWORD BY PETER KINDFIELD

When I began my study of Taiji Quan, I had no interest in fighting or weapons. I explained to my teacher Danny Gordon, a student of Master Hsu Fun Yuen, that when I was younger and interested in fighting, I had done Karate, but that now I was more interested in matters of health and spirit. Danny explained that to truly get the health, spiritual, or martial arts benefits from Taiji Quan, I would need to do more than simply learn a Taiji Quan form (i.e., a fixed sequence of movements that instantiate Taiji Quan principles). I would also need to learn how each movement of the form could be applied in a fight, and I would need to do push hands, a two-person practice for learning how to respond to an opponent's incoming energy. I practiced as instructed by my teacher but was still not interested in Taiji fighting or weapons.

Upon moving to New Jersey, I began studying with Master Zhang Yun, who was, at that time, a twenty-year student of Grandmaster Wang Peisheng of Beijing. About a year later, Master Zhang Yun began teaching the Taiji *jian* (straight double-edged sword) to our class. Not without reservations, I began my initiation into Taiji weapons. At the time it was somewhat less than clear to me how waving weapons around was going to be good for my health. And, while I had already begun to integrate into my spiritual practice Taiji ideas like relaxing, paying attention to others' energy, and following an incoming force, training to skewer people with sharp objects did not seem particularly aligned with my general preference toward practicing compassion toward all beings. Since then, I have learned many things through weapons practice.

As a beginning Taiji student and like many people who don't know much about Taiji Quan, I thought of it as a slow and gentle martial art. Some of my early teachers practiced Taiji this way and each added other practices (such as Xingyi or Western boxing) to complement their Taiji. When I first began training with Master Zhang Yun, my misperception of Taiji continued. Master Zhang, a gentle man himself who taught us a beautiful form that we practiced very slowly and gently, mentioned one day that we should try to study with other members of his gongfu family in addition to him. He told us that we would learn that Taiji could be practiced with many different personalities. He explained that his way of doing push hands was to let people get in to the point where they would think they were about to throw him off balance. At this point, he would let his opponents fall into emptiness by making a subtle change in his movements so that his opponents, rather than he, became unbalanced. His brother, Master

Lu Shengli, on the other hand, would direct opponents to the floor as quickly as possible. Yet both men followed the same Taiji principles taught to them by Grandmaster Wang Peisheng in their practices.

I still haven't had the opportunity to push with any of Master Zhang's brothers. While I continue to look forward to that opportunity, we are all fortunate that there are other ways to get some feel for the many personalities of Taiji Quan. One such way is through learning how to use the various weapons that are part of training in the Yin Cheng Gong Fa system founded by Grandmaster Wang and developed and taught by Master Zhang. As with different members of our gongfu family, each weapon has a different personality.

The *qiang,* or spear, is a long weapon that we practice quickly with room for improvisation in the form. The spear has the personality of a swimming dragon. When we practice the spear, its movements should be very smooth, nimble, changeable, and mysterious. The spear is like a thief coming and going silently, unseen and unheard. This makes it difficult to defend against. A skilled spear attack can happen without the defender's even knowing that it has occurred. Thus, practicing with and against a spear can help us learn to be fast and nimble and how to modify our movements based on our internal feeling.

The *jian* is the scholar's sword. It has the personality of a phoenix. Its movements should be very natural, beautiful, unrestrained, light-hearted, and lively. Its light weight and sharp double-edged tip make this sword suitable for small, precise movements. Practicing the *jian* is like practicing with a gentleman. This kind of practice can help each of us learn how to move gently with great fluidity. A *jian* fight might take awhile, each successful strike rendering your opponent a little less able to continue.

The *dao,* or broadsword or saber, is the warrior's sword. It has the personality of a tiger. Its movements should be brave, hard, quick, and powerful. Practicing with the *dao* helps us develop courage and internal strength. Its sturdier construction and single-edged design lend themselves to more aggressive attacks and defenses. Practicing the *dao* can help us learn how to practice Taiji aggressively and assertively. A real *dao* battle would likely end quickly, with the first strike disabling your opponent.

Practicing with each of these weapons helps us learn the many different personalities of Taiji Quan, and learning these different personalities helps illuminate the deep, grand, unifying principles of this incredible art. It is not that Taiji is slow and gentle. Taiji can be slow or fast and hard or soft. Its forms can be completely fixed or somewhat improvisational. Its movements can be small and precise or large and magnificent.

Taiji Quan is first and foremost an internal martial art. This means that the focus of the training is on internal practice. For example, we train how to listen to an opponent's incoming force to determine the direction, strength, and speed of that force (called *ting jin* in Chinese) and how to use that force to our own advantage. Through these internal practices, Taiji players learn how to relax, listen, follow, and respond to another's energy in a way that subtly changes that energy to our own advantage. We also learn how to integrate our movements; be stable and agile; move slowly, smoothly, and evenly; know ourselves from the inside out; and read others from the outside in.

Practicing the Taiji *dao* is especially useful in dispelling the misconception that Taiji Quan is a slow and gentle martial art. It highlights, instead, the true nature of Taiji Quan as an internal martial art that focuses on the ever-changing balance of *yin* and *yang,* each of which always contains some of the other.

May learning the warrior's sword complement your current knowledge of Taiji Quan and help you understand the powerful principles that underlie the many personalities of Taiji Quan.

Peter Kindfield, Ph.D.
Summertown, TN
May 7, 2008

AUTHOR'S PREFACE

Chinese swordsmanship includes the use of two different swords, *jian* and *dao*. *Jian* blades are double-edged and straight, while *dao* blades are normally single-edged and curved. Each sword has distinctive features, and the practices of each follow different principles and training methods. Characterized by grace and elegance, *jian* skills are agile and subtle, devoid of hard blocks or strikes. The quick and nimble skills of *dao*, by contrast, should be delivered with great strength and courage. It is said that "*jian* is like a flying phoenix and *dao* is like a ferocious tiger." High-level skills can be developed with either type of sword, and most martial artists train with both in order to get the unique benefits of each.

Traditional Chinese martial arts are generally considered today to include both weapons and empty-hand training, in which only the human body is used. Ever since the invention of tools, however, martial arts practice has focused primarily on the use of weapons; of all the weapons developed before the appearance of firearms, which are usually classified as "cold" weapons, *dao* have been the most popular.

Often translated as broadsword or saber, *dao* have appeared in almost all cultures throughout history, and *dao* skills have been practiced in almost every school of martial arts. In some groups, these skills were specialized and developed to a very high level. Although all *dao* practice follows similar principles, many features of the weapon, such as its shape and length, have been modified over time. There have also been many changes in *dao* techniques.

Most of the variations in *dao* features and techniques have resulted from advances in the field of metallurgy. While the earliest *dao* were made of stone, careful research and persistent efforts to improve manufacturing processes eventually led to the production of high-quality metal swords. Swords of bronze, iron, and steel appeared in successive historical periods, and each advance in metallurgy improved the quality and usefulness of *dao*.

In recent times, martial arts expertise is no longer important in warfare or as a means by which to establish one's honor or superiority. *Dao* swords and skills have, for the most part, been rendered irrelevant by modern, high-tech weapons. Most modern-day practitioners engage in traditional martial arts as a sport rather than as preparation to deliver lethal force against an enemy. As practiced today, martial arts are usually pursued to improve health and mental discipline, to mount public performances, and to gain a deeper understanding of the cultures from which these arts have emerged. Weapons practice has, for the most part, been replaced by empty-hand training.

Although the primary purpose of martial arts training has changed over the years, such training still yields many benefits. Taiji Quan, for example, holds a very special place among Chinese martial arts, now as in the past, and remains a highly challenging physical and mental discipline. Like any serious martial arts practice, Taiji Quan training promotes significant increases in physical strength, flexibility, and overall fitness, and because it incorporates many traditional health practices like qigong, Taiji Quan also improves the functioning of various internal systems.

Traditional Taiji Quan requires practitioners to accomplish their purposes in the most efficient way possible, not only when they take part in competition or in combat but also in their daily activities. Improved control over physical and mental functioning is a major training goal of Taiji Quan, and the diligent study of Taiji Quan can also further practitioners' understanding of traditional Chinese philosophy. This, in turn, can sharpen one's insights into nature's patterns and the deeper meanings of life.

Finally, founded on very special principles and practices, Taiji Quan training promotes responses that conflict with one's natural instincts and reduces the tendency to rely on habitual but inefficient reactions. Taiji Quan principles direct, for example, that a smaller force be used to oppose a large incoming force even though one's habits urge the exertion of a greater force. A constant state of mindfulness, attention to detail, and a powerful but deeply calm focus eventually lead to the replacement of instincts and habits by more effective physical and emotional responses. Taiji Quan practice transforms not only one's fighting skills but also one's character.

In a complete Taiji Quan training system, weapons practice retains some importance even today. Because weapons skills can be delivered with greater speed and power than empty-hand skills and because they are more difficult and complex to use and defend against, weapons practice always has the effect of advancing one's skill level and increasing understanding of martial arts. As these changes occur, the commitment to martial arts study typically intensifies. Martial artists who enjoy Taiji Quan practice and want to gain additional benefits from their training should consider weapons practice, and Taiji Dao has always been an excellent first choice.

The practice of Taiji Dao holds a special place in the Taiji Quan group. While the feeling developed through the practice of Taiji Jian is very similar to that of Taiji Quan empty-hand training, Taiji Dao practice arouses quite a different set of feelings that allow practitioners to experience the basic principles and skills of Taiji Quan from a new vantage point. As a distinctive set of sword skills that uses a specially designed Taiji sword, Taiji Dao provides very useful training for advancing one's Taiji Quan practice. Practitioners must exercise great care in this training, however, to ensure their own safety and the safety of their practice partners.

The first four chapters of this book introduce the history and development of the *dao* as a weapon, as well as the principles, basic skills, and training methods that make Taiji Dao skills unique. The middle section of the book, Chapter Five, is devoted to a comprehensive presentation of the thirteen-posture Taiji Dao form and applications. This thirteen-posture form has been practiced in the Taiji Quan group for more than a hundred years. Although its precise origins are unknown, the thirteen-posture form is the main focus of *dao* training in most modern-day Taiji groups.

Although most of the skills of the thirteen-posture form are executed with only one hand holding the sword, the Taiji *dao* can also be wielded with two hands. The special two-handed Taiji Dao form is described in Chapter Six. Taiji Dao fighting applications and the principles that underlie them, along with many practice examples for defending against a variety of weapons, are presented in Chapter Seven.

Just as the principles and applications of empty-hand Taiji Quan skills are radically different from other styles of martial arts, Taiji Dao application skills and training methods—as well as the foundational principles and even the shape of the *dao* weapon—are very different from those of other sword styles. Careful attention should be paid to these distinctions, and each unique feature should be attentively studied. All these differences will be explained in detail in this book. It is important that one's training follows a correct course and that a Taiji *dao* not be used as though it were a regular broadsword or saber.

My own interest in martial arts began when I was a young boy. As a teenager, I practiced Chinese wrestling, Shaolin Quan, Baji Quan, Xingyi Quan, Tongbei Quan, and some weapons technique. Through these practices I acquired good foundation skills, but not yet an understanding of the core principles and meanings of traditional martial arts.

When I was sixteen, I began my study of Taiji Quan with Master Luo Shuhuan. One year later, Master Luo sent me to my grandmaster, Wang Peisheng, one of the most outstanding martial artists in China, to get intensive training. I was very fortunate that Master Luo had given me this opportunity to learn high-level martial arts from a top-level master; during almost thirty years with Master Wang, my training focused on Taiji Quan and Bagua Zhang. I also learned Xingyi Quan, Tantui, qigong, and weapons techniques.

Grandmaster Wang Peisheng practicing sword technique

Taiji Dao was the first set of weapons skills that I studied with Master Wang. When I began this training, I had not yet achieved a full understanding of Taiji Quan. Consequently, I could not fully appreciate the deeper meaning of Taiji Dao skills. As my knowledge of Taiji Quan grew, I was able to incorporate Taiji Quan principles into my weapons training and gain a clearer understanding of Taiji Dao skills, as well as the difference between these skills and those of regular *dao.*

Initially, I used a regular broadsword to practice Taiji Dao, but it was difficult to develop strong internal feelings with this sword because broadswords are both shorter and wider than Taiji *dao.* A longer sword is always preferable for projecting *qi* to the tip of the weapon, as well as for expanding one's mind, strengthening *shen,* and creating a feeling of circular expansion in the body. A Taiji *dao* also allows for the execution of some two-handed skills that are difficult or impossible to perform with regular swords. Among these two-handed skills are most of those that require the use of the pommel ring to control the movements of the Taiji *dao.*

Master Luo Shuhuan and Zhang Yun practicing broadsword technique

When I received my first Taiji *dao* in 1982, the feelings I experienced in training were very different from those I had been used to. I had been able to develop hard, powerful skills with my regular broadsword, but training with a Taiji *dao* increased my awareness of the more refined and subtle characteristics of sword skills. I could, for example, discern more clearly the flow of the internal components *shen, yi* (mind), *qi,* and *jin,* as well as the agile, free, spontaneous, and wily aspects of sword skills. These new feelings opened my mind and had a strong influence on the way I thought about *dao* techniques. They raised the level of my practice and enriched my understanding of Taiji Dao and Taiji Quan.

After almost thirty years of study and practice, I believe that traditional Taiji Dao expresses profound Taiji principles and promotes the development of many useful skills. It is a highly beneficial addition to martial arts training, especially for practitioners interested in Taiji Quan. In writing this book and sharing my experiences, I hope to pass on to others the knowledge of Taiji Dao and Taiji Quan that I inherited from Master Luo and Master Wang. My wish is that the traditional art of Taiji Dao will bring its rewards to many future generations of martial artists.

Zhang Yun
Pittsburgh, PA
March 30, 2008

AUTHOR'S NOTES

The book *Iron and Steel Swords of China* by Huang Fujiang offers a clear and detailed description of the history and features of ancient Chinese swords. It is one of the best reference books I have found for the study of Chinese swords and served as an important source of information for the materials presented in Chapter One. The many beautiful pictures in the book come from the personal collections of the author and his friends, and from many famous museums around the world.

Because there are no English equivalents for many Chinese terms, more than one word or even a sentence is sometimes used to describe the meaning of these terms. To convey a precise understanding of the Chinese terms for the concepts, skills, and weapons of Taiji Dao, all such terms are presented first in Pinyin (the international standard transliteration system for Chinese characters using phonetic English spelling), then in Chinese characters, and finally in English. The goal of this three-part system is to give readers access to information in several forms so that they can make their own judgments about the full meaning of these terms.

For Chinese terms that cannot be simply translated into English, an explanation is provided the first time the term appears in the text, but, subsequently, only the Pinyin word is used. *Shen,* for example, is defined initially as "spirit, attention, or mentality," but the definition is not repeated thereafter.

Most Pinyin terms are italicized upon first reference in order to distinguish them from regular English words, but terms such as Taiji Quan and Bagua, which have been used and accepted in English for many years, are capitalized and presented in regular font.

Different Chinese characters may have the same or similar pronunciations. As a result, identical Pinyin terms will be used for these characters even though the meanings of the characters are different. When written in Chinese, for example, the characters for the Pinyin term *quan* are pronounced the same but have different meanings: one character means "fist," while the other means "circle." It is important that readers pay careful attention to the context of Pinyin terms when considering the meaning of these terms. It should also be noted that because no distinction is made in Pinyin between singular and plural nouns, nouns such as *dao* can refer to one or more items.

Chinese characters can also be combined to form one word by joining together the letters of two or more originally separate Pinyin terms. Examples include the characters for concepts such as Taiji; for the parts of a *dao,* such as *daobing;* for the names of skills, such as *zhengwo;* and for acupoints, such as *yanglingquan.*

Acupuncture is one of the core aspects of traditional Chinese medicine, and knowledge of acupuncture points, or acupoints, is very important in the practice of internal martial arts. Many acupoints are used in Taiji Dao training, but because the acupuncture system is extensive and complex, the text does not include descriptions of the exact locations and significance of each acupoint mentioned. The only information provided for these points are their Pinyin names. We hope that readers who are interested in this kind of information will seek other sources.

For ease of reading, *dao* and Taiji *dao* are often referred to in this book simply as "swords." Regular *dao,* also known as broadswords or sabers, should not be confused with Taiji *dao.* The latter are specialized swords used only in the Taiji Quan group.

The use of capitals and italics in the words Dao and *dao* highlights an important difference between these two words. The capitalized but non-italicized word refers to a set of skills; the italicized but not capitalized word refers to the specialized sword. This distinction will be repeated again in Chapter Two as a reminder to the reader.

Because the principles and skills of Taiji Dao are the same as, or very similar to, those of Taiji Quan and Taiji Jian, readers who are already familiar with Taiji Quan or Taiji Jian will find that a close reading of Chapters Two and Three may not be necessary.

Chapter One

The History and Features of *Dao*

Today most people associate the term "martial arts" with empty-hand fighting skills. Historically, however, the major focus in martial arts training has always been on weapons skills. Whenever the use of deadly force is involved, whether on the battlefield, in civilian law enforcement, or for personal self-defense, it is always dangerous to be unarmed.

Unlike modern or "hot" weapons that use gunpowder, the traditional weapons that are called "cold" weapons in China are very simple in their operating principles. Most were designed to act as physical extensions of a fighter's arms or legs. The more primitive the weapon, the more work the user had to exert to provide the necessary destructive power and speed and to achieve maneuverability and accuracy. As a result, a high degree of physical skill was required to wield traditional cold weapons effectively. Typically, the foundation skills needed for advanced mastery of cold weapons have been developed primarily through empty-hand training.

Historical records indicate that a wide diversity of cold weapons have been used in China throughout the ages. *China's Ancient and Modern Military Weapons Illustrated* (中华古今兵器图考; Pei Xirong, Han Minghua, Jiang Songyou, People's Sport Press, 1999), for example, lists 124 types of broadswords.

Cold weapons have been classified into many categories distinguished by features such as size, shape, and function. These categories are not defined by strictly established standards but rather by traditional conventions. As a common example, cold weapons have been divided on the basis of shape into eighteen groupings and, as a result, are sometimes referred to as "eighteen category weapons." Different martial arts groups, however, categorize cold weapons in different ways and, ordinarily, more than eighteen categories are used. This system is only one of several used to identify the differing shapes of cold weapons. Over the years, martial arts groups have adopted varied systems for making shape distinctions.

Other cold weapons categories include: hard weapons such as swords and spears; soft weapons such as whips and ropes; projectile weapons such as bows and arrows; and throwing weapons such as darts and stones. In addition, many unique cold weapons have been developed by a wide variety of martial arts groups. For traditional martial arts practice, hard weapons are hand-held, made of firm materials, and have shapes that, unlike those of soft weapons, do not change during use. Hard weapons are the most frequently used weapons in martial arts practice.

In general, hard weapons have traditionally been divided by size into long weapons and short weapons. With no standard measure for distinguishing the two categories, long weapons such as spears and staffs are usually considered to be those that are more than five feet in length and are gripped with both hands. Short weapons, such as swords and daggers, are those that can be readily used with only one hand.

The four skills that make up the majority of hard weapons skills are the long-weapon thrusts (*zha* 扎) and strikes (*da* 打) of the spear (*qiang* 枪) and staff (*gun* 棍), respectively, and the short-weapon chops (*pi* 劈) and hits (*ji* 击) of, respectively, the broadsword/saber (*dao* 刀) and straight double-edged sword (*jian* 剑). Given the widespread use of these four skills, most martial arts groups include spear, staff, broadsword, and straight double-edged sword in their training curricula. It is said that if you achieve mastery with these four weapons, you will be able to easily learn the skills of all the other hard weapons.

The weapon featured in this book is a specialized short weapon known as Taiji *dao.* Detailed consideration will be given to the principles from which *dao* skills derive and the training methods used to develop these skills. First, however, the history and characteristics of the varied class of weapons known as *dao* will be presented.

History and Development

Translated into English as "broadsword" or "saber," the term *dao* refers to a single-edged sword or knife with a blade that is usually curved. *Dao* is one of the most widely used weapons in Chinese martial arts.

While *dao* refers to a single-edged, curved sword, the term also has a variety of additional usages. It can also refer to the set of skills that can be executed by *dao,* the separate techniques that comprise each *dao* skill, a style of *dao* skills, and an approach for using the *dao* weapon. When the term is used to refer to these skill-related aspects of practice, it is always capitalized but not italicized. When the term refers to the *dao* weapon, itself, it is always italicized but is capitalized only if it appears at the beginning of a sentence. As an example of this distinction, if your opponent tells you that he or she will give you three Dao, your opponent means that he or she will attack you three times using three *dao* techniques.

The English word "sword" denotes a class of weapons that contains many different varieties, including the single-edged sword that, in Chinese, is referred to as *dao.* For ease of reading, when techniques are described later in this book, the word "sword" will be used and, unless otherwise modified, should be understood as referring to *dao.*

History

Swords of many shapes and sizes have been found in almost all cultures throughout history. This section presents a brief historical review of the popular Chinese sword known as a *dao.*

Pre-Qin Era

Dating back more than five thousand years, *dao* were originally made of stone, and the metal *dao* used by soldiers and martial artists were produced much later. Figures 1-1 and 1-2 show jade *dao* made during the Xia Dynasty (2100–1600 BC). The holes on the jade were used for binding the blade of the *dao* to a staff.

Fig. 1-1: Two-hole jade sword from the Xia Dynasty

Fig. 1-2: Four-hole jade sword from the Xia Dynasty

Bronze *dao* (figs. 1-3, 1-4, and 1-5) first appeared in China during the Shang Dynasty (1600–841 BC) at the start of the Bronze Age. A straight double-edged sword called *jian* appeared during the Zhou Dynasty (841–221 BC) when the Bronze Age had reached full maturity. By the end of the Zhou Dynasty, well-made bronze jian had become very popular, but bronze *dao* were still relatively rare because bronze—a heavy, soft metal that had to be cast—could not easily be fashioned into curved *dao* blades that were both sufficiently strong and suitably long. As a result, early bronze *dao* tended to be short, usually only thirty to fifty centimeters (about twelve to twenty inches) in length. Figure 1-6 shows bronze *dao* from the Zhou period.

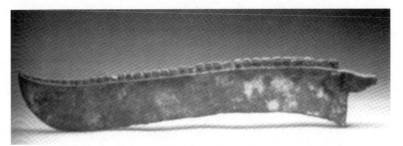

Fig. 1-3: Shang Dynasty bronze sword

Fig. 1-4: Shang Dynasty bronze sword

Fig. 1-5: Horse-head bronze sword from the late Shang Dynasty

Fig. 1-6: Zhou Dynasty bronze sword

Swords made of iron first appeared in the middle of the Zhou Dynasty, the so-called Spring and Autumn period (770–476 BC). Because the technology necessary for ironwork was still primitive during this time, however, iron swords were not initially popular. So far, only a few fragmentary remains of iron jian and no remains of iron *dao* have been discovered from this period. Not only were iron swords relatively rare during the Zhou Dynasty, but they also corroded much more quickly than bronze swords from the same period.

Fig. 1-7: Fragmentary remains of an iron sword unearthed from Shan County of Henan Province in 1957.

Qin Dynasty

From the Warring States Period (476–221 BC) during the Zhou Dynasty, China entered into the Iron Age. Then, during the Qin Dynasty (221–206 BC), iron swords came into more widespread use and began to replace bronze swords. The advantage of iron was that unlike bronze, it could be forged into many different shapes without compromising the strength of the metal. This manufacturing technique made possible the creation of many different types of weapons during the Qin period. Only a few incomplete iron *dao* have been recovered from this period, however, because of the metal's susceptibility to corrosion.

The growth in popularity of *dao* during the Qin Dynasty was due in large part to the increasing use of the cavalry in warfare. For the purposes of mounted soldiers, a single-edged curved sword with a thick back had many advantages over a double-edged straight sword like a jian. Foremost among these was the fact that the chopping skill was the cavalrymen's most effective method of attack. As a result, *dao* replaced jian as the preferred weapon by cavalry soldiers. *Dao* were subsequently adopted for use by infantrymen as well.

Han Dynasty

Although bronze swords of astonishing strength were still being used as late as the Han Dynasty (206 BC–220 AD), they fell out of favor when techniques for converting iron to steel were improved. Iron and steel *dao* blades from this period were thin and straight or just slightly curved, and the ring pommel that first appeared at this time quickly became a very popular *dao* feature. Swords with ring pommels, also known as *huan shou dao* (环首刀) or ring head swords, were exported in large quantities to Japan and evolved eventually into the Japanese sword we know today.

Fig. 1-8: A ring pommel iron sword from the Han Dynasty

Iron-working techniques continued to improve throughout the Han Dynasty. Archaeological digs from 1957 to 1958 in the city of Luoyang in Henan Province unearthed iron *dao* from twenty-three Han Dynasty tombs. The lengths of these swords varied from eighty-five centimeters to 114 centimeters (about thirty-four to forty-five inches). In 1962, a Chinese *dao* of the same type dating to 184–189 AD was discovered in an ancient grave in Nara, Japan.

Since the 1970s, more Han Dynasty iron and steel *dao* have been found in various locations. Most swords from this period were about three centimeters wide (about one and a quarter inches) and the thickness of the back could be as thin as seven millimeters (a little more than one quarter inch). Archaeological research suggests that *dao* longer than eighty centimeters (thirty-two inches) were used in the cavalry, while shorter *dao* were used in the infantry. The longest Han Dynasty *dao* measured 120 centimeters (forty-eight inches). One such *dao* is the lower of the three iron swords pictured in figure 1-9.

Fig. 1-9: Three Han Dynasty iron swords

Fig. 1-10: A short iron sword from the Han Dynasty

Fig. 1-11: Three swordsmen from a Han Dynasty brick sculpture

During the middle period of the Han Dynasty, the technology of making iron and steel swords was developed to a very high level. Advanced techniques allowed iron to be "folded" many times in the forging sequence that also included heating and hammering. In the forging process, carbon was added to iron to transform the metal into steel, and the number of folds, varying between thirty and fifty or even more, provided a measure of the steel's eventual quality.

In another popular technique developed at this time, batches of steel with different amounts of carbon content were combined to produce high-impact blades that could also maintain hard cutting edges despite long and intensive use. Quenching technology used to cool the steel after folding was also advanced during the middle Han Dynasty. The significance of timing and temperature control in working with metal was better understood, and polishing and sharpening skills were vastly improved. Expert polishing made visible a blade's veins, the result of multiple folds during the manufacture of the metal.

From these veins, an experienced master can discern many of the attributes of a sword. This skill is called *xiang dao* (相刀) or *xiang jian* (相剑). Here, *xiang* means "observing" and involves determining the intrinsic quality of an object by observing its visible attributes. People well versed in this skill were in high demand and were accorded a high level of respect. The beautiful patterns etched into sword blades by the veins in the metal incited imagination, and such swords were often given elegant, literary names. Modern testing has revealed that the quality of these swords is superior even to twentieth-century military swords produced during the 1940s in factories using highly developed metallurgic methods and machinery.

Three Kingdoms Period

The production of high quality *dao* became common during the Three Kingdoms Period (220–280 AD), and the ring pommel sword was the most popular style. Long-handled *dao* became popular, especially for use by the cavalry, and it was during this time that *dao* generally replaced jian as the most common weapon for soldiers, while jian became the weapons of choice for officers. *Dao* were used as indicators of rank in the royal court settings and at ceremonial functions. Among martial arts groups, they remained one of the most popular weapons for practice.

Historical records of the Three Kingdoms Period contain entries describing the King of Wei's placing an order for a Five-Treasure *Dao*. The order specified *bailian liqi* (百炼利器)—a sharp sword that had been forged one hundred times.

In conversational Chinese, characters like *bai* (a hundred), *qian* (a thousand) or *wan* (ten thousand) are often used to signify an unspecified but very large number. It is possible, therefore, that the word *bailian* in these historical records may actually indicate a number higher than one hundred.

The distinctive steel that became the ideal material for sword production is referred to as *bailian jinggang* (百炼精钢), or "a hundred-times-forged high quality steel." The metallurgic method of heating, hammering, folding, and quenching produced a blade that was sharp, hard, and elastic. A *dao* made using this method can also be called *baizhe dao* (百折刀)— "a hundred-times-folded *dao.*"

Fig. 1-12: Two steel swords from the Three Kingdoms Period

From the Jin Dynasty to the South and North Dynasty

Civil wars were widespread throughout China during the three hundred years following the Three Kingdoms Period. These wars accelerated the development of sophisticated weaponry, including changes to the shape of *dao*. *Dao* blades became wider and more curved; the length was shortened to less than one hundred centimeters (forty inches); and the back was made thicker. It is thought that these changes were a response to the development of the saddle and stir-rup, both of which made it possible for horsemen to move more flexibly astride their horses. The shortened *dao* were well suited to the execution of a variety of highly effective skills.

Fig. 1-13: A *dao* with a shorter and wider blade

Fig. 1-14: A straight ring pommel *dao* with a modified ring

Sui Dynasty and Tang Dynasty Period

The Sui Dynasty (581–618 AD) brought to a close the long period of chaos caused by incessant warfare, and, during the Tang Dynasty (618–907 AD) that followed, economic and military power in feudal China reached its zenith. The technology of sword manufacturing advanced to a very high level and influenced weapons production in many neighboring countries. Because of their high qual-ity, straight *dao* were still in use, and many types of *dao* with varying shapes were developed for special purposes.

Fig. 1-15: Two Sui Dynasty straight *dao* with scabbards unearthed from the royal tomb in Luoyang City, Henan Province, in 1929

Fig. 1-16: A Sui Dynasty straight *dao* with a tip shape that resembles a jian

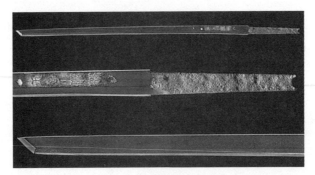

Fig. 1-17: A Sui Dynasty *dao* with engraving that dates the sword from 616 AD, preserved in the Shitenno Temple in Osaka Prefecture, Japan

Carried on the waist, *heng dao* (横刀), a *dao* with the short, narrow features of swords from earlier eras, and *mo dao* (陌刀), a specialized long-handled *dao*, first appeared during the Tang Dynasty. Both of these *dao* were popular in the army. Historical documentation indicates that about 80 percent of soldiers in the army used *heng dao*.

Fig. 1-18: Two Tang Dynasty *heng dao,* 100 centimeters (about 40 inches) and 110 centimeters (about 44 inches) long

Dao with a sharp edge on each side of the tip appeared during the Tang Dynasty. The two-edged *dao* tip was a recurring feature in the evolution of the sword.

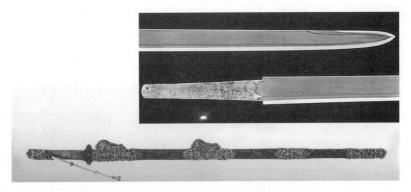

Fig. 1-19: Tang Dynasty *dao* preserved in the Shosoin Depository in Nara, Japan

Song Dynasty

The period known as the Five Dynasties and Ten Kingdoms (907–960 AD) followed the Tang Dynasty. During this time, chaos and conflict became widespread, and the government changed hands many times. There was no centralized authority capable of imposing order. The civil disarray resulted in decreased cultural development until the Song Dynasty, when China was once again unified.

During the Song Dynasty (960–1279 AD), a large variety of *dao* with different shapes and sizes were produced. Straight *dao,* although still in use, were no longer as popular as they had been in the past. *Shou dao* (手刀) or hand swords exemplified the trend toward wider, shorter, and curvilinear blades.

Two swords with wider, straight blades are shown in figure 1-20. The lower sword was unearthed from Zhenjiang, Jiansu Province, and the engraving on it indicates that it was made in 1270 AD. Figures 1-21 through 1-23 show a variety of *shou dao* blades.

Fig. 1-20: Two Song Dynasty straight ring pommel *dao*

Fig. 1-21: A Song Dynasty *shou dao* with a narrow curved blade

Fig. 1-22: A Song Dynasty *shou dao* with a wide curved blade

Fig. 1-23: Three *shou dao* blades from the Song Dynasty

Pu dao (朴刀) became very popular during this time. At about three to four feet long, the handle of a *pu dao* is shorter than the handle of a *da dao* or "big" *dao,* but longer than the handle of a "short" *dao.* Because of its intermediate length and its relative ease of use, the *pu dao* was preferred by infantrymen. Another popular special-purpose sword from this era was the *zhan ma dao* (斩马刀), a short sword designed to be held with both hands and used to chop the legs of horses. It is thought to have been designed by General Yue Fei (岳飞, 1103–1141 AD) specifically to counter the armored and chain-linked cavalry of the invading Jin army.

Fig. 1-24: Chop-horse sword from the Song Dynasty

The quality of swords manufactured during the Song Dynasty was very high. The blades of these swords were typically about three to four inches wide. Descriptions of the process by which these blades were made can be found in the *Mengxi Journal* (梦溪笔谈) by Shen Kuo (沈括, 1031–1095 AD). Shen Kuo is arguably the most famous scientist, statesman, and military strategist in Chinese history.

Fig. 1-25: Brick engraving from the Song Dynasty showing a swordsman holding a *dao* as he stands behind an officer

Ming Dynasty

The Song Dynasty was brought to a violent end by Mongolian invaders who, once in power, established the Yuan Dynasty (1279–1368 AD). In order to ensure its dominance, the Yuan government applied tight restrictions on all martial arts activities. This prevented the development of innovation in martial arts until the Ming Dynasty ushered in a change of regime.

Martial arts principles and training methods became very refined during the Ming Dynasty (1368–1644 AD). Many of today's most prominent styles and schools can be traced to this era. Variations in *dao* shape continued to appear, and most of these are still in use today.

Fig. 1-26: Ming Dynasty ring pommel *dao* called *yun kou dao,* or "cloud head" sword

Fig. 1-27: Two *yan chi dao*—goose-wing swords from the Ming Dynasty

Fig. 1-28: A *yan ling dao*—goose-feather sword and scabbard from the Ming Dynasty

Fig. 1-29: A *ma dao*—short cavalry sword from the Ming Dynasty

Historical events taking place in Japan had a large impact on the development of the Chinese *dao,* both the weapon and the set of skills associated with it. Beginning in the Han Dynasty, the Japanese had been learning Chinese sword skills and production techniques. With a supportive social system, Japanese sword smiths from the warrior caste spent centuries refining the Chinese *dao.* Their modifications eventually resulted in the emergence of the distinctive Japanese samurai sword.

Meanwhile in China, the prototypical Chinese swords with long, narrow blades had gradually been falling into disuse since the Song Dynasty. At the start of the Ming Dynasty, this type of *dao* was no longer being produced in China, and after awhile people came to believe that it had always been made in Japan but never in China. Because the swords made in Japan during the Ming Dynasty were of very high quality and were highly regarded by the Chinese, the manufacture of similarly shaped *dao* was reinstituted in China.

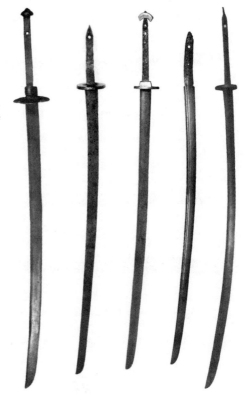

Fig. 1-30: Several Ming Dynasty *dao* modeled on the Japanese sword

At the conclusion of the major civil wars that had taken place in Japan, many samurai warriors on the losing side found themselves homeless, jobless, and often persecuted by the new government. Finding life impossible on the main islands of Japan, and lacking any skills other than soldiering, many of them became pirates and moved to small islands off the coast of China. These highly trained and professional pirates plagued residents along the eastern and southeastern coasts of China for many years.

During the extended period of peace in China after the Chinese civil wars, most generals had little if any occasion to gain combat experience, and soldiers lacked training, discipline, and weapons of even moderate quality. As a result, there was no organized opposition to the Japanese pirates plundering the Chinese coastal areas until General Qi Jiguang (戚继光, 1528–1587 AD) and Yu Dayou (俞大猷, 1504–1580 AD) were placed in charge of the situation.

Facing the unprecedented challenge of fighting an enemy of elite professionals with only a regular conscription army, General Qi made systematic changes to the training, tactics, and weapons used by the Chinese troops. As part of this effort, he used the Japanese sword as a model for recreating the long, narrow Chinese *dao*. With his acute appreciation, acquired on the battlefield, for the various features of Japanese swords, General Qi researched and refined the design of the Chinese *dao*. He also systematized the sword skills of the Japanese and emulated their training methods, and then created the useful skills and highly efficient training methods of Chinese swordsmanship.

Combining intense realistic training, innovative group tactics, and improved weaponry, General Qi's troops fought hard against the Japanese for twelve years and were finally able to put an end to the one hundred years of piracy that had plagued China. Called the Qi Family Army, General Qi's soldiers became justly famous, and the long, narrow *dao* once again became popular in China. With only minor modifications, these swords were used by the Chinese army throughout most of the Qing Dynasty.

Fig. 1-31: Swords for two-handed grips used by Ming Dynasty imperial guards

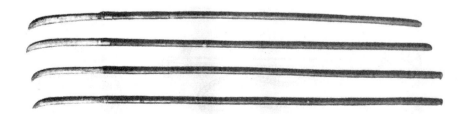

Fig. 1-32: Long-handled swords used by Ming Dynasty imperial guard

Fig. 1-33: Painting of Ming Dynasty imperial guards holding *dao*

Fig. 1-34: Painting of Ming Dynasty imperial guards holding long-handled *dao*

Qing Dynasty

Dao was the most popular weapon during the Qing Dynasty (1644–1911 AD). *Yao dao* (腰刀), or waist swords, so-called because they were worn on the waist, were common. Many different types of *dao* of various lengths were used by different services within the military.

Fig. 1-35: A Qing army officer carrying a *yao dao*

Fig. 1-36: A Qing soldier carrying a *yao dao*

Fig. 1-37: Emperor Kangxi's long-handled sword with a wide blade and scabbard

Fig. 1-38: Long-handled sword with a narrow blade and scabbard

Fig. 1-39: Chuanwei *dao*—boat-tail sword

Fig. 1-40: Long-handled swords

Dao were used not only for fighting but also to signify a bearer's rank and class. Strict and detailed rules dictated the type of *dao* and decorations that could be worn by people of differing ranks. Figures 1-41 to 1-44 show several different types of waist swords worn by emperors, kings, nobles, officers, and soldiers. The shapes of most of the swords in these pictures are of the goose-feather type. The pictures also indicate that a sharp edge on the back of the head of the sword was a common feature of *dao* during this time.

In the early Qing Dynasty, the ancient art of Chinese sword production reached its height. Emperor Qianlong (乾隆, 1711–1799) placed an order for three groups of thirty swords each. The groups were called heaven (*tian* 天), earth (*di* 地), and man (*ren* 人). It took forty-seven years to fulfill this order of ninety swords, fashioned to the highest quality possible.

The No. 17 sword from the Heaven series, called *Baoteng* (宝腾), is shown at the top of figure 1-41. It was sold for 46,040,000 Hong Kong dollars (about 6 million US dollars) at a Sotheby auction held in Hong Kong during the spring of 2006.

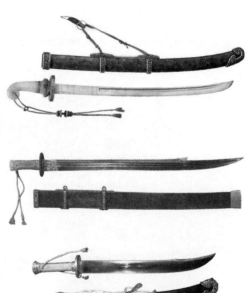

Fig. 1-41: Three *yao dao* and scabbards for Emperor Qianlong

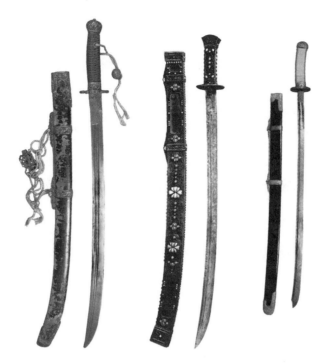

Fig. 1-42: *Yao dao* and scabbards for kings (left), princes (middle),
and women in the royal family (right)

Fig. 1-43: *Yao dao* for high-ranking officers (three on the left)
and low-ranking officers (two on the right)

Fig. 1-44: *Yao dao* for soldiers from different military services

From the Ming Dynasty on, the Chinese military began to use "hot" weapons, or firearms, in addition to cold weapons. Firearms became increasingly popular in the military during the Qing Dynasty, especially after the reign of Emperor Qianlong, and the government's support for sword-making waned as demand for high-quality swords decreased. As a result, the technologies and skills involved in sword production began to decline.

Traditional martial arts, however, went through a period of rapid development among the civilian population. Many new ideas emerged, and new skills and styles were created. *Dao* principles and skills continued to be systematized and refined. Most of the styles developed during the Qing Dynasty are still in practice today. Figures 1-45 and 1-46 show several different Qing Dynasty swords used by the army and by martial arts groups.

Fig. 1-45: Chopping *dao* for the army and martial artists

Fig. 1-46: Several *dao* used by martial arts groups during the Qing Dynasty

Twentieth Century

Throughout history, *dao* have been the most common weapons used in the Chinese army. Although most traditional cold weapons were phased out by the military during the first half of the twentieth century, *dao* remained in use until the 1940s. During World War II, they were highly regarded as effective weapons for hand-to-hand combat.

Fig. 1-47: A Chinese soldier holding his chopping sword in the late 1930s

Although jian were initially more prevalent than *dao* because of the relative ease of their manufacture, *dao* eventually became the better known and more widely used sword. Employed in large-scale organized warfare since the beginning of the Iron Age, high quality *dao* became increasingly easy to produce, and *dao* skills were also easy to teach, learn, and use. For these reasons, *dao* remained the most popular sword in the cold weapon arsenal.

Dao in the Army and Martial Arts Groups

In Chinese military history, high-level individual martial arts were generally considered to have very little importance. General Qi Jiguang, an outstanding leader on the battlefield, was also exceptional for his dedication as a researcher and expert practitioner of martial arts skills and training methods. He consulted with many martial arts masters in his extensive travels and had a deep understanding of all aspects of the martial arts. He clearly understood that martial arts training had to be very different for soldiers than it was for professional martial arts practitioners, and he elucidated these key differences in his book, *The New Book of Efficient Training Methods* (纪效新书).

In his work, he emphasized that because warfare involves fighting between organized groups, the success of an army depends on its ability to function as a unit. He held that the most important elements of such functioning were cooperation and discipline and that discipline should be the foremost focus of military training. In General Qi's view, the skill level of one soldier in an army of a thousand soldiers was not nearly as critical as the ability of all soldiers to maintain their proper place in formation and to move as a coordinated unit.

Martial arts training for soldiers was regarded mainly as a method to improve physical conditioning and basic skills. From years of experience, General Qi had observed that even soldiers with extensive martial arts training quickly forgot their difficult and high-level skills when faced with a well-armed and highly motivated enemy. They tended, instead, to react instinctively using only a few of their most rudimentary skills. To correct this tendency, General Qi organized his army into fighting groups in which each soldier mastered only a few carefully chosen simple skills that complemented those of the other soldiers within the group.

Overall, the skills that are most useful for battlefield combat are those that are easy to teach, easy to learn, and easy to remember and use under conditions of even extreme stress. Basic *dao* skills fit these criteria perfectly and this match accounts for the fact that, historically, *dao* and qiang (spears) were the most commonly used weapons in the Chinese army. While short *dao* were typically carried by infantrymen, both short *dao* and long-handled *dao* were used in the cavalry. Usually, soldiers carried a *dao* in one hand and a shield in the other.

妙．力用牌．右用此　埋　人關下畔金
頂刀不如勢　伏　莫為藏頭雞
開尖能有進　勢　變難進之畔
急將脫鎗步　．　刀當步勢頭
進牌手戳甚　　鎗　如最勢
絕借．在速　　牌　風為．

一
四
六

Fig. 1-48: *Dao* postures from General Qi's book

Off the battlefield, in one-on-one encounters between professional martial artists, the primary predictor of success is skill level. The goal of training is to attain a high degree of skill, and this level can be developed only through long periods of full-time, dedicated, and specialized practice. As in any other field that has been highly developed, a large body of hard-won knowledge is accumulated slowly through the contributions of countless generations of masters. A high-level skill, by definition, is not one that can be taught to large groups of people with average talent in a short period of time. Only practitioners with deep commitment and the prerequisite talent can, under favorable circumstances, achieve mastery of high-level skills.

Although originally created for battlefield combat, *dao* skills were further developed to a high degree among martial arts groups. The training in this civilian arena was even more complex and demanding than in the military, and weapons skills advanced to an ever higher level of sophistication.

During the Ming Dynasty, the famous martial arts master Cheng Chongdou (程冲斗, 1561–?) studied traditional Chinese *dao* for many years and then learned high-level Japanese sword skills from Master Liu Yunfeng (刘云峰), who had trained directly with Japanese masters. Cheng incorporated many Japanese sword skills into traditional Chinese sword practice and described them in his highly regarded book *A Selection of Single-Sword Skills* (单刀法选). Most *dao* postures from Master Cheng's book are still used today in many martial arts groups.

上弓刀势　　　　　左提撩刀势　　　　　飞刀势

Fig. 1-49: *Dao* skills from Master Cheng's book

During the early Qing Dynasty, another outstanding master, Wu Shu (吴 殳, 1611–1695), wrote the seminal spear classic *Arms Journal* (手臂录). This work contains a chapter describing *dao* skills, including how to use *dao* to defend against spear attacks. It also introduces new ideas for *dao* use. The *dao* skills presented in Master Wu's book are, like the postures from Master Cheng's book, practiced in many martial arts groups to this day.

拗步撩刀势　　　　　入洞势　　　　　担肩势

Fig. 1-50: *Dao* skills from Master Wu's book

As the theory and practice of *dao* skills became more refined and clearly understood among martial arts groups, the distilled knowledge was recognized by the military and integrated into its training systems. Often during times of need, famous martial arts masters were invited to train the troops. Based on the requirements of combat, appropriate skills that were easy to learn and use were incorporated into training and tactics. Lessons learned on the battlefield led, in turn, to further understanding and to improved martial arts practices. Historically, this continual cycle of information exchange between the military and martial arts groups helped advance the development of *dao* skills to ever higher levels.

The latest example of this cycle occurred during World War II. Responding to the needs and constraints of the Chinese armed forces, several famous masters, including the Baiyuan Tongbei Quan grandmaster Li Zhendong (李振东), a martial arts instructor for many years in the twenty-ninth army, distilled a few simple but extremely useful *dao* skills and taught them to the soldiers of the famous Big Chopping-Sword Brigade (*da dao dui* 大刀队). This brigade earned renown in the War of Resistance against Japan from 1937 to 1945. This brigade and many others like it throughout the Chinese resistance forces were widely feared by the enemy for their *dao* skills.

Fig. 1-51: Soldiers of the Big Chopping-Sword Brigade carrying their swords as they march to the front

Fig. 1-52: Soldiers of the Big Chopping-Sword Brigade preparing to charge

Fig. 1-53: Soldiers of the Big Chopping-Sword Brigade preparing to charge

Other *dao* masters contributed to the war effort by composing training manuals. Bagua master Yin Yuzhang (尹玉章) wrote *The Practice Method of Chopping-Sword Skills* (砍刀术练习法). Although the production quality of the book was poor due to wartime conditions, the content was invaluable and the book became famous during that time. Figures 1-54 and 1-55, taken from this book, show Master Yin demonstrating chopping-sword skills.

Fig. 1-54: Master Yin Yuzhang holding his big chopping sword

Fig. 1-55: Master Yin Yuzhang demonstrating his big chopping-sword skill

Classification

The *dao* sword is a curved, single-edged weapon that has undergone many variations throughout history. Some of these variations were designed by the military for specific wartime purposes; others were developed by martial artists to emphasize or combine particular principles or skills. Specialized design variations often make special skills possible.

There are perhaps more variations of *dao* than there are of any other cold weapon. *Dao* blades can vary by shape, length, and width, and *dao* handles can vary by length and shape. *Dao* are generally classified as short, or *duan dao;* medium, or *pu dao;* and long, or *da dao.*

Dao or *Duan Dao* (短刀)—Short *Dao*

Usually, the term *dao* refers to a short *dao,* commonly translated as a broadsword or saber. The blade length of a short sword can range from one foot to four feet; the handle length can range from half-a-foot to two feet. A short weapon, *duan dao* is typically held with one hand, but both hands can be used if additional power is needed. A short *dao* can be wide or narrow, thick or thin, heavy or light. Its blade may be more or less curved; some blades have scabbards, while others do not. Several of the most common short *dao* are described in this section.

Yao dao (腰刀)—waist sword: a short, light *dao* with a scabbard; usually carried on the waist. Because *yao dao* is light, the skills associated with it are quick and easily changed. The handle of a *yao dao* is usually no longer than one foot, and *yao dao* blades can be of many different shapes and widths.

Fig. 1-56: Two *yao dao* with scabbards

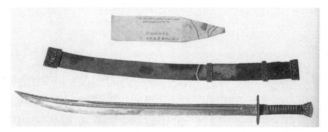

Fig. 1-57: *Yao dao* and scabbard used by Nurhachu, first Qing Dynasty emperor

Since the beginning of the Ming Dynasty, the most popular *yao dao* have been *yan ling dao* (雁翎刀), the goose-feather sword; *liu ye dao* (柳叶刀), the willow-leaf sword; and *niu wei dao* (牛尾刀), the oxtail sword. The names of these swords derive from the shapes of the blades, and each blade has additional distinguishing features.

The width of a *yan ling dao* blade is almost constant except at the head of the sword and at the tip, which narrows sharply. The body of the blade is almost straight but curves slightly at the tip, and the handle is straight.

Fig. 1-58: *Yan ling dao*—goose-feather swords

The willow-leaf shaped *liu ye dao* blade narrows gradually from the base or "root" of the blade to the tip. The body of the blade is slightly curved but becomes more sharply angled at the tip.

Fig. 1-59: *Liu ye dao*—willow-leaf swords

Niu wei dao or oxtail sword blades widen gradually from the base or root to the tip. The head, or widest part of the tip, can be about twice as wide as the root. The blade is curved, as are most *niu wei dao* handles.

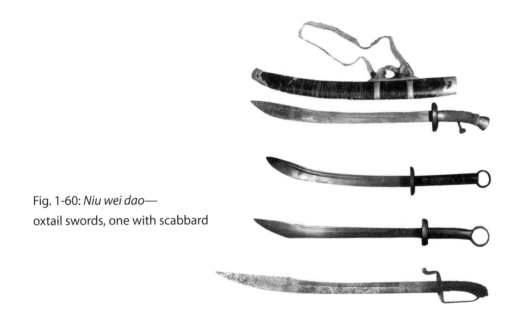

Fig. 1-60: *Niu wei dao*—
oxtail swords, one with scabbard

The three differently shaped *yao dao* were commonly used by martial artists and guards during the Ming and Qing Dynasties. *Yao dao* is the type of *dao* most frequently used in martial arts schools today.

Da kan dao (大砍刀)—big chopping sword: a wide, thick and heavy, short *dao*. Because its back is thick, *da kan dao* can be effectively used for powerful blocks. Its weight makes it suitable for powerful chops.

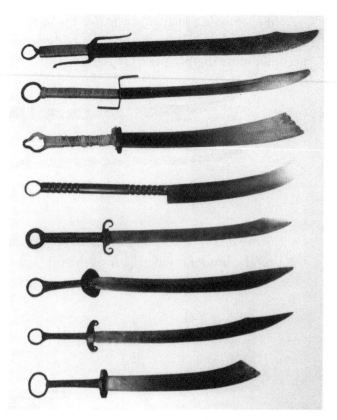

Fig. 1-61: Several different
Qing Dynasty *da kan dao*

Da kan dao skills are very simple and thus easy to learn and use. Popular among soldiers, this sword is too heavy to be conveniently carried at the waist, so it is usually slung across the bearer's back.

Fig. 1-62: A soldier carrying a *da kan dao*

Because its blade is wide and thick, a *da kan dao* can be manufactured without relying on high quality steel or advanced techniques. As a result, its price is often much lower than the price for other kinds of swords. During the latter years of the nineteenth century and well into the twentieth century, China was a relatively poor nation with a primitive and very small industrial base. The production of traditional Chinese swords waned during this period of economic depression. Because of the ease, convenience, and low cost of their manufacture, however, *da kan dao* became a popular weapon for both the military and the militias during World War II. *Da kan dao* were produced in large quantities and required neither highly technical manufacturing facilities, nor advanced knowledge or adherence to exacting standards.

During World War II, many Chinese armies organized their own Big Chopping-Sword Brigades. Each soldier in the brigade carried a big chopping sword as well as a gun. The sword was used only for close hand-to-hand combat. In these frequently occurring situations, *da kan dao* proved to be vastly superior to bayonets fixed to rifles. Although *da kan dao* are most often held with one hand, some soldiers preferred a more powerful variant with a long handle that allowed for more forceful two-handed grips.

Fig. 1-63: A short-handled big chopping sword used in World War II

Fig. 1-64: A long-handled big chopping sword used in World War II

Miao dao (苗刀)—long and narrow *dao:* The Chinese character *miao* has two meanings. As an adjective, it means "long and slender"; as a noun, it refers to a small ethnic group in Southwest China in which every man customarily carries a long, narrow sword. The term *miao dao* can be interpreted either as a "long, narrow sword" or as a "Miao style sword." The first interpretation is generally preferred because most Chinese people belong to the Han, rather than the Miao ethnic group, and archaeological evidence indicates that the Han people had used this sword since the Han Dynasty (206 BC–220 AD).

It was during the Han Dynasty that the long and narrow ring pommel sword first appeared. The design of *miao dao* is widely believed to have been inherited from this period, and the subsequent development of these swords indicates that their features were adopted from the Han swords and then improved upon. Because its blade is long and narrow and has to meet exacting standards, these swords were difficult to manufacture on a large scale during ancient times.

Fig. 1-65: A Qing Dynasty *miao dao*

As mentioned previously, the long and narrow *dao* fell out of favor after the Song Dynasty but was redesigned by Ming Dynasty General Qi Jiguang. The newly designed sword borrowed various features from the Japanese and Chinese swords in use at the time, and it has been used by both the military and martial arts groups ever since.

Although the derivation of the name *miao dao* is not known with certainty, it is generally thought to have originated during the Qing Dynasty. During that period, a Miao Dao martial arts style, in which practitioners focused their training almost exclusively on skills associated with this type of sword, became widely known. In other groups, such as Tongbei style, *miao dao* are used only to practice regular single *dao* skills.

Fig. 1-66: Strider Clark practicing Tongbei Dao

Dan Dao and *Shuang Dao*—Single *Dao* and Double *Dao*

There are two basic categories of short *dao* practice: *dan dao* (单刀), a single *dao* style, in which only one sword is used; and *shuang dao* (双刀), a double *dao* style, in which two swords are used. The most common style by far is *dan dao.* Many groups combine *dan dao* practice with the practice of other weapons, such as a shield, a whip, or hidden weapons.

Fig. 1-67: Master Luo Shuhuan practicing single *dao*

It is not clear when double *dao* skills were first developed, but Ming Dynasty records include mention of famous double *dao* masters. The most famous of these was General Washi, a woman warrior who used double *dao* and led an army of thousands against the Japanese pirates. She is renowned for leading charges with a sword in each hand and always from the front.

Fig. 1-68: Clayton Shiu practicing double *dao*

Fig. 1-69: Patrick Ingram practicing double *dao*—
butterfly swords commonly used in southern China

Da Dao (大刀)—Big *Dao*

Da dao, a big or long-handled sword, has a handle that can be five feet or more in length and is usually more than twice as long as the sword's blade. Big sword blades come in many different shapes. There are two kinds of *da dao:* an extremely heavy sword used only for practicing basic skills, and a lighter sword well-adapted for fighting. Historically, the lighter sword was used primarily by mounted fighters. When combined with the momentum of a charging horse, the qualities of this sword made extremely quick and powerful attacks possible. Mounted opponents had difficulty defending against these attacks because they were unable to change position quickly enough.

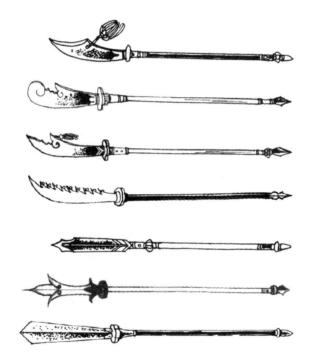

Fig. 1-70: Different types of *da dao*

Martial arts groups favor the very heavy *da dao* for basic gongfu training because the extra weight increases the difficulty of mastering real fighting skills. This sword, however, cannot be manipulated easily and quickly enough for effective use in actual combat. A very popular type of big sword is the *qinglong yanyue dao* (青龙偃月刀), more commonly known as *guan dao* (关刀). It is said that Guan Yu (关羽), probably the most celebrated general in Chinese history, used a big sword that weighed eighty-two *jin,* according to ancient measurements, or around sixty to seventy pounds according to current standards.

During the Ming Dynasty, Master Cheng Ziyi (程子颐) wrote *A Brief Discussion of the Key Points of Martial Preparation* (武备要略), a well-known book in which one chapter was devoted to big sword skills (大刀法). In this chapter, Master Cheng advised that big swords should be used for mounted combat only after big sword skills had been practiced on foot and thoroughly mastered.

檐前滴水刀势　　　　　　勾斫刀势

Fig. 1-71: Some *da dao* skills from Master Cheng's book

Fig. 1-72: Master Zhang Yun practicing *da dao*

Pu Dao (朴刀), or *Shuang Shou Dai* (双手带)

Pu means simple, and a *pu dao,* also called *shuang shou dai*—sword for two hands—is as useful as it is simple. Although there is some disagreement about the exact shape of the early *pu dao,* they are widely considered to have been of medium length. A *pu dao* blade is usually equal in length to its handle and similar in length to a *yao dao* blade, which is approximately three feet. *Pu dao* were in widespread use by the military, especially the infantry, during the Song Dynasty.

Fig. 1-73: A Qing Dynasty *pu dao*

Fig. 1-74: Josh Hehr practicing *pu dao*

General Features of the Single *Dao* Skills

Because Taiji *dao* belong to the single *dao* category, a discussion of the general features of all single *dao* skills is included in this introductory chapter. Subsequent chapters will focus on the special principles, skills, and training methods of Taiji Dao practice.

It Is a Hard Weapon

It is said that "*dao* is the most reckless and daring of all weapons" (刀为百兵之胆). When you hold a *dao,* you should fear nothing. Another common expression is that "*dao* is like a ferocious tiger" (刀如猛虎), which means that the chop of a *dao* must be powerful like a tiger; nothing can stand in its way. These expressions describe the basic principle of all *dao* skills. The *dao* is a hard, powerful weapon that demands a strong spirit and ample courage from the fighter who wields it. He must be full of determination and vigor, surging ahead bravely with quick and nimble steps.

It Is a Short Weapon but Must Be Used Like a Long Weapon

The injunction to "use a short weapon as a long weapon" (短兵长用) indicates that the goal of single *dao* skills is to extend the reach of the short weapon as far as possible. An important part of the training for any type of weapon is learning how to use that weapon against other weapons likely to be encountered, and the main challenge for anyone with a short weapon is learning how to use it successfully against a long weapon. Theoretically, it should be impossible to meet this challenge because the fighter with the long weapon can always reach farther than the fighter armed with a short weapon.

Of all long weapons, the spear is the most difficult to defend against. In addition to its great length, it is highly maneuverable, and so its motions can be changed very quickly and nimbly. For these reasons, the spear is known as the king of all weapons. Learning how to use a *dao* to defend against a spear is a central goal of *dao* practice and a most difficult skill to acquire. In Chinese swordsmanship lore, it is said of the use of short weapons versus the long that only if your mind remains calm and clear and your movements quick and accurate will you have any chance to prevail. It is also said that you must be able at any moment to exploit every opportunity that may arise, no matter how small and fleeting it may be.

The Importance of Empty-Hand Skills in Dao Practice

It is said that "in single *dao* practice, one should always watch the practitioner's empty hand" (单刀看手). By watching the hand that is not holding the sword, it is possible to assess accurately the level of a practitioner's single-sword skill. The empty hand can be used for a variety of purposes: to balance the force of the sword strikes; to add power to the sword; to grab the opponent's weapon or execute other offensive and defensive skills; to wield additional weapons; or to divert an opponent's attention. Executing a sword skill properly is often largely dependent on your empty-hand skills, so single *dao* practice must include a focus on these skills as well as on sword skills. These empty-hand concepts are used widely in Chinese swordsmanship, and we will return to these concepts often in later chapters.

Insubstantial and Substantial

Xu (虚)—insubstantial—and *shi* (实)—substantial—are common concepts in martial arts and are always used together when describing skills. Because this pair of words has two different sets of meanings, there has been considerable confusion in the martial arts literature about these concepts. A clear understanding of xu and shi is vital for success in fighting.

In the first set of meanings, *xu* is translated as weak, feeble, or poor and *shi* as strong, powerful, or rich. In the second set of meanings, *xu* is translated as false, fake, deceptive, changeable, illusory, virtual, or uncertain and *shi* as true, real, unchangeable, fixed, sure, or corporeal. Each pair of meanings forms the basis for a central tenet of military strategy.

The first tenet advises to "avoid shi and attack xu" (避实击虚) and is based on the first pair of translations in which *shi* refers to strength and *xu* to weakness. The instruction, put forth in Sun Zi's *Art of War* (孙子兵法), is to stay clear of your enemy's main force and attack at your enemy's weak point. If, for example, your opponent uses a heavy weapon, its movements will be very powerful and will be considered to be shi. You should avoid shi by not blocking his blow directly with your sword and, instead, attack at a vulnerable point like the wrist or ribs, which would be considered your enemy's xu parts.

The second tenet counsels to "avoid xu and attack shi" (避虚击实). This statement is based on the second set of translations, in which *xu* means false or fake and *shi* means true or unchangeable. This instruction warns you to avoid being duped by your opponent's feinting movements and to try instead to attack his unchangeable part. If, for example, your opponent wields a spear, he can change the movements of his spearhead very quickly and confuse you with many false attacks. Here, the spearhead is considered xu, and it will be very difficult for you to judge which of its movements might signal a real attack. If you concentrate on this xu point, you will be likely to make a mistake. Compared to the quickly moving spearhead, however, your opponent's front hand and the shaft of his spear can be moved and changed only slowly, so it is these shi parts that should become the focus of your attention and attack. Careful practice is needed to learn how to use your sword to chase these shi parts.

Moving and Stillness

Dong (动)—movement—and *jing* (静)—stillness—are used to describe internal and external feelings. It is said that there is stillness within motion and motion within stillness. When there is external movement or dong, no matter how fast or complex in your body or weapon, you should maintain an internal state of stillness or jing. Qi should continue to flow smoothly, and your mind should remain calm, clear, and focused. In a state of jing in which only small, if any, external movements are occurring in your body or weapon, your internal feeling should be dong, a state of excited anticipation of movement that might arise at any moment. Dong and jing must always exist in balance with each other.

Dong and jing can also be used to describe the relationship between you and your opponent. You should "use stillness to control movement and movement to control stillness" (以静制动 以动制静). Whenever your opponent's body or weapon moves, you should maintain a state of inner stillness. If you let yourself be emotionally drawn in by your opponent's movements, you are likely to become confused. No matter how fast your opponent's movements are, your mind must remain quiet. You must be patient and able to sense clearly your opponent's intentions and skills. This is expressed in the traditional adage: "When he is busy, I must wait quietly" (彼忙吾静待).

When, on the other hand, your opponent is quiet and focused, you should move your body or weapon to confuse and harass so that your opponent loses concentration. You should divert your opponent's attention so focus will be directed to a point of your choosing. This will lead your opponent to make mistakes. The traditional expression of this injunction is: "When he is quiet, I must agitate and disturb him" (敌静我扰).

Hard and Soft

Gang (刚)—hard—and *rou* (柔)—soft—refer to the internal trained force used in fighting. Some skills are hard and others are soft, but no skill is pure. Each must contain the other within itself. Hard must have some soft, lest it be too easily broken, and soft must include some hard, lest it be too weak. In sword skills, both hard and soft internal trained forces should extend into and move through your sword.

In fighting, you can use a hard skill before your opponent releases a hard attack against you or a soft skill when your opponent's hard force arrives. Hard and soft qualities can be combined and can complement each other by remaining in constant flux. A skill that appears to be hard can actually be soft and vice versa. Learning how to combine hard and soft qualities and how to change each to the other from inside your body will allow you to control the rhythm of your movements and will greatly improve your fighting skills

In this chapter, the history and general features of single *dao* have been discussed. The following chapters introduce a specialized type of *dao* called a Taiji *dao* and describe in detail the principles, skills, and Taiji Dao training system for this unique kind of sword.

Chapter Two

Taiji Dao

While the general history and features of regular *dao* were described in Chapter One, this chapter focuses on the distinctive characteristics, skills, and training methods of the specialized sword known as Taiji *dao*. Similar to the difference between the terms *dao* and Dao, Taiji *dao* refers to the specially designed sword used by Taiji Quan practitioners, while Taiji Dao refers to the skills associated with this specialized type of sword.

In traditional Taiji Dao, only one sword is used and referred to as *dan dao*, or single-sword skill. Over time, some Taiji Dao practitioners developed *shuang dao*, or double-sword skills, in which one sword is held in each hand and the swords are used in a coordinated way. In this book, only traditional *dan dao* skills will be considered.

The most important distinction between Taiji Dao and other Dao skills is that Taiji Dao follows Taiji Quan principles. Only if you are guided by these principles, can you consider yourself to be practicing Taiji Dao, regardless of how excellent your sword skills may be. For this reason, it is important that you have a thorough understanding of Taiji Quan principles and practices before beginning your study of Taiji Dao. The foundation for Taiji Dao training should include an understanding of the fundamental Taiji philosophical concepts and a thorough familiarity with the internal components and external movements of Taiji Quan as well as knowledge of its fighting principles and methods.

This chapter introduces the main features of the Taiji *dao* weapon and the basic principles of Taiji Dao.

Taiji Dao Sword

Before discussing Taiji Dao skills, we will describe the basic features of a Taiji *dao*, including its shape, length, width, weight, and balance, and the names for each part of the weapon. Given the traditional view that a held weapon is considered to be an integral part of the bearer's body, you should be familiar with each of the weapon's aspects and have a deep understanding of its qualities and movements.

The Shape of Taiji *Dao*

There are three separate parts of a Taiji *dao* (fig. 2-1): *dao* (刀)—the sword; *dao-qiao* (刀鞘)—the scabbard of the sword; and *daocai* (刀彩)—the tassel of the sword, which is used occasionally for demonstrations but not often in regular practice. The following discussion will focus only on the first part, the sword itself.

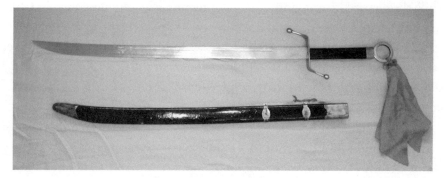

Fig. 2-1: A Taiji *dao*

The shape of a Taiji *dao* is special and relates to how the sword is used. Each part of the sword has been named so that the skills associated with it can be more easily learned and remembered (fig. 2-2).

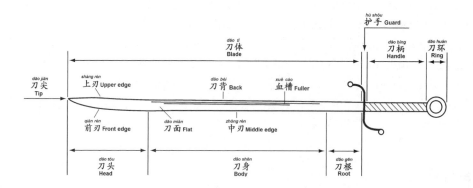

Fig. 2-2: The parts of a Taiji *dao*

There are four basic parts of a Taiji *dao: daoti*—the blade; *hushou*—the guard; *daoba* or *daobing*—the handle; and *daohuan*—the ring.

Daoti (刀体)—the blade of the sword: A Taiji *dao* blade is long and narrow, usually more than three feet long and one and a half to two inches wide. It includes three parts, and each is associated with different kinds of skills.

Daotou (刀头)—the head of the sword: The head of the sword begins at the tip of the blade and extends six to twelve inches down. Called *daojian* (刀尖), the tip or point of a Taiji *dao* differs from the tip of other swords in that both edges of a Taiji *dao* are sharp. The upper sharpened edge is called *shangren* (上刃) and its length can be from half a foot to two feet, depending on the practitioner's preference. Because the upper edge makes the head of a Taiji *dao* resemble the blade of a jian, the other name for a Taiji *dao* is *dan bei jian* (单背剑), or single-back jian.

The lower or front sharpened edge of a Taiji *dao* is called *qianren* (前刃). It extends the length of the head.

Daoshen (刀身)—the body of the sword: Daoshen is the middle part of the blade. The side of the sword that extends down from the upper edge is called *daobei* (刀背). This section, which is referred to as either the back of the sword or the spine of the blade, is dull rather than sharp. *Zhongren* (中刃), the middle edge, refers to the side of the blade that extends down from the front edge of the sword. Like the front edge, it is sharp and, as a result, the middle edge and the front edge are often referred to as one continuous section called *daoren* (刀刃), or the edge of the sword.

The flat side of the blade is called *daomian* (刀面) or the flat of the blade. On both flat sides of the sword, there may be one or two grooves to accommodate the blood flowing from a wounded opponent. This groove is called *xuecao* (血槽), which can be translated as "blood groove" or "fuller." A second function of the groove is to lighten the blade while allowing it to retain its strength and stiffness, similar to the effect produced by a steel I-beam.

Daogen (刀根)—the root of the sword: Below daoshen is daogen, the root or ricasso of the sword. This four-to-six-inch-long part of the blade is the strongest part of the sword. It can be used for hard blocks because, first, its edge is blunt rather than sharp, and, second, it is the part of the blade that is closest to your hand.

Hushou (护手)—the hand guard of the sword: Shaped like an "S," the hand guard of a Taiji *dao* is unique. Its special shape allows the sword to be used not only to block an opponent's weapon but also to catch it by hooking onto it. Consequently, the number of guard skills possible with a Taiji *dao* is much greater than the number possible with a regular *dao*.

Daoba (刀把)—the handle of the sword: The handle of a Taiji *dao* is referred to as either *daoba* or *daobing*. Because it is ten to twelve inches long, longer than the handles of most other single swords, a Taiji *dao* can be used with both hands.

Daohuan (刀环)—the ring of the sword: The pommel of a Taiji *dao* is a ring with a usual diameter of about three inches. The pommel's shape dates from about two thousand years ago, and many Taiji Dao skills rely on its unique features. These will be described in a later section.

Length, Weight, and Balance

It is very important in weapons practice that you find a comfortable weapon that suits you well. Characteristics such as your height, weight, strength, and overall conditioning should be taken into account. In addition to its quality, the length, weight, and balance of your Taiji *dao* are important. A good sword can help you develop correct feelings and master skills more easily. An unsuitable sword may hurt your qi and create incorrect feelings that can lead your practice in a wrong direction.

Taiji *dao* come in a variety of lengths. The length you choose should depend on your height. If you stand straight and hold your sword vertically with the tip touching the ground in front of your body, the center of the ring should be at the level of the *tanzhong* acupoint in the center of your chest (fig. 2-3). This is considered the standard length for a Taiji *dao*.

Some practitioners prefer swords that are longer than the standard length. In this case, two situations need to be carefully considered. Be careful that when you hold your sword in a natural way and drop your sword arm, the tip of your sword does not touch the ground (fig. 2-4).

Be careful, too, that the tip does not touch the ground when you turn your wrist outward to hold your sword vertically along the side of your body with the tip pointing down (fig. 2-5). If your sword is so long that the tip does touch the ground in either of these two circumstances, some skills will be difficult or impossible for you to execute.

Fig. 2-3   Fig. 2-4   Fig. 2-5

The weight of your sword will have a direct influence on the execution of your skills. Heavy swords are more effective for simple skills like chops but disadvantageous for making smooth and quick changes once you have initiated a movement. Also, if your sword is too heavy for you to manipulate comfortably, you will have difficulty developing correct feelings. In years past, when wars were fought with swords, soldiers preferred heavy swords because only simple and powerful skills were required for battlefield combat. Martial arts practitioners usually prefer lighter swords because these swords are better suited to the practice of more refined skills.

Balance is the most important feature of Taiji *dao*. If the balance is good, you will be able to hold your sword comfortably and remain relaxed. A well-balanced sword will also feel lighter than its actual weight. This, in turn, will increase your control of the sword and make it more flexible in your hand. Different practitioners prefer different balance points depending on the skills they use most often.

The ideal balance point of a Taiji *dao* is four to six inches from the guard, but because a Taiji *dao* is long, the balance point is often too far forward. In this circumstance, the head of the sword will feel heavy and this will make your wrist tired and your sword difficult to control. Your qi will not flow smoothly, and your *jin,* or trained force, will be interrupted. It is said of this situation that "the sword snatches your qi."

While a good sword that suits you well can help develop your skills, a sword that is not satisfactory can impede your progress. Finding the right sword is not easy, so it is wise to test a sword before you buy it. To evaluate a sword, hold it in the variety of hand positions to be shown in Chapter Three. Swing it in different circles to assess whether its length, weight, and balance are well matched to your size, strength, and style. The sword should be very comfortable for you to hold, and you should be able to control it very well with a relaxed hand. If you cannot find the perfect sword and have to make some compromises, give consideration first to the sword's balance, then to its weight, and finally to its length.

It is important to understand the shape of the Taiji *dao* because many of the sword skills are based on this singular feature. The unique shape of a Taiji *dao* has evolved over many years and has undergone various modifications by Taiji Quan practitioners. As can be seen from the illustrations in Chapter One, each design feature of Taiji *dao* has its own history and derives from characteristics of earlier traditional swords. No clear record exists today indicating when Taiji Dao skills originated within the Taiji Quan community, nor who was responsible for the Taiji *dao*'s design. It is common knowledge, however, that by the end of the nineteenth century, this sword was being used in the Beijing Taiji Quan group.

Because Taiji *dao* are so special, they have never been easy to acquire. The highly skilled sword makers who produce them must meet rigorous and specialized standards. Such sword makers are rare because the market for this kind of sword is small, and very few craftsmen have the necessary training. Even in nineteenth century Beijing, only one small mill produced high quality Taiji *dao*.

As a result of the current shortage of qualified sword makers, the price of a Taiji *dao* is high, and, consequently, many practitioners choose to practice Taiji Dao skills using regular broadswords or sabers. It is important to recognize that this choice can easily cause considerable confusion and misunderstanding. The special details of many Taiji Dao skills may not be performed correctly when a regular *dao* is substituted for a Taiji *dao,* and some skills may be completely impossible to execute.

Ideally, you will be able to find a suitable Taiji *dao* (sword) for your Taiji Dao (skill) practice, but if this is not possible, and you have to use a regular sword, it is very important that you understand clearly the ways in which the two kinds of swords are similar and different. Only then will you have a chance to make your practice effective and raise your level of expertise.

Taiji Quan and Taiji Dao Skills

Although Taiji Dao retains many of the skills of other Dao forms and Taiji *dao* share some basic physical features with other *dao*, Taiji Dao practice must follow the same Taiji principles as Taiji Quan. In fact, Taiji Quan and Taiji

Dao skills are often considered to be essentially the same, given that the *dao,* when expertly used, is viewed as an extension of your body. From a high-level perspective, the correct practice of Taiji Dao embodies all the skills and principles of Taiji Quan.

Applying Taiji principles with a weapon in hand is in many ways more difficult than applying the same principles using empty-hand skills. For this reason, empty-hand Taiji Quan practice serves as the foundation for Taiji Dao practice. Traditionally, at least three years of dedicated training were required before a student could be considered to have acquired a rudimentary knowledge of Taiji Quan skills. During that time he or she would not even have been put in a position to touch a sword, no less encouraged to train with one.

With a bow to tradition, we will review the philosophical concepts upon which Taiji Quan is based and explore both the basic features of Taiji Quan skills and also the process by which Taiji principles are applied in the martial art of Taiji Quan. Only then will we turn to a consideration of the principles and practices of Taiji Dao.

Review of Basic Taiji Principles

Taiji is a concept represented by the symbol in figure 2-6. In Chinese cosmology, the beginning state of the universe is *wuji,* a homogenous, undifferentiated, or chaos state of being. Wuji then begets the state of *taiji* in which the forces of *yin* and *yang* appear and begin to separate, but are still in one entity. The *liangyi* state emerges from taiji when yin and yang become fully separated and can be clearly identified as two independent entities. If you were counting, wuji would be zero, taiji would be one, and liangyi would be two. From a philosophical perspective, wuji is basically inert and without content or meaning; taiji is the first meaningful state. All changes start from this state.

 Fig. 2-6: Taiji symbol

In Chinese culture, the concept of *yin* and *yang* expresses the oppositions found in all natural and social phenomena. *Yin* represents qualities such as negativity, femaleness, passivity, subordination, internality, softness, fullness, quietness, substantiality, and darkness. It also characterizes objects like the moon and earth. *Yang* represents the opposite qualities of positivity, maleness, initiative, leadership, externality, hardness, emptiness, movement, insubstantiality, and light, and characterizes objects like the sun and sky.

It is commonly said that "taiji is yin and yang." Given the definitions provided above, however, this statement is not sufficiently precise because the same could be said of the state of liangyi. Taiji exists only when yin and yang occur together in a unified whole; neither can exist independently of the other. They are complementary and each can be transformed to the other. A correct understanding of Taiji Quan skills requires that the distinction between yin and yang be as specific as possible.

At a fundamental level, all forms of martial arts focus on the application of force, and, in this respect, most martial arts styles follow the liangyi principle in which the two forces can be used separately: a yin force for defense and a yang force for attack or counterattack. In Taiji Quan, however, defense and offense are always combined and the yin and yang forces are always presented simultaneously. As in the taiji principle, yin and yang coexist and each force always contains some of the other. Neither force is ever static. Each is in constant flux, and, as a result, the taiji state in which both arise is also dynamic.

In the famous Taiji symbol, yin and yang appear to be in perfect balance. This depicts the inherent tendency in the taiji state toward balance. The relationship between yin and yang varies from moment to moment; sometimes the yin component is greater than the yang component, and sometimes the reverse is true. Since they are part of the same entity, a momentary change in one force automatically implies and causes a simultaneous change in the other. The two forces always complement, replenish, support, and transform each other.

Basic Taiji Quan Principles

Taiji Quan is a traditional internal martial arts style that includes both empty-hand and weapons training. Commonly thought of as synonymous with the term "Taiji Quan," empty-hand training includes basic form training to develop fundamental abilities and skill training, like push hands, to develop proficiency in fighting.

The principles, tactics, and skills of Taiji Quan are radically different from those of the much greater number of external martial arts styles. Although all martial arts styles are designed to be effective in combat, the internal martial arts styles, and Taiji Quan in particular, emphasize efficiency as much as effectiveness. Efficiency is measured by the ability to achieve success by using the absolute minimum amount of effort necessary.

The main fighting principles of Taiji Quan are *yin jin luo kong* (引进落空), or luring an opponent into an empty place, *si liang bo qian jin* (四两拨千斤),

or using four ounces of force to manipulate one thousand pounds of force, and *jie li da li* (借力打力), or borrowing the opponent's force to defeat his force.

Luring an opponent into an empty place, the main Taiji Quan tactic, is analogous to setting a deadfall trap. Your opponent is encouraged to take what seems to be a safe step into a stable situation only to find that the ground underneath seems to disappear. As a result, your opponent loses balance, and while falling down, your opponent's own weight supplies most of the force that defeats him or her.

The adage of "using four ounces of force to manipulate one thousand pounds of force" is a hyperbole in which "four ounces" denotes a very small force, and "one thousand pounds" signifies a very large force. This fighting principle defines the ideal level of efficiency as one in which a fighter supplies only the smallest amount of the force needed to defend successfully against a forceful attack from an opponent.

Efficiency can be maximized by applying the third main principle, "borrowing the opponent's force to defeat his force." In order for a fighter to borrow an opponent's force and conserve his or her own, the fighter must first understand everything about the opponent's force, including its amount, direction, duration, and the timing of its acceleration and deceleration. Only if these attributes are known in detail can a fighter manipulate them to his or her advantage. The ability to assess these attributes depends on the sensitivity a fighter develops through training.

To achieve highly efficient skills, acute sensitivity can be developed through training of the four basic Taiji Quan skills: *zhan* (粘), *nian* (黏), *lian* (连) and *sui* (随). These skills, in turn, depend on the basic abilities to execute relaxed, integrated, stable, nimble, changeable, and lively external movements and to coordinate these movements with what will be referred to throughout this book as the internal components of *shen* (神), *yi* (意), and *qi* (气). Efficiency requires that fighters concentrate shen, focus yi, strengthen qi, and are able readily to change jin.

Of these foundational abilities, relaxation is the first that should be given careful attention in practice. In martial arts, relaxation has a meaning different from the usual meaning in everyday life, where instinctive resistance to a large incoming force typically involves exerting an equal or larger force in the opposite direction. While this instinctive approach may often be effective, it is far from being efficient. Instead of a struggle directly against the incoming force, the correct response in Taiji Quan is to first follow the incoming force and then, at an appropriate moment, skillfully redirect the incoming force using only the smallest amount of force necessary to lure the opponent into emptiness and defeat.

Another major ability that increases the efficiency of skills is *he* (合), or harmony or integration. In internal martial arts, *he* is defined as the combination of *waisanhe* (外三合)—three external integrations—and *neisanhe* (内三合)—three internal integrations. Usually, this combination is referred to as *liuhe* (六合), or six integrations, a term that describes how the internal and external parts of the body can work together to achieve maximum efficiency.

All of these skills are included in both empty-hand training and also in weapons training. If you have already practiced empty-hand Taiji Quan, you will already be familiar with them. After transferring the basic skills from your hands to your weapons, you can apply these skills in combat based on the main Taiji fighting principles. It is important that all the skills you practice and the principles you follow in your Taiji Dao practice derive from traditional Taiji Quan philosophy. If they do not, you will not be practicing Taiji Dao skills, however proficient a martial artist you may be.

Basic Skills of Taiji Quan as Applied to Taiji Dao

Through many years, Taiji Quan has evolved into a unique technical system embodying Taiji principles. Within this system, zhan, nian, lian, and sui are the skills upon which all Taiji Quan techniques are founded. Each of these skills requires that the movements of the practitioner be characterized by relaxation, integration, and sensitivity.

The defining feature of the Taiji Quan approach is the use of minimum force. The skills of zhan, nian, lian, and sui provide ways to express force that are consistent with Taiji principles and are equally applicable to Taiji Quan and Taiji Dao. Taiji Quan and Taiji Dao incorporate the same basic techniques, all of which employ zhan, nian, lian, and sui.

Zhan means sticking to something, usually from above. In fighting, zhan causes your opponent to feel glued to you at the point of contact. If you initiate movement at that point, your opponent will have no choice but to move in the same direction. This will create an unbalanced force in your opponent's body, and, without your having to grip him or her, your opponent's momentum will cause him or her to fall down.

Nian also means to stick or adhere. In this case, your opponent will feel as though you are sticking to him or her and that no matter what he or she does, he or she cannot escape your touch. Whatever movements your opponent makes, you will be able to maintain contact and follow, and, at the same time, continuously give your opponent a little bit of trouble at the contact point.

Lian means to link. When using this skill, no matter what your opponent does, you are able to follow his or her movements as if the two of you were linked together. Like nian, lian requires that you maintain contact with your opponent so that he or she cannot escape, but unlike nian, lian does not require that you give your opponent trouble.

Sui means to follow. With sui, whatever your opponent does, you follow in the same direction. You constantly follow your opponent so that his or her force cannot reach your body and give you trouble. It is as if your opponent's motion causes you to move, but, because you are relaxed, your opponent cannot direct any force into your body, even though you are in contact with him or her.

While these four skills can be theoretically analyzed separately, they are not separable in practice. Flowing seamlessly together, they are the basic elements of all Taiji Quan and Taiji Dao skills.

Internal and External Training of Taiji Dao

Given that Taiji Quan and Taiji Dao are internal martial arts, all of their skills involve not only physical movements but also the internal components. Through training, external movements strengthen internal feelings, and, subsequently, the internal feelings direct the external movements required for the successful application of skills. Finally through training, internal and external processes are integrated, and the practitioner's natural abilities are transformed. Because all skills develop through internal and external training, it is important to understand what these two kinds of training involve and how they proceed.

Internal Training

Practitioners should have a thorough understanding of the internal components if they wish to achieve high-level mastery of Taiji Quan and Taiji Dao. Sometimes these internal components are very difficult to understand because they are not tangible. Most of the time, practitioners must be very attentive in order to recognize them and feel their effects internally. Each component might involve a different kind of internal feeling. Knowledge of these components and the internal feelings they create is important for mastering the Taiji Dao skills that will be described in the remaining chapters.

Shen—Spirit, Attention, or Mentality

Shen (神) is usually translated as spirit, attention, or mentality, but while this definition is reasonable, it does not capture all meanings of the original Chinese word. Very difficult and perhaps impossible to render precisely, shen can be thought of as a subjective feeling that is essentially nonverbal but that can be sensed internally when it occurs. Sometimes, it is expressed through one's gaze and is likened to the stare of an animal ready to spring at its prey. Shen is the internal component that directs or leads all the other internal components in every movement and at all moments of your practice. Yi, qi, jin, and all physical movements follow the direction and flow of your shen.

Generally speaking, shen is the reflection of what is in *xin* (心), the Chinese term for the heart or the innermost component of the self. It cannot be seen directly, but its contents, the thoughts and feelings associated with it, can be manifested outwardly through the eyes. If your eyes reveal only a blank, lethargic, out-of-focus stare, your mental activity will be unsynchronized with your physical activity even though you may be executing an external movement correctly. Your movement will be devoid of spirit. The intensity of your shen has a profound impact on the final quality of your movements. A strong spirit can invigorate you and lend you great strength.

The internal components of yi, qi, and jin flow from shen, so shen is the most important internal component to master in Taiji Quan and Taiji Dao. It is also the most difficult to learn and so is usually the last element to be mastered in practice. When executing a technique, shen should be projected outward. You should strive to enhance and intensify this feeling in your training so that you can gain greater control of it and use it to achieve optimal results.

Yi—Mind

Usually, *yi* (意) is translated as "mind," but more precisely, it refers to the cognitive aspects of the mental process. Yi is the explicit instruction or decision that flows naturally from xin or shen. While feelings are often difficult to specify and fully comprehend, intentions are usually relatively clear and useful for making operational decisions. In the Taiji Quan Classics, many references are made to the functions of yi, including the following examples: "The mind is the commander"; "First in the mind, then in the body"; "*Jin* (trained force) may be broken, but mind is still intact"; "Use mind instead of physical force."

In Taiji Quan and Taiji Dao practice, high-level skill must be matched by a mindset that functions at an equally advanced level and can provide an appropriate starting point for all the action that may follow. If a state of liuhe exists in which all components are linked together flawlessly, any change in mindset, no matter how small, will be instantaneously translated into appropriate and correct physical action. This is how yi, deriving naturally from xin and shen, functions in actual competition or combat.

When something is natural, it is done without any conscious thought. When you perform a physical movement without any conscious thought, you are using your natural mindset of the moment. Because mental activity must be well matched to physical skill in order to achieve an effective and efficient outcome, Taiji Quan and Taiji Dao training must be initially guided by new uses of yi that are consciously directed.

If, for example, you are trying to learn a new technique for dealing with an incoming force at a particular pressure point, Taiji principles require that you direct your yi to a spot where there is no incoming force. This is not the usual or natural response, but by consciously applying your mind to the task and focusing it away from the point of attack, the part of your body that receives the incoming force will be able to follow that force more naturally. After repeating this initially unnatural mental reaction many times in your training, it will become a new natural response of yi.

Only by fulfilling the Taiji principle of using yi instead of physical force can real Taiji Quan skill be developed. If you fail to train yi, you will have no choice but to be led mindlessly by whatever force is imposed upon you.

Qi

This is a familiar term to many people but an especially difficult one to define clearly. *Qi* (气) has been described variously as breath, vital energy, or a special kind of feeling. The existence of qi has not yet been scientifically documented, perhaps because instruments capable of measuring it do not yet exist and because sufficient research has not yet been done. There is, however, considerable anecdotal support suggesting that it is not only a real phenomenon but also a very common one.

Sometimes qi seems to be an objective and real physiological process, while at other times it seems to be more like a spiritual or metaphorical phenomenon. It can move inside the body or be extended through a weapon. Because it is difficult to describe and subtle to feel, and because its traditional definition is not very precise, the concept of qi is often viewed skeptically. Despite general skepticism, martial artists and many others believe qi to exist. They are familiar with methods for feeling, strengthening, and applying qi and have found that although it is invisible, qi can be sensed, controlled, and effectively used.

Common physical indicators of qi during Taiji Quan and Taiji Dao training are warmth, heaviness, and a slight swelling and/or pulsating sensation in your body. As training advances, qi becomes stronger and, similarly, your body will feel stronger and more stable and more nimble. Your breathing will remain regular and relaxed, even after vigorous movements.

For three thousand years, Chinese people have applied qi in many disciplines, especially in medicine where the strong and unimpeded flow of qi and blood throughout every part of the body is thought to be essential for general well-being. Many methods for increasing the intensity and flow of qi have been developed. These methods have been described in detail in the system known as Qigong or Neigong. The practices of Qigong and Taiji Quan produce similar health benefits.

In terms of fighting, qi is a general feeling of physical energy and power. The steady and free movement of qi throughout your body makes all your movements robust and quick. If your qi is strong, your physical force will likewise be strong. Qi's smooth movement downward creates stability; its movement upward creates nimbleness.

The most efficient way to train your qi is to practice the form and to remain relaxed and focused throughout. Your form movements should be correct in every detail, and the form should be practiced daily and with great attentiveness. It is very important to avoid conscious attempts to direct or control your qi. Instead, let it emerge and intensify naturally. Remember that qi flows freely from *yi,* and that, as the Taiji Quan Classics admonish, you should "focus on the mind, not on qi; if the primary focus is on qi, stagnation will result."

One of the most important aspects of qi practice concerns the fields of qi, collectively known as *dantian* (丹田). The three qi fields in your body are upper (higher), middle, and lower. The upper dantian is located inside your head at the vertex of the *baihui* and *xuanguan* points. The middle dantian is inside your abdomen, one third of the way between the *shenque* and *mingmen* points. The lower dantian is at your perineum or *huiyin* point. Usually, when people talk about dantian, they are referring to the middle dantian. Different systems or styles may locate dantian in different places, and this difference will lead to variations in training methods. In all systems, however, qi is considered to be collected, concentrated, developed, and refined in dantian.

Jin—Trained Force

Perhaps more than any other martial arts style, Taiji Quan makes very detailed distinctions between *jin* (劲), or trained force, and *li* (力), or raw physical strength. In Taiji Quan, li refers to the natural force produced from simple muscle activity. Jin, on the other hand, can be acquired only through special training. There are thirty-six variations of jin and two broad categories: external jin and internal jin.

Although all martial arts styles rely on the use of jin, this force provides the basis for an important distinction between the external and internal styles of martial arts practice. External martial arts focus primarily on external jin; internal martial arts use both external and internal jin, but internal jin plays the more critical role in competition or combat.

The two categories of jin differ in terms of how force is generated, how much of it can be produced, and how it is ultimately applied. The two types also have different advantages and disadvantages. In general, external jin generates more force and, so, can cause heavy damage to your adversary, while internal jin is ideally suited for controlling your adversary. In internal martial arts where efficiency is of paramount concern, internal jin is used first to provide control of your opponent, and then external jin is used to bring your attack to a successful conclusion.

Both external and internal jin are more effective and efficient than li, their untrained counterpart. Unlike li, jin requires that all muscles of the body work together to create integrated movements. This feature significantly reduces the amount of work that must be exerted by any one muscle or muscle group. Because jin is expressed by your whole body, it can be released in all directions, whereas li can be released in only the direction dictated by the particular muscle or muscle groups that generate it.

A second, and perhaps more important consequence of the fact that jin uses all the muscles of the body and each to only a minimum degree, is that much greater relaxation can be maintained throughout your body than when only isolated muscles or muscle groups are used and must be exerted to their maximum capability. This fact illustrates the close relationship that exists between your ability to use jin and your ability to relax.

Jin is also directly related to yi. While untrained force derives directly from natural reflexes, jin's development is guided by the newly acquired or new natural reactions that result from specialized yi training.

After li has been transformed to jin through form training, your next task is to learn each of the thirty-six types of jin and how to use them. Students of all martial arts should gain as much knowledge as possible about jin in all its varieties. The most important elements for proficiency in the use of jin are relaxation, timing, direction, yi, and an understanding of yin and yang. A thorough familiarity with jin and all its elements is critical for the development of high-level skill.

Combining the Internal Components—the Three Internal Integrations

The internal components comprise a sequence in which shen leads and is followed in order by yi, qi, and jin. If shen does not lead correctly, yi cannot follow, and the sequence cannot proceed. When yi does follow, shen must move on to the next point as soon as yi arrives. If shen and yi remain at the same point, a state of double-weightedness results.

Following shen, yi, in turn, leads qi. The movement of yi to a point of contact between you and an opponent will cause qi to flow through your body to the contact point. If in fighting or competition, your opponent touches you at two different points, you should focus yi on the lighter of the two touch points in order to avoid becoming double-weighted. If there is only one touch point, as often happens in Taiji Dao fighting, you should imagine a second touch point and direct yi to it. It is important to follow these guidelines even if there is no touch point at all but only a point that is simply thought of as having been touched.

With training, qi will be able to follow yi smoothly and freely throughout your body. When qi moves, jin will follow and can then be released at any point of contact you choose. This release is referred to as *fajin* (发劲).

The order in which the internal components should be learned and mastered is the reverse of the sequence just described. Jin develops first as the movements of the form are learned and perfected. The ability to feel, control, and develop qi increases throughout this process, and as qi intensifies, an awareness of yi arises. Finally, shen emerges and can be used to lead the entire sequence.

When this level of practice has been achieved, you have only to reach out with your shen to accomplish your goal because as soon as your shen is projected to a point, the rest of the sequence will naturally and immediately unfold. Whenever you practice the applications of Taiji Quan or Taiji Dao, you should strive to direct all the internal components to the point identified by your shen. Your ability to extend all the internal components simultaneously to a given point provides a direct measure of your gongfu.

As your training becomes advanced, you will no longer need to pay specific attention to your movements. You can forget them, which means they will have become your new natural movements that can be expressed without conscious effort. At this stage of training, you can limit your focus to shen, yi, qi, and jin. As you continue to advance, you will be able to forget jin and focus your training only on shen, yi, and qi. With concentrated practice, you may be able to forget qi and focus only on shen and yi. Finally, yi can be forgotten. Because movements are the slowest component, followed in descending order by jin, qi, yi, and finally shen, which is the fastest, your skills will increase in speed as you progress through this sequence of forgetting.

Finally, at the highest level of Taiji Quan and Taiji Dao practice, only shen is necessary. There is no need to concentrate on anything else. This does not mean that you do not have to know about or use any of the other components but, rather, that after a sufficient amount of repetition, you will be able to correctly and automatically do whatever is required at any time without consciously directing the process. At the highest level, you will need to concern yourself only with the movement of shen; everything else will follow naturally. All your responses will be fully consistent with the principles of Taiji Quan, and you will have achieved the highest level of mastery.

External Training

While the emphasis in internal martial arts is on internal training, external training must also be included. Correct external training promotes the development of strong internal feelings, while incorrect external training impedes this process. External training in Taiji Quan practice is different from such training in other martial arts because Taiji Quan is based on a particular set of philosophical principles, and, despite some superficial similarities to external martial arts styles, its techniques are also different. This section presents descriptions of some of the most important external training concepts used in Taiji Quan. All of them also apply to Taiji Dao training.

Relaxation

Song (松), or relaxation, is one of the most important foundational abilities in Taiji Quan. Maintaining a state of physical relaxation does not require that you avoid the use of all force but only extra or unnecessary force. The goal of relaxation is to use the minimum force needed to accomplish your purpose. Relaxation increases not only the efficiency of all actions but also the smooth flow of qi throughout your body. Relaxation can indirectly increase stability by allowing qi to move freely downward and similarly increase nimbleness by allowing qi and *jingshen* (mind and spirit) to move freely upward.

In competition or fighting, relaxation increases the chance of escape from your opponent's control. It allows you to conserve energy and release more powerful force. It also increases the comfort of all body positions. Relaxation is the first ability that must be understood and perfected if you hope to master Taiji Quan and Taiji Dao.

Relaxation is much easier to describe than to achieve. It is difficult to acquire partly because so much attention and effort must be directed to learning how to use the physical movements and four internal components of the Taiji Quan form. In the form, relaxation results from the ability to sense and expend only the amount of physical energy necessary to move correctly from one posture to the next. In push-hands practice, relaxation requires that you forget or ignore the point of contact with your opponent. The ability to use minimum force and the ability to ignore the touch point of your opponent's attack are difficult to learn because neither is a natural response. In fact, habits and past training in other physical disciplines tend to promote the opposite response, the use of as much force as possible. Consistent reinforcement through thoughtful training is necessary to overcome this habitual reaction.

Smoothness of Movement

The quality of smoothness has two important aspects. First, all movements must follow an arc or curve. This characteristic is called *yuan* (圆)—circling. Curvilinear movements not only increase relaxation, flexibility, and changeability but also strengthen and set in motion the flow of qi.

The second aspect of smoothness, called *yun* (匀), or evenness, requires that all movements be performed at a steady, even pace. Even more important than maintaining the continuity of movements, however, is the maintenance of an uninterrupted flow of shen, yi, and qi. This is especially important in Taiji Dao practice because some sword skills contain pauses between movements. These apparent breaks in the flow of external movement are not a problem if the internal components of shen, yi, and qi remain uninterrupted. As the Taiji Quan Classics instruct: "Do not make movements that are interrupted, broken, or uneven. If the movements are broken, do not allow yi to be interrupted. If the yi is interrupted, then use shen to provide continuity." Adherence to this instruction when practicing Taiji Quan or Taiji Dao will afford many benefits, including a strengthening of your shen, yi, and qi.

Nimbleness and Liveliness of Movement

A famous Taiji Quan prescription for *qingling huobo* (轻灵活泼), or nimbleness, advises the practitioner to "move like a great river." Nimble movements flow seamlessly throughout the body with currents that can quickly change speed and direction. Other Taiji Quan precepts instruct that "whenever a body moves through space, there is no part of that body that does not also move"; one should "walk like a cat"; and one must "suddenly appear and suddenly disappear."

Nimble and lively movements are light, agile, and quick. They may be so large that your opponent cannot follow them or so small that your opponent cannot sense them. Whatever the case, nimbleness and liveliness will allow you to follow and control the movements of your opponent and confound his or her attempts to follow or control your movements. Nimbleness and liveliness make it possible for qi to move with agility, and this, in turn, ensures that all movements will embody the principle of sudden appearance and disappearance, a quality that is especially important in combat. If qi is nimble, jin will be nimble, and if jin is nimble, your movements will also be nimble.

If you achieve overall nimbleness, your opponent will be easily confused by the apparent suddenness with which your qi and jin seem to appear and disappear. This will make it difficult for your opponent to keep his or her qi and jin unbroken and shen and yi quiet and focused.

To practice nimbleness and liveliness, imagine at all times that the baihui point on the top center of your head is suspended from above. This feeling will keep your mind calm and your qi moving actively throughout your body.

Stability

According to principle, a Taiji Quan practitioner should "be as still as a mountain." This quality of stability, called *wen* (稳), requires that your body be upright and comfortable so that it can withstand force from any of the eight directions. (In Chinese, "eight directions" refers to all directions around you.) A related precept advises against leaning in any direction.

Stability requires that your body remain centered, a condition referred to as *zhongding* (中定), or neutralization. In push hands or fighting, it is impossible to maintain balance if you lose your center. Maintaining stability does not require that you stop moving but rather that you remain stable while in motion. If you achieve stability and your movements are correct, your qi will sink down to dantian and you will feel as though your feet extend deeply into the ground like the roots of a tree.

Just as yin always contains yang and yang always contains yin, stability always includes a sense of nimbleness and nimbleness always includes a feeling of stability. Because most of the movements of Taiji Dao skills are larger than those comprising empty-hand Taiji Quan skills, stability will be more difficult to achieve and maintain in Taiji Dao.

Emptiness

Kong (空), or emptiness, is the highest-level skill in Taiji Quan, and always increases nimbleness and power. In solo practice, kong is usually felt as a drawing back of your body that creates a sense that something solid has disappeared and left a vacuum in its place. This feeling of emptiness will cause other parts of your body to extend or expand. In "empty chest" *(kongxiong),* for example, as you draw your chest back, your back and arms should expand and extend.

In fighting, kong will create an uncomfortably odd feeling in your opponent, as though something strange has suddenly happened to him or her. Your opponent will feel confused and unsure of his or her response. Your opponent's yi will lose continuity, his or her heart may pound and movements will become stiff and awkward. Overall, your opponent will feel as though he or she has just stepped on a deadfall trap and fallen through. This sensation is called "stepping on an empty place."

To use kong effectively, you should lure your opponent into the belief that he or she can touch and control you and defeat you easily. Timing and direction are the critical factors for the successful application of the kong skill.

When your opponent commits to a movement, your kong will create the sensation in him or her that there really is no contact between the two of you. This will cause a break in your opponent's qi, yi, and shen. Your opponent's body will stiffen, and he or she will lose balance. This moment provides you with your best opportunity to redirect your opponent's incoming force and turn it back against him or her. This use of kong is called *yin jin luo kong* (引进落空), or "lure into emptiness."

External Integrations or Harmony

He (合) refers to integration or harmony and means that all parts of your body are working together. External integration refers to the integration or coordination of your physical movements and to their harmoniousness. *He* conserves energy and thereby allows you to maintain a relaxed and powerful internal trained force.

To fulfill the requirement of high efficiency, all Taiji Quan skills must involve coordination of the whole body, and unnecessary force must be avoided. Each muscle should exert only a small amount of force, and all the muscles should share in generating the overall effort. With all the muscles working together, relaxation is possible, and each movement becomes more forceful. Clearly, the force that can be exerted when the muscles throughout your body work together is greater than the force that can be generated when the muscles of only one part of your body are used.

In the skills of everyday life, this precept generally receives little, if any, attention, especially when only small amounts of force are needed to achieve a particular purpose. When, for example, you take a drink of water, you do not generally use as little force as possible to lift the glass, place it under the faucet, and tip the rim to your lips. Usually, you perform the entire action sequence without much, if any, conscious thought and use only a small group of muscles, in this case, the muscles of your arm and hand. A Taiji Quan practitioner, however, should be keenly aware of each movement and of the minimum amount of force that is needed to accomplish each action. He or she should coordinate all the muscles of the body so that the force for the action sequence is generated by small exertions of every muscle rather than by larger exertions of only the muscles of the arm and hand.

As in Taiji Quan practice, Taiji Dao mastery requires complete coordination of all the muscles throughout your body. Led by your mind, the movements of your Taiji *dao* must also be integrated with the movements of your whole body.

Joints separate many parts of your body from one another, and the most movable body parts are your arms and legs. If your arms and legs are integrated, the other less mobile parts of your body will naturally follow the movements of your limbs, and greater overall coordination will be possible. To take advantage of this fact, training for external integration focuses on your arms and legs.

The three-external-integrations method is the traditional system used to train external integration. The three integrations, each of which can be practiced in many different ways, are shoulder and hip integration; elbow and knee integration; and hand and foot integration. One common way to practice these integrations is to use your mind to lead the coordination between one arm and the opposing leg. Although, in training the three external integrations are practiced in individual arm-leg pairings, the final goal is to achieve simultaneous and natural integration throughout your body.

Internal and External Integration—Six Integrations

To achieve integration, you should practice *liuhe* (六合), or the six integrations. Through the practice of liuhe, which involves careful attention to acupuncture points, your movements will become relaxed, smooth, coordinated and complete and will more fully reflect shen, yi, qi, and jin. The integration of all the Taiji Quan components will make your responses consistent from one situation to the next.

In traditional martial arts, all parts of the physical body are considered to be outside, or external; whereas shen, yi, qi, and jin are considered to be inside, or internal. The six integrations include the three external integrations of shoulder-to-hip, elbow-to-knee, and hand-to-foot; and the three internal integrations of shen-to-yi, yi-to-qi, and qi-to-jin. In practicing Taiji Quan, the sequence of internal integrations is as follows: shen should lead or direct yi, yi should lead qi, and qi should lead jin. Ultimately, jin should lead your movements. Through the proper practice of this sequence, your movements will come to reflect fully all the internal components.

To ensure that this sequence is followed, you must be very attentive during your practice. At every point in the form, you should know where to direct your shen, yi, qi, and jin and how to position your body. You should also be able to assess your degree of relaxation. Because this kind of knowledge does not come naturally to most people, it must be practiced with thoughtfulness and dedication.

Integration in empty-hand practice should be achieved before you begin your practice of Taiji Dao because Taiji Dao training includes the added task of integrating an external object, the sword, into the sequence of internal and external components. Your sword must come to feel like a natural extension of your arm, and your sword's movements must become integrated with all the movements of your body. This process of extending integration to include your sword requires that your shen be enlarged, your yi become stronger, your qi move with greater smoothness, your jin grow more powerful and reach farther, and your movements become quicker, more nimble and stable, more easily changed, and more relaxed.

Only when your shen and sword have become fully integrated will you be able to attain high-level sword skills. Integration training is much more difficult to accomplish than it is to describe. It depends not only on concentrated practice but also on deep thought about the fundamental principles of Taiji. It requires alertness to every detail until all your movements can be executed with such ease that they seem to be flowing naturally from the feelings in your heart. It is said that during training, the performance of correct external physical movements leads the acquisition of correct internal feelings but that during fighting, the external movements are, themselves, led by the internal feelings developed through practice.

Features of Taiji Dao Skills

Although all the features of regular Dao are inherited by Taiji Dao, Taiji Dao skills are different from those of regular Dao in two special ways. Some skills are specialized because they depend on the unique shape of the Taiji *dao*. All are special in that they embody Taiji Quan principles.

Taiji Dao Includes All Basic Sword Skills

Although there are many *dao* skills, this type of sword is used mainly for chops. Other common *dao* skills, such as *shan* (煽), *kan* (砍), *pi* (劈), *duo* (剁), *jie* (截), *dai* (带), *liao* (撩), *mo* (抹), and *zha* (扎), all of which are described in detail in Chapter Four, are foundational skills practiced in all styles, including Taiji Dao. Because Taiji Dao skills incorporate Taiji Quan principles, however, these skills tend to be lighter and more changeable than the powerful skills used in styles that involve direct collisions between weapons.

The Taiji Dao Shape Determines the Basic Taiji Dao Skills

The shape of a Taiji *dao* is generally narrower and longer than that of a regular single sword and consequently, a Taiji *dao* is not well suited to forceful and simple skills, like powerful chops. Instead, it is effective for the development and application of more refined skills, like soft parries or slides. The emphasis on these techniques encourages Taiji Dao practitioners to focus their practice on high-level skills.

The special design of the Taiji Dao guard and ring allow for additional specialized uses of Taiji *dao*. These features increase the flexibility and changeability of Taiji Dao sword skills.

The Long Handle of the Taiji Dao Allows for One- or Two-Handed Skills

Swords with short and light handles promote skills that are quick, nimble, and changeable; those designed to be held with two hands are longer and heavier and promote the use of more powerful skills. The Taiji *dao* allows for both kinds of skills because both one- and two-handed grips are possible.

Usually, a Taiji *dao* is held with only one hand and the second hand is used only when necessary. The option of holding the sword with one or two hands makes possible many specialized Taiji Dao skills. The ring at the end of the Taiji *dao* handle, for example, allows for unique two-handed variations of several Taiji Dao skills. Chapter Six presents a detailed discussion of two-handed Taiji Dao skills, including those using the end ring.

Because the Taiji *Dao* Is Used in Taiji Quan Groups, All Taiji Dao Skills Must Follow Taiji Quan Principles

Taiji Quan seeks the most highly efficient skills, and, consequently, its principles and practices are very different from those of other martial arts styles. Taiji Dao and Taiji Quan practitioners use special training methods to modify or change their original abilities and master special techniques in order to reach the goal of maximum efficiency set forth by Taiji Quan principles.

The Main Skills of Taiji Dao Are Designed for Defense against Spear Attacks

The spear is the most dangerous weapon in martial arts practice. Its great length and maneuverability make the task of defending against spear attacks very difficult. For this reason, most Taiji Dao skills are designed to defend against the spear. Although, theoretically, a swordsman will be at a considerable disadvantage when facing an opponent armed with a spear, long and careful practice and a deep understanding of Taiji principles will increase the swordsman's chance to win.

Practicing Taiji Dao

Taiji Dao practice begins by learning how to manipulate your sword and how to perform the movements of the Taiji Dao form. Gradually, this training promotes the development of internal feelings and as correct internal feelings grow stronger, they begin to lead the physical movements. This cycle brings many benefits.

The Basic Training Sequence

Before learning the Taiji Dao form, you should thoroughly and diligently practice the empty-hand Taiji Quan form. This training will deepen your understanding of essential Taiji Quan principles and will strengthen your basic abilities. Given that eventually your sword should function as an extension of your arm, the ability to use your arm well in empty-hand practice is a prerequisite for effective manipulation of a sword.

To understand real Taiji Dao fighting skills, you need to practice Taiji Quan push hands, and you must always bear in mind that Taiji Dao skills follow Taiji

Quan principles. Push-hands practice is critical for deepening your understanding of Taiji Quan. Without push-hands practice, it is impossible to master Taiji Quan skills, and without Taiji Quan skills, mastery of Taiji Dao skills will be similarly impossible.

Before learning the Taiji Dao form, you should practice some basic Taiji Dao skills. You should, for example, understand how to hold and manipulate your sword comfortably and adeptly. There are some simple and basic techniques that can help you develop this ability and increase your sword control. As you acquire sword-handling skills, you will be able to execute ever more detailed skills, and your form practice will become more enjoyable.

Basic skill practice is always the first step in Taiji Dao practice. You should perfect ways to hold your sword and change grips quickly and comfortably so that you can correctly perform the many different sword movements that comprise Taiji Dao practice. You should be able to hold your sword very flexibly so that its angle and thrust, especially at the edges, can be deftly changed. An understanding of the application of a single skill can be very helpful at this point in your training.

In your study of Taiji Dao form, you should first learn each movement of the form in great detail. The ability to perform the movements correctly is basic to the development of all the other skills. It is usually best to practice the form many times from beginning to end at increasing levels of detail. After you have learned the basic movements, you should focus your attention on footwork and stances and then on controlling the range, direction, and level of your movements.

When your movements are correct and can be performed smoothly, you should turn your attention to the training of the internal components of shen, yi, and qi. Through this training, your movements will increasingly reflect your internal feelings. Fighting skills can be introduced into your practice at this point. They will increase your awareness of your internal feelings.

This phase of your training requires a lot of time and discipline. Do not rush or become impatient. Practice regularly and with devotion, and take one step at a time. It is not wise, and can even be dangerous, to seek shortcuts. There are none to be found, and the futile search for shortcuts will distract you and make it much more difficult for you ever to achieve high-level expertise.

When you can perform the form well, you should focus on one section of the form and research the applications of each skill in that portion. You will need a partner to help you in this phase of your training. Your partner, playing the role of your opponent, should use different kinds of weapons to attack you in different ways so that you can learn to use your Taiji Dao skills to defend against a wide variety of attacks. You will need to pay great attention to the angles, directions, and timing of the movements of both your sword and your opponent's weapon.

The two-person stage of your training must extend for a long period of time in order for you truly to understand Taiji Dao skills. Throughout your training, always remember that your ultimate goal is not to master and apply individual skills but to understand high-level Taiji Dao practice and principles. As with Taiji Quan practice, your deepening understanding of Taiji Dao will foster new abilities and a growing sense of naturalness and ease in all your movements. At this stage, you will no longer need to focus on any particular skill but will be able to achieve any desired outcome in a completely spontaneous and natural way.

Finally, always maintain your study of Taiji and Taiji Quan principles. These provide the essential foundation for Taiji Dao skills, and if you do not understand them, high-level mastery will be unattainable.

The Benefits of Practice

If you are a Taiji Quan enthusiast seeking to improve your practice, you should begin your study of weapons as soon as your empty-hand form practice has reached a satisfactory level. Weapons practice will always enhance your understanding and abilities.

Usually, a short weapon should be learned first. Although both Taiji *dao* and Taiji jian belong to the short weapon category, there are significant differences in the forms and practices associated with each of these two Taiji swords. The movements of the Taiji Dao form, for example, are generally more nimble and flexible than those of the Taiji Jian form. As a consequence, Taiji Dao practice is especially helpful for developing the qualities of nimbleness and flexibility. Compared to Taiji Jian, Taiji Dao practice also involves more exclusive attention to fighting skills and so can be of particular benefit in developing these skills.

These comparisons are drawn only to indicate some of the notable benefits of Taiji Dao practice and not to suggest that Taiji Jian practice does not have unique benefits of its own. The practice of both Taiji Dao and Taiji Jian have the obvious advantages of promoting your internal training, health, and character as well as improving your understanding of Taiji Quan tenets and Taoist philosophy.

First among the many benefits of Taiji Dao practice is a more profound understanding of the principles and practices of Taiji Quan. This benefit derives from the fact that Taiji Dao skill is more complex than empty-hand Taiji Quan skill. The increased number of touch points and the continuously changing nature of yin and yang in Taiji Dao practice contribute to its greater complexity. It is this complexity that can augment your knowledge of Taiji principles.

In Taiji Quan push hands, there are usually two or more touch points that can be used by you and your opponent. Yin and yang can be separately associated with each of the points, and changes in yin and yang can be clearly distinguished. In Taiji Dao fighting, however, there is typically only one touch point between you and your opponent, and both yin and yang center on this singular point. In this situation, there are two ways to create balance. One is to use your empty hand and your mind to create a second touch point so that yin and yang can be separately associated with the actual and imagined touch points. Creating the second touch point and distributing yin and yang correctly requires and promotes a sound understanding of Taiji Quan principles.

The second way to create balance is to separate yin and yang at the actual touch point. Because even a tiny touch point occupies a finite area, it is always possible to separate yin and yang at that point. It is not easy to develop the ability to distinguish between yin and yang under such a circumstance. Taiji Dao practice can enhance the acute sensitivity and attention to detail that promote this development and, by so doing, can be of great benefit in fostering a more nuanced understanding of Taiji principles.

A second benefit of Taiji Dao practice is an increase in internal feeling. In studying the fundamentals of Taiji Quan, you will have acquired some internal feeling, but your practice of Taiji Dao will strengthen all the internal components. Because Taiji Dao movements have greater range, speed, suddenness, variation of rhythm, and energy extension than the movements of the empty-hand Taiji Quan form, Taiji Dao training will make your jin more changeable. Your qi will become smoother in its flow and farther in its reach. Also, the circles of your yi will grow larger, and your shen will be projected out to a greater distance. All of these alterations will not only refine your fighting skills but also directly enhance Qigong practice designed to promote and maintain good health. When your internal components are intensified, your spirit and concentration will increase and your mastery of details will be greatly improved.

A third benefit of Taiji Dao practice is an increase in the coordination and integration of your physical movements. Because the movements of the sword form are more difficult than those of the empty-hand form, Taiji Dao practice can facilitate correct timing in all your movements. The necessity of holding and manipulating a sword will also lead to improvements in the complexity of your hand skills and stepping skills.

Although you may feel somewhat awkward and uncomfortable at the outset of your Taiji Dao training, the challenges of Taiji Dao practice will gradually lead to a marked improvement in your skills and in the coordination of your movements. Improvement in your physical movements will yield clear and quite rapid increases in the strength of your shen, yi, qi, and jin. Through Taiji Dao training, the integration of external and internal components will also improve, and your sword will come to feel more and more like a natural extension of your arm.

Fourthly, Taiji Dao practice yields special benefits for your legs and waist. Many central features of Taiji Dao training, like footwork and the larger range of motion required, are more difficult to master than similar elements in the empty-hand form. Taiji Dao's more demanding set of challenges will encourage you to exert greater focus and effort in your training and will lead to significant improvements in your overall skill level.

The fifth benefit of Taiji Dao practice is an improvement in stability and nimbleness. While the Taiji Quan empty-hand form is very effective for improving stability of motion, it does not typically lead to equally great increases in nimbleness. Taiji Dao practice, in contrast, requires many complex step changes and intensive training of the internal components. These demands make Taiji Dao practice more effective than the empty-hand form for promoting liveliness of movement.

Finally, the fighting skills in Taiji Dao practice will improve your mental training. Historically, martial arts practice was always carried out with the knowledge that death might await the practitioner in any fight. A swordsman would understand keenly the difficult and dangerous situation faced when confronting a spear master, and the question of how to succeed against such an experienced adversary would be foremost in the swordsman's mind. This is the spirit in which you should conduct your Taiji Dao practice.

You must be able to focus your shen intensely in order to take advantage of any opportunity your opponent gives you. Your mind must remain calm so that you can make correct decisions. When you face danger, you must be focused but not nervous, patient but not hesitant, brave but not careless, and steady but not flustered. All of these qualities rely on a strong mind and a state of psychological balance. Both of these crucial characteristics can be gained through the diligent practice of Taiji Dao.

Chapter Three

The Foundation Movements of Taiji Dao

Foundation movements are the basis of all skills and they must be thoroughly learned before skill training can be effective. The ability to execute foundation movements correctly is essential for success in competitions or combat.

How to Hold Taiji *Dao*

The first step in Taiji Dao training is to learn how to hold your sword properly. In this section, the different types of hand positions and grips will be described. Because these positions and grips have a direct influence on the effective application of skills, you must be very familiar with the relationship between your sword and your hand. You should be able to change the various grips and sword positions smoothly and easily at any time so that your sword moves as though it were a natural extension of your arm.

Here, we introduce several common methods for holding your sword, all of which can be varied in many ways. Because most applications involve combinations of these single methods, your grip and hand positions should be flexible and changeable in a lively, fluid way so that you can take advantage of the variations that such combinations allow. Many of these combinations will be described in Chapter Four.

Types of Grips

Wodao (握刀)—grip sword: *Wodao* refers to any method for gripping your sword. It defines the relationship between your sword and your sword hand. Throughout this book, it is assumed that you are right-handed and that you will use your right hand to hold your sword for major skills. In most cases, the descriptions provided here can be quite easily adapted for use by left-handed practitioners.

Zhengwo (正握)—standard grip or blade-forward grip: In zhengwo, the tiger mouth, which is the area between the thumb and index finger of the sword hand, faces the tip of the blade. This is the most common grip for holding the sword in the dominant hand, i.e., the right hand for right-handed practitioners and the left for left-handed practitioners. In the zhengwo grip, there are two methods for holding the sword: *quanwo* and *banwo*.

Quanwo (全握)—full grip: Quanwo is a full grip in which the four fingers grip upward from the lower side of the handle and the thumb grips downward from the upper side of the handle. The thumb should extend over the index finger (fig. 3-1-1).

Fig. 3-1-1

Banwo (半握)—half grip: Banwo is a half grip or loosened grip. Starting from a quanwo grip, banwo involves loosening the control of the thumb and relaxing the index and middle fingers so that the sword drops down and forward (fig. 3-1-2).

Fig. 3-1-2

Alternatively, after loosening the control exerted by the thumb, banwo can be achieved by relaxing the ring and little fingers to allow the tip of the sword to move up and back in a vertical circle (fig. 3-1-3).

Fig. 3-1-3

Fanwo (反握)—reverse grip: In fanwo, the tiger mouth of the sword hand faces the ring at the end of the sword's handle. This is the most common grip when the sword is held in the nondominant hand. In fanwo, as with zhengwo, there are full-grip and half-grip methods for holding the sword.

Fan quanwo (反全握)—reverse full grip: Fan quanwo is a full grip in which the index finger rests on the side of the handle that extends below the sharp edge of the blade, while the middle, ring, and little fingers grip the side of the handle that extends from the blunt back edge of the sword. The thumb is placed on the upper part of the sword guard, and the ring and little fingers touch the side of the guard (fig. 3-1-4).

Fig. 3-1-4

Fan banwo (反半握)—reverse half grip: Fan banwo is a half or loosened grip. Starting from a fan quanwo position, the index finger is loosened and placed alongside the other fingers. The thumb remains on the upper part of the guard, while the middle, ring and little fingers grip the edge of the guard on the lower side of the sword (figs. 3-1-5a, b).

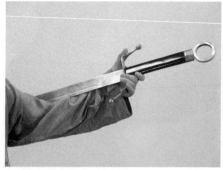

Fig. 3-1-5a

Fig. 3-1-5b

Hand Positions

When the sword is held, the relationship of the hand, body, and sword is called *bawei* (把位), or hand position.

Here, we introduce eleven of the most common variations of hand position for a zhengwo grip.

• *Zhengba* (正把): In this hand position, the sharp edge of the sword faces down (fig. 3-1-6) or forward (fig. 3-1-7). The zhengba position is the most natural and comfortable position for holding a sword.

Fig. 3-1-6

Fig. 3-1-7

- *Fanba* (反把): Fanba is the opposite of the zhengba position. Here, the sharp edge of the sword faces up (fig. 3-1-8) or inward (fig. 3-1-9), and the arm and wrist of the practitioner are turned so that the palm of the sword hand faces the opposite direction from that in zhengba.

Fig. 3-1-8

Fig. 3-1-9

- *Yinba* (阴把): In this hand position, the palm of the sword hand faces up (fig. 3-1-10). In Taiji Quan, an upward-facing or inward-facing palm is called "yin palm." It should generate soft power.

Fig. 3-1-10

- *Yangba* (阳把): In this hand position, the palm of the sword hand faces down (fig. 3-1-11). In Taiji Quan, a downward-facing or outward-facing palm is called "yang palm." It should generate hard power.

Fig. 3-1-11

- *Neiba* (内把): In this hand position, the palm of the sword hand faces your body (fig. 3-1-12). *Nei* means inward, internal, or inside.

Fig. 3-1-12

- *Waiba* (外把): In this hand position, the palm of the sword hand faces away from your body (fig. 3-1-13). *Wai* means outward, external, or outside.

Fig. 3-1-13

- *Shangba* (上把): In this hand position, the sword is raised above chest level (fig. 3-1-14). *Shang* means higher or upper.

Fig. 3-1-14

- *Xiaba* (下把): In this hand position, the sword is held below chest level (fig. 3-1-15). *Xia* means lower or down.

Fig. 3-1-15

- *Heba* (合把): This hand position involves gripping the handle of the sword with both hands (fig. 3-1-16). *He* means to unite or combine together.

Fig. 3-1-16

- *Zhengti* (正提): In this hand position, the tip of the sword points to the ground, and the sharp edge faces the body (fig. 3-1-17). *Ti* means to hold something up.

Fig. 3-1-17

- *Fanti* (反提): In this hand position, the tip of the sword points to the ground, sharp edge facing away from the body. There are two variations of fanti.

- *Zhengshou fanti* (正手反提): In this hand position, the palm of the sword hand is rotated inward and faces outward (fig. 3-1-18).

Fig. 3-1-18

- *Fanshou fanti* (翻手反提): In this hand position, the palm of the sword hand is rotated outward and faces outward (fig. 3-1-19).

Fig. 3-1-19

In a fanwo grip, the back of the sword usually remains in contact with the arm of the sword hand. This contact limits the number of fanwo variations that are possible.

- *Yinba* (阴把): In this hand position, the palm of the sword hand faces upward (fig. 3-1-20).

Fig. 3-1-20

- *Yangba* (阳把): In this hand position, the palm of the sword hand faces slightly downward. The downward turn of the palm must be carefully limited to prevent the sharp edge of the sword from cutting your arm as you rotate your sword hand (fig. 3-1-21).

Fig. 3-1-21

- *Neiba* (内把): In this hand position, the palm of the sword hand faces the body (fig. 3-1-22).

Fig. 3-1-22

- *Waiba* (外把): In this hand position, the palm of the sword hand faces away from the body. The turn of the palm must be very limited when the arm is rotated outward (fig. 3-1-23) and is not possible at all when the arm is rotated inward.

Fig. 3-1-23

- *Shangba* (上把): In this hand position, the sword is raised above chest level (fig. 3-1-24).

Fig. 3-1-24

- *Xiaba* (下把): In this hand position, the sword is held below chest level (fig. 3-1-25).

Fig. 3-1-25

- *Heba* (合把): In this hand position, both hands grip the handle of the sword, one hand from above and the other from below (fig. 3-1-26).

Fig. 3-1-26

All of the many zhengwo and fanwo variations are foundational. In actual practice, most techniques may require combining two or more of these basic grips.

Fanshou Dao (反手刀)
—Sword-Practice Method Using Reverse-Hand Grip

Fanshou dao is a special, rarely used Taiji Dao practice method in which the sword is held with a type of grip called *fanshou*. *Fan* means reverse and *shou* means hand and, taken together, fanshou, sometimes called fanwo, means to grip the sword with your hand in a position that is the reverse of the position used for the regular zhengwo grip. The term *fanshou dao* refers to the sword skills and practice method in which the sword is held in the reverse-hand grip.

Either hand can be used in *fanshou dao* practice. The tiger mouth of your sword hand should face the ring of the sword, and the root of your palm should make firm contact with the sword guard. The blade of the sword in *fanshou dao* extends from the pinky end of your hand rather than from the thumb end as it does in the zhengwo grip. The blunt back edge of the sword is positioned close to the outside of your forearm so that the edge of the sword faces outward.

Fanshou is usually a full grip in which your four fingers grip downward from the lower side, or front edge, of the handle and your thumb grips upward from the upper side of the handle and extends over your index finger (fig. 3-1-27). This arrangement of fingers and thumb is the same as that in the zhengwo grip.

Fig. 3-1-27

When holding the sword in this way, your wrist should be flexible so that the blade can be manipulated quickly and smoothly. Most of the time the back of the blade should touch your elbow. This contact increases your ability to control the sword and adds power to the sword's movements (fig. 3-1-28). When the sword is used for *fanshou dao* practice, the tip and edge can be used for close distance fighting (fig. 3-1-29) or, in a high position, for frequently used thrust skills (fig. 3-1-30).

| Fig. 3-1-28 | Fig. 3-1-29 | Fig. 3-1-30 |

Although not commonplace in Taiji Dao, *fanshou dao* is a more central focus of training in several other schools of sword practice. Some groups have developed forms specifically to practice the special skills that this method makes possible. *Fanshou dao* skills are not included in the Taiji Dao form described in this book, but they are not complex. They can be practiced in your individual training if you want to use them should the opportunity ever arise.

Empty-Hand Shape

As has been described, Taiji *dao* can be held with either one or two hands. In the former case, the empty hand can be used for many other purposes. For this reason, it is very important to develop empty-hand skills. The shapes that can be formed by the palm and fingers of the empty hand in relation to the wrist and arm comprise the foundation for empty-hand skills.

Shouxing (手形)—**Hand Shapes**

Li zhang (立掌)—standing palm: In this hand shape, the wrist of the empty hand is bent upward so that the lower edge of the palm faces forward. The four fingers are held close together and point straight up, and the thumb is bent inward toward the center of the palm. The edge of the palm near the wrist should feel as though it is being stretched downward or "sitting down," while the four fingers should feel as though they are being stretched upward or "standing up" in the opposite direction (fig. 3-2-1).

Fig. 3-2-1

Ping zhang (平掌)—flat palm: This hand shape is formed by holding the four fingers and thumb close together and pointing them straight ahead with an open flat palm (fig. 3-2-2).

Fig. 3-2-2

Waleng zhang (瓦楞掌)—tile palm: In this hand shape, the four fingers are slightly separated and allowed to bend naturally. The tiger mouth is open and rounded (fig. 3-2-3).

Fig. 3-2-3

Gou (勾)—hook: This hand shape is formed when the thumb touches the first joint of the index finger and the other fingers bend toward the center of the palm. In forming a hook, the fingers can point either down (fig. 3-2-4) or up (fig. 3-2-5).

Fig. 3-2-4   Fig. 3-2-5

Quan (拳)—fist: This hand shape is formed when the four fingers are bent inward toward the palm until the tips of the fingers touch the palm. The thumb should be placed on top of the index and middle fingers. In Taiji Quan, the center of a fist always remains empty, meaning that even though the tips of the four fingers touch the palm, the fingers should not be squeezed tightly inward. Space should be left between the pads of the fingers and the palm as though an invisible object like a pen were inserted through the center of the fist (fig. 3-2-6).

Fig. 3-2-6

Wo biao zhang (握镖掌)—holding-*biao* palm: Originally, the term *biao* referred to a metal bar that was part of a chariot horse's mouthpiece. Early records suggest that it might have been common practice for chariot drivers to remove this bar from a horse's mouthpiece so that it could be used to ward off robbery attempts. Since the bar could be thrown at an attacker, it was called *fei biao* (飞镖) or "flying biao." Over time, the term *biao* has come to mean a hidden weapon.

Since *dao* is a short weapon that can be wielded with one hand, a fighter frequently uses another weapon in conjunction with his or her *dao*. In the army, *dao* are most popularly used with shields, but in martial arts groups, many different weapons can be used in combination with *dao*. Biao, or any of a variety of other hidden weapons, are a common choice. Usually, these weapons are very small and can be hidden somewhere on your body, often in a small pouch hanging close to your side where your opponent cannot readily see them.

There are many types of biao. Five that are used very commonly are: *fei biao* (飞镖), or flying dart, which is shaped like a spear head; *fei dao* (飞刀), or flying dagger or flying knife; *jin qian biao* (金钱镖), or golden coin dart; *shi hui bao* (石灰包), or lime powder packet; and *fei huang shi* (飞蝗石), or flying locust rock, which is actually a collection of small rocks. The physical and flight characteristics of different kinds of biao require different types of throwing methods and different palm shapes. In Taiji Dao practice, fei biao and jin qian biao are the most commonly used hidden weapons. Figure 3-2-7 illustrates how to hold a flying dart, and figure 3-2-8 shows how to hold a flying dagger.

Fig. 3-2-7

Fig. 3-2-8

In ancient China, coins were produced in many different shapes. Eventually, the dominant shape became a round coin with a square hole in the center. Coin size varied from one to one and a half inches. Figure 3-2-9 illustrates how a golden coin dart should be held, and figure 3-2-10 shows two coins used to make these darts. The edges of golden coin darts were sharpened to cause injury on impact.

Fig. 3-2-9

Fig. 3-2-10

Stance

A stance refers to the static posture of legs and feet. To execute a skill properly, the stance must be stable, and the practitioner's movements must be nimble. Stability is achieved by stance practice, and nimbleness depends on stepping ability. Because a step always begins and ends with a stance, the quality of one's stances will directly affect stepping ability. In this section, some of the basic stances used in Taiji Dao practice will be described. In Chinese martial arts, all stances are referred to as *buxing*.

All Taiji Dao stances are based on the Taiji Quan empty-hand form, and the descriptions of their sizes follow standard methods of measurement. Despite standard measurement, stance length, or the distance between the feet, can vary for a given stance. The stances used in form practice, for example, are often longer than standard specifications require. These longer stances lower the postures and thereby strengthen the body and present more of a challenge during the learning process. In real fighting situations, however, stances are usually shorter than those recommended by the standard specifications, and postures are correspondingly higher in order to increase nimbleness.

Buxing (步形)—stance: In all stances, the legs and feet remain static. Different stances are needed to create a comfortable position when using different skills. Every stance must allow for stability, nimbleness, and the ability to make quick changes while also generating power and promoting the smooth flow of energy throughout the body.

Several basic Taiji Dao stances are not included in Taiji Dao form practice. These stances should be practiced individually or in combination with sword skills practice.

Bingbu (并步)—feet-together stance: In *bingbu*, or feet-together stance, the feet are close to one another and parallel, and the weight of the body is evenly distributed between the legs. In this stance, the feet are said to be "closed." Despite the equal weight distribution, your mind should be focused on only one leg at a time to prevent "double-weightedness." The two common variations of bingbu stances are straight-leg stance and bent-leg stance.

• *Zhili bingbu* (直立并步)—feet-together stance with legs straight (fig. 3-3-1).

Fig. 3-3-1

• *Quxi bingbu* (曲膝并步)—feet-together stance with legs bent (fig. 3-3-2).

Fig. 3-3-2

Gongbu (弓步)—bow stance: In a gongbu, or "bow" stance, the front leg is bent like a bow and bears the full weight of the body while the back leg is straight and empty. There are three main variations of gongbu: standard bow stance, wide bow stance, and side-bow stance. The bow stance can be either high or low.

• *Zheng gongbu* (正弓步)—standard bow stance: In a standard bow stance, the toes of both feet point forward, and the feet are placed one foot-length apart horizontally and one or one and a half foot-lengths apart from front to back. In zheng gongbu, one should feel ready to charge quickly forward (fig. 3-3-3).

Fig. 3-3-3

- *Yu gongbu* (隅弓步)—wide bow stance: The wide bow stance is the same as the standard bow stance except that the feet are placed one and a half foot-lengths apart horizontally and about one-half foot-length apart from front to back. In yu gongbu, the practitioner should feel ready to dodge and then charge forward (fig. 3-3-4).

Fig. 3-3-4

- *Ce gongbu* (側弓步)—side-bow stance: The side-bow stance is commonly called the lay-down stance *(pubu).* In this stance, as in the other bow stances, one leg is bent and the other is straight. The feet are parallel to each other and placed about two and a half foot-lengths apart. The bent leg bears the full weight of the body while the straight leg is empty. The two variations of the side-bow stance, high and low, differ only in the degree to which the weight-bearing leg is bent.

  ○ *Gao pubu* (高仆步)—high side-bow stance: In this stance, the hip of the weight-bearing leg is higher than the knee of that leg. The height of gao pubu is usually comparable to that of the standard bow stance (fig. 3-3-5).

Fig. 3-3-5

◦ *Di pubu* (低仆步)—low side-bow stance: In this stance, the hip of the weight-bearing leg is the same as or lower than the knee of that leg. The straight leg drops down as far as possible, ideally until it almost touches the ground (fig. 3-3-6).

Fig. 3-3-6

Zuobu (坐步)—sitting stance: In *zuobu,* or sitting stance, the back leg is bent and bears the full weight of the body. In this position, the practitioner seems to be sitting on his or her back leg as though it were a stool. The front leg is straight and empty with the heel touching the ground and the toes pointing upward.

• *Zheng zuobu* (正坐步)—standard sitting stance: In the standard sitting stance, the distance between the feet is the standard distance of one foot-length horizontally and one foot-length from front to back (fig. 3-3-7). Because the foot positions in a standard sitting stance are the same as those in a standard bow stance, the two stances can be exchanged just by shifting the weight distribution.

Fig. 3-3-7

- *Yu zuobu* (隅坐步)—wide sitting stance: A wide sitting stance is the same as a standard sitting stance except that, in the former, the feet are placed in the wide distance position, which is one and a half foot-lengths apart horizontally and about one-half foot-length apart from front to back (fig. 3-3-8). These two stances can be exchanged just by redistributing the weight, given that the foot positions of the two stances are the same.

Fig. 3-3-8

Mabu (马步)—horse-riding stance: In *mabu,* or the horse-riding stance, both legs are bent, and the insides of the thighs and crotch form an arch.

- *Zheng mabu* (正马步)—standard horse-riding stance: In the standard horse-riding stance, both legs are bent, and each knee should be directly above the toes of the corresponding foot. The feet are parallel to each other or slightly wider apart at the toes than at the heels, and they are separated by about two and a half foot-lengths. In horse-riding stances, the weight is evenly divided between the legs, but your mind should always be focused on only one leg (fig. 3-3-9).

Fig. 3-3-9

- *Ban mabu* (半马步)—half horse-riding stance: In the half horse-riding stance, one foot points forward and bears 60 percent of the body's weight, while the second foot points to the side. The distance between the heels is about two feet (fig. 3-3-10).

Fig. 3-3-10

Xubu (虚步)—insubstantial stance: In *xubu,* or insubstantial stance, the back leg is bent and bears all or almost all of the body's weight. The foot of this leg is flat on the ground. The front leg, which is called the "empty" or "insubstantial" leg, is also bent and carries little or no weight. The knee of the empty leg should be slightly raised, as should the heel so that only the toes of this foot touch the ground (fig. 3-3-11). Technically, sitting stances and insubstantial stances are differentiated by the fact that, in the former, the heel of the front foot touches the ground, while, in the latter, the toes of the front foot touch the ground. Sometimes, however, no distinction is drawn between these two stances, and they are referred to interchangeably.

Fig. 3-3-11

Hougenbu (后跟步)—following stance: In *hougenbu,* or following stance, the front leg is bent and bears all or most of the body's weight. The foot of the weight-bearing leg should be flat on the ground. The back leg, which is the empty or insubstantial leg, is also bent but carries little or no weight. The heel of the back leg should be raised so that only the toes of this foot touch the ground (fig. 3-3-12). Usually, the distance between the back foot and the front foot is less than one foot-length.

Fig. 3-3-12

Xiebu (歇步)—resting stance: In *xiebu,* or resting stance, the legs are crossed and bent. The front foot is always pointed away from the body and bears almost all of the body's weight. The front foot should be flat on the ground. The back leg, also bent, carries little or no weight. Only the toes of the back foot should touch the ground. The knee of the back leg should touch the back of the front leg.

Figure 3-3-13 shows a low resting stance. When correctly done, this stance gives the impression that the practitioner is sitting on his or her front leg and letting the back leg rest. In a high resting stance (fig. 3-3-14), the front leg is bent only slightly, and the back leg is almost straight.

Fig. 3-3-13

Fig. 3-3-14

Gaibu (盖步)—covering stance: In *gaibu*, or covering stance, the legs are crossed. The front foot is always pointed outward. One leg is bent and bears most of the body's weight while the other leg is almost straight.

• *Qian gaibu* (前盖步): In a front covering stance, most of the body's weight is on the front leg (fig. 3-3-15).

Fig. 3-3-15

• *Hou gaibu* (后盖步): In a back covering stance, most of the body's weight is on the back leg (fig. 3-3-16).

Fig. 3-3-16

Dulibu (独立步)—single-leg stance: In *dulibu,* the single leg or balance stance, one leg is raised off the ground, and the full weight of the body is balanced on the other leg (fig. 3-3-17). There are many variations of this stance. The leg that supports the body can be straight or bent, and the raised leg can assume a variety of positions. Single leg stances can be very helpful for developing an awareness of internal force and for increasing one's ability to use internal force more skillfully. In general, this stance is used in training to build a good foundation rather than for direct application in fighting situations.

Fig. 3-3-17

Steps

When armed with a short weapon such as a Taiji *dao* and defending against a long weapon such as a spear, one's footwork will be a very important factor in determining the final outcome of the fight. The footwork must be nimble enough to allow you to dodge attacks effectively and quick enough to allow you to take advantage of any opportunity to approach the opponent. It must also be stable enough for you to release your force and to maintain good balance.

Bufa (步法)—step: The term for footwork is *bufa,* which means method of stepping. Steps can be described as dynamic postures of the legs and feet and are the most important basic components of all Taiji Dao skills. In form practice, larger steps are generally preferred to smaller ones, but in fighting situations, step size can vary freely depending on the particular circumstances. Some basic steps used in fighting do not occur in the Taiji Dao form and so should be practiced individually or as part of sword skills training.

Shangbu (上步)—step forward with the back foot: Starting from a bow stance with the front foot fixed, a *shangbu* is a step in which the back foot moves forward and is placed in front of the fixed foot. As the back foot moves forward, it follows a curved path, first being placed alongside the fixed foot and then moving forward to a position ahead of the fixed foot. The distance between the feet at the end of the step is either one or one and a half foot-lengths, depending on the stance. Because shangbu is a big step, it should be taken slightly more slowly than smaller steps and used only when it is necessary to move far forward. Figures 3-4-1 through 3-4-3 show a shangbu with the left foot moving from a right bow stance to a left bow stance.

Fig. 3-4-1

Fig. 3-4-2

Fig. 3-4-3

Chebu (撤步)—step backward with the front foot: Starting from a bow stance with the back foot fixed, *chebu* is a step in which the front foot moves back so that it is behind the fixed foot. The moving foot should follow a curved path, moving first alongside the fixed foot and then to the back and side of the fixed foot.

Like shangbu, chebu is a large, slow step used to move back a long distance. Figures 3-4-4 through 3-4-6 show a chebu with the right foot in which the stance is changed from a right bow stance to a left bow stance.

Fig. 3-4-4

Fig. 3-4-5

Fig. 3-4-6

Jinbu (进步)—step forward with the front foot: *Jinbu* is a step in which the front foot moves further forward and the back foot usually just follows. It is a frequently used quick step for situations that require swift forward movement. Figures 3-4-7 through 3-4-9 show a jinbu with the left foot.

| Fig. 3-4-7 | Fig. 3-4-8 | Fig. 3-4-9 |

Tuibu (退步)—step backward with the back foot: *Tuibu* is a step in which the back foot moves further back and the front foot usually just follows. Like a jinbu, it is a quick, commonly used step but, unlike a jinbu, it is used for situations that require swift backward, rather than forward, movement. Figures 3-4-10 through 3-4-12 show a tuibu with the right foot.

| Fig. 3-4-10 | Fig. 3-4-11 | Fig. 3-4-12 |

Hengkaibu (横开步)—step sideways: Used very often for moving quickly to the side, *hengkaibu* is a step in which the left foot moves to the left while the right foot follows, or the right foot moves to the right while the left foot follows. Figures 3-4-13 through 3-4-15 show a hengkaibu with the left foot.

Fig. 3-4-13   Fig. 3-4-14   Fig. 3-4-15

Ceshanbu (侧闪步)—dodge sideways step: Used when it is necessary to dodge quickly to the side while moving forward or backward, *ceshanbu* involves moving the left foot to the left and forward or backward while the right foot follows, or moving the right foot to the right and forward or backward while the left foot follows. Figures 3-4-16 through 3-4-18 show a ceshanbu for dodging to the left and moving forward. Figures 3-4-19 through 3-4-21 show a ceshanbu for dodging to the left and moving backward.

Fig. 3-4-16   Fig. 3-4-17   Fig. 3-4-18

Fig. 3-4-19   Fig. 3-4-20   Fig. 3-4-21

Daochabu (倒插步)—back insert step: In *daochabu,* one foot moves forward or sideways and is positioned behind the other foot. Figures 3-4-22 and 3-4-23 show a daochabu starting from a right bow stance. Before the left foot has passed the right foot, the right foot is moved a half-step forward and is turned on its heel so that the toes of this foot point inward. Then, the left foot is inserted behind the right foot with only the ball of the left foot touching the ground. A daochabu always ends in a rest stance.

Fig. 3-4-22   Fig. 3-4-23

Figures 3-4-24 through 3-4-26 show a daochabu that starts from a horse-riding stance and involves a 180-degree turn of the body. In this daochabu, the right foot is moved behind the left foot until it reaches the left side of the left foot. Only the ball of the right foot should touch the ground. As soon as the ball of the right foot touches the ground, you should turn on the ball of that foot and simultaneously on the heel of your left foot so that your body makes a 180-degree turn and again assumes a horse-riding stance.

Fig. 3-4-24   Fig. 3-4-25   Fig. 3-4-26

Gaibu (盖步)—covering step: *Gaibu* is a step in which the back foot moves forward, passes in front of the front foot, then turns outward and finally comes to rest alongside the fixed foot where it is placed flat on the ground. This step can result in a rest stance in which most of the body's weight is carried on only one leg or in a covering stance in which the weight is usually divided more evenly between the legs. Gaibu is a fast step very often used for moving forward and turning quickly to the side. Figures 3-4-27 through 3-4-29 show a gaibu with the right foot.

| Fig. 3-4-27 | Fig. 3-4-28 | Fig. 3-4-29 |

Koubu (扣步)—buckle step: *Koubu* is a step in which the back foot moves forward, touches the ground heel-first, and then turns so that the toes of that foot point slightly back toward the other foot. This places the toes of the feet closer to each other than the heels. Your knees should be close to one another and may even touch. Koubu is a quick step used frequently for turning the body inward. Figures 3-4-30 and 3-4-31 show a koubu with the left foot.

| Fig. 3-4-30 | Fig. 3-4-31 |

Baibu (摆步)—swing step: In *baibu,* the back foot moves forward, then swings to the outside and touches the ground heel-first. The toes of this foot point outward so that the heels of the feet are at right angles to each other. Baibu is a fast step very commonly used for turning the body outward. Figures 3-4-32 and 3-4-33 show a baibu with the right foot.

Fig. 3-4-32   Fig. 3-4-33

Dianbu (垫步)—preparatory and replacement step: In *dianbu,* a small step with one foot is used to connect two big steps either forward or backward with the other foot. The small step is a preparatory step for the two bigger steps. A common and quick step that is very useful for the development of nimble foot-work and for maintaining your posture as you move, a dianbu should smoothly connect the two larger steps.

Figures 3-4-34 through 3-4-37 show a forward dianbu in which the left foot moves forward and the right foot follows in a preparatory step that leads to the left foot's immediately moving forward again. Figures 3-4-38 through 3-4-41 show a backward dianbu in which the right foot moves backward and the left foot follows in a preparatory step that immediately leads to the right foot's moving backward again.

Fig. 3-4-34   Fig. 3-4-35   Fig. 3-4-36

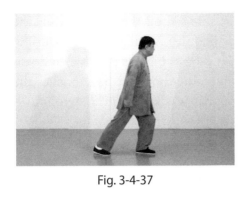

Fig. 3-4-37

Fig. 3-4-38

Fig. 3-4-39

Fig. 3-4-40

Fig. 3-4-41

Jianbu (箭步)—lunge: *Jianbu* is a lunge in which the front foot takes a large step quickly forward and the back foot follows as though being pulled along behind the front foot. Jianbu can be repeated several times in a continuous sequence. Figures 3-4-42 through 3-4-44 show a jianbu with the left foot.

Fig. 3-4-42

Fig. 3-4-43

Fig. 3-4-44

Tiaobu (跳步)—jump: In *tiaobu,* one foot is raised off the ground while the other leg is bent, and then the knee of the bent leg is quickly raised, causing the body to spring upward. The jump should be as high as possible, and you should remain in the air as long as possible. The foot that first touches the ground after the jump should be the foot that was raised off the ground to initiate the tiaobu.

Figures 3-4-45 through 3-4-51 show a tiaobu in which the right foot and knee are initially raised. This movement is immediately followed by the left knee moving quickly upward, causing the left foot to leave the ground in a jump in which both feet are high in the air. The right foot lands first, followed by the left.

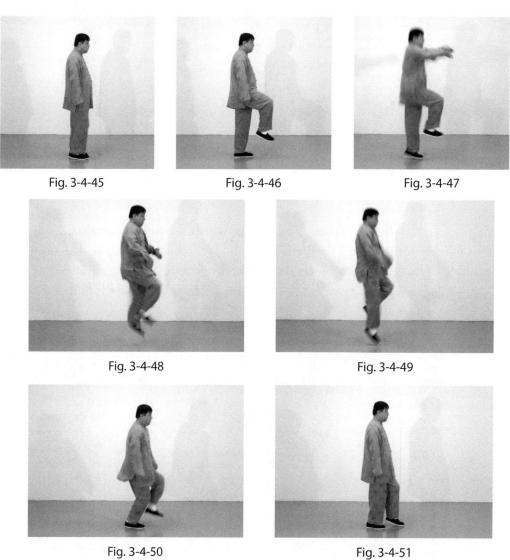

Fig. 3-4-45   Fig. 3-4-46   Fig. 3-4-47

Fig. 3-4-48   Fig. 3-4-49

Fig. 3-4-50   Fig. 3-4-51

Diantiaobu (点跳步)—toe hop: *Diantiaobu* is a series of hopping steps done in quick succession on the toes of alternating feet. The hops are not high but must be very nimble and lively. Diantiaobu is commonly used to dodge attacks to the lower body from long weapons. Figures 3-4-52 through 3-4-57 show a diantiaobu in which the first hop with the right foot is followed by several hops using alternating feet.

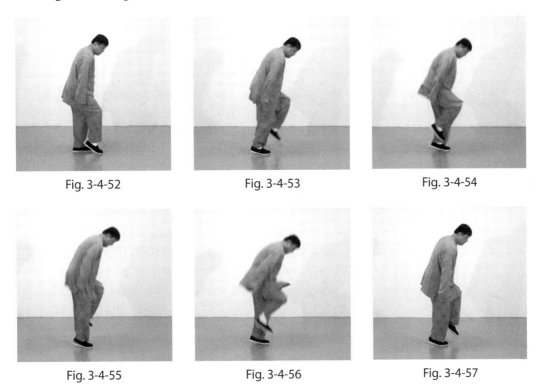

Fig. 3-4-52   Fig. 3-4-53   Fig. 3-4-54

Fig. 3-4-55   Fig. 3-4-56   Fig. 3-4-57

Body

Shenfa (身法)—body movement method: *Shenfa* specifies the basic movement requirements for each part of the body in all Taiji Quan training methods, whether empty-hand form, push hands, or weapons practice using saber, straight double-edged sword, staff, or spear. Without good shenfa, it is not possible to perform any Taiji Quan skills well.

Tiding baxiang (提顶拔项)—suspend head and neck from above: *Tiding* means to suspend the head from above, and *baxiang* means to straighten the neck, so *tiding baxiang* means to hold the head erect as though it were suspended from above. This is one of the most important Taiji Quan principles, and it must be correctly observed if your skills or techniques are to be effective. Tiding baxiang enhances the development of shen, yi, and qi and improves alertness and nimbleness. It also adjusts balance and increases one's mental focus on the acupoints.

The key acupoint for the skill of tiding baxiang is baihui. Baihui is at the top of the head and is aligned with the huiyin acupoint midway between the sexual organs and the anus. The *shenfa* requirement for tiding baxiang specifies that you focus on baihui and imagine that your whole body is suspended from this point.

Chenjian zhuizhou (沉肩坠肘)—sink shoulders and drop elbows: *Chenjian* (also called *songjian*) means to relax and sink the shoulders; *zhuizhou* means to drop the elbows. If the shoulders relax, the arms will also become more relaxed, and qi and internal force will be able to extend through the arms. If the shoulders are not relaxed, the muscles of the arms and hands will tighten and make it difficult to move with strength and fluidity. The key acupoints for chenjian are the *jianjing* points on the shoulders.

Dropping the elbows will allow qi and internal force to extend to the hands, and, as a result, the wrists will acquire greater power and move more nimbly. Dropping the elbows will also increase the integration of one's movements. The key acupoints on for zhuizhou are the *quchi* points on the elbows.

Hanxong babei (含胸拔背)—hollow the chest and straighten the back: *Hanxiong* means to empty the chest, and *babei* means to straighten the back as if it were being pulled up from the top and down from the bottom. You can "empty" your chest by drawing it slightly back to create a feeling of hollowness or concavity on your torso. This will cause qi to sink smoothly and easily down to dantian along *renmei*, the acupuncture meridian that is the centerline on the front of the torso. It will also improve your footwork. For hanxiong, one should focus on the tanzhong acupoint, which is at the center of the chest.

The back must always be kept straight, never hunched forward or swayed backward. Proper alignment of the back will help qi ascend smoothly and easily along *dumei*, the acupuncture meridian that is the centerline on the back of the torso. When combined with hanxiong, babei will allow qi to move around the body in a circle, extending from the head down to the toes and back up again. This circular movement of qi facilitates the release of internal force and is the most important element in basic internal training. You should focus on *jiaji*, the key babei acupoint located at the center of your back, to help align this part of your body.

A traditional adage suggests that a hunched back signifies a high level of skill. This assertion refers to a very special and complex case that is beyond the scope of this book.

Songyao choukua (松腰抽胯)—relax the waist and draw in the hips: *Songyao* means to relax the waist, and *choukua* means to draw in the hips. Songyao is an extremely important principle because it involves the waist, which is the center of the body and the locus of control for all movements. If one's waist is tight, it will not be possible to relax any other part of the body. Qi will not move smoothly through the body, internal force will not be sustained, limbs will not be flexible, and footwork will not be nimble. The key acupoints for relaxing the waist are mingmen at the center of the lower back and *shenque* on the navel. Your focus should alternate between these two points.

Choukua refers to the feeling that, as you take a step, the hip above the unweighted leg (the leg that moves) is being placed on top of the hip above the weighted leg. This will make your footwork quick, nimble, stable, and powerful. In choukua, the key acupoints are the *huantiao* acupoints on the hips. When taking a step, you should focus on the unweighted hip.

Guodang liutun (裹裆溜臀)—rounding the insides of the thighs and crotch, and tucking in the buttocks: *Guodang* means to round and expand the arch formed by the inside of the thighs and crotch, and *liutun* means to tuck the buttocks in so that they are aligned with the lower back. In guodang, the line created by the inner thighs should be curved, and there should be a feeling of expansiveness to this arc. These adjustments will help qi sink and move smoothly to the legs without becoming dissipated. Guodang will also increase one's root, nimbleness, and the power of the legs. The key acupoints for guodang are the *yanglingquan* points on the knees. Focusing on these acupoints will help curve and expand the crotch correctly and will ensure that each knee is aligned directly above the toes of the corresponding foot.

In liutun, the lower spine should be aligned so that the buttocks do not protrude. This alignment allows the waist to remain relaxed and shen to rise. The key acupoint for liutun is *weilu*, on the tailbone. Weilu should be positioned above an imaginary horizontal line connecting the heels.

Tixi kongzu (提膝空足)—lift the knee and hollow the center of the sole: *Tixi* means to raise the knee, and *kongzu* means to hollow or empty the center of the sole of the foot. These shengfa specifications concern footwork and the feelings that accompany footwork. In tixi, the focus should be on relaxing a hip and then raising a knee as high as possible. This allows qi to both sink down in the weight-bearing leg, making it very stable, and also to ascend in the empty leg, increasing nimbleness.

In kongzu, the center of the sole of each foot should feel hollow, and each foot should be thought of as gripping the ground whenever contact is made. This will increase stability by allowing qi to sink down. Similarly, a feeling of hollowness, as though each foot is ready to embrace an object whenever it leaves the ground, will increase nimbleness by helping qi ascend. Tixi and kongzu should be done in unison. The key acupoint for both is *yongquan* at the center of the sole of each foot.

Chapter Four

Basic Skills of Taiji Dao

There are two major sets of basic Taiji Dao skills: those relating to the use of the sword itself and those that enhance both attack and defense sword skills by the proper use of your empty hand and your feet. The most common cause of defeat in actual combat situations is incomplete mastery of these sets of skills. It is important to focus your practice on basic skill movements before attempting to learn particular techniques.

The two key points for basic skills training are understanding the meaning of each skill and coordinating the movements of all parts of your body with each other and with your sword. Each basic skill should be repeated a hundred or even a thousand times until it can be performed in a completely natural way and until you feel as though your sword has become part of your body. The key points apply to all your external movements and to shen, yi, qi, and jin, referred to in this book as the internal components. With diligent and correct practice, the movements of your sword will follow your shen wherever it leads, and your jin will be able to move to any part of your weapon. The flow of the internal components will ensure the effectiveness of your applications. When you have achieved this degree of mastery, you will begin truly to understand real sword skills.

In some cases, skills that use different parts of the sword have the same name because the principles on which they are based are the same or very similar. It is important to recognize and understand the specific factors that distinguish these skills. The distinguishing factors often concern the amount of force that each skill requires.

Sword Blade Skills

Taiji Dao encompasses many different kinds of sword skills. Some are general skills used in a variety of situations; others are used only in special cases; and still others are designed to defend against particular weapons. For example, the *jia* (架) skill can be used effectively to block a wooden spear staff but not directly to block another sword, especially a heavy one. Many of these basic skills are inherited directly from regular *dan dao,* single-sword skills.

The part of the sword that is most often used for attack and defense is the blade. As discussed in Chapter Two, the blade consists of the tip; the edge, which itself can be divided into the upper edge, the front edge, and the middle edge; the back; the flat surface; and the root. The term "edge" without other specification should be understood as referring to the middle edge. When the description of an external movement indicates, for example, that "the edge faces the ground," the edge referred to is the middle edge.

The Head of the Sword

Daotou (刀头)—The head of the sword refers to the uppermost six inches of the blade and includes the tip and the upper and front sections of the edge. Because the top six inches on both sides of the blade are very sharp, the skills that rely on this part of the sword do not have to be hard or powerful. More often, they are light, quick, and easily changed. Compared with other kinds of single-sword skills, Taiji Dao skills do not often require that you turn your wrist over because both edges at the top of your *dao* are sharp. As a result, Taiji Dao daotou skills are more efficient and easier to execute than other single-sword skills. The most common daotou skills are listed below.

Ci (刺)—thrust, pierce: *Ci* is a thrust skill in which the tip of the sword moves straight ahead and extends quite far forward toward a relatively distant target. Although many daotou skills are not hard and powerful, ci is an exception—its power is similar to that of a spear thrust.

There are several variations of ci, each of which uses a different blade position. Figures 4-1-1 and 4-1-2 show *zhici,* a straight thrust in which the blade is vertical and the edge faces the ground.

Fig. 4-1-1

Fig. 4-1-2

Zha (扎)—plunge: *Zha* is a thrust skill in which the tip of the sword is plunged forward at a target that is only a short distance away. The effectiveness of the zha skill depends more on speed and suddenness than it does on power.

There are several variations of zha skills. They are differentiated by the position of the blade. Figures 4-1-3 and 4-1-4 show *pingzha,* a plunge in which the blade is horizontal and the edge faces to the left.

Fig. 4-1-3   Fig. 4-1-4

Ci and zha, the most important daotou skills, are very similar to each other, varying only by the distance at which each is optimally used. There is no clear way to specify the defining distance that differentiates the two, and usually practitioners do not concern themselves with this distinction. Occasionally, the skill is considered to be ci if your whole arm is involved in the movement and zha if only your forearm is involved.

Dian (点)—peck or snap down: *Dian* is a downward strike using the tip of the sword to pierce a small point on your opponent's body. It is a quick but not a hard skill. The movement required for dian is small and usually involves only a quick flick of your wrist (figs. 4-1-5 and 4-1-6).

Fig. 4-1-5   Fig. 4-1-6

Beng (崩)—poke up: *Beng,* a strike upward with the tip of the sword, is the opposite of dian. Like dian, however, beng is quick rather than hard and requires only a small movement of your wrist (figs. 4-1-7 and 4-1-8).

Fig. 4-1-7   Fig. 4-1-8

Hua (划)—slice: In *hua,* the tip of the sword is used to slice or make a linear cut in the target. It is a quick but not a particularly powerful movement (figs. 4-1-9 and 4-1-10).

Fig. 4-1-9   Fig. 4-1-10

Liao (撩)—upward cut: *Liao* is an upward cut that can be forceful or light. In liao, the sword is swung forward and up to make a curved cut to the target. One variation of liao, called *zhengba liao* (figs. 4-1-11 and 4-1-12), uses the upper edge of the sword to create the upward cut up; a second, called *fanba liao* (figs. 4-1-13 and 4-1-14), uses the front edge of the sword to accomplish the same result.

Fig. 4-1-11   Fig. 4-1-12

Fig. 4-1-13

Fig. 4-1-14

Tiao (挑)—flick upward: *Tiao* combines a thrust with an upward slice. It is important that the thrust and slice be smoothly connected to form a single movement (figs. 4-1-15 and 4-1-16).

Fig. 4-1-15

Fig. 4-1-16

Huo (豁)—thrust and rip: *Huo* requires first that the tip of the sword be thrust into your target and then pulled quickly upward and back to rip the target in a curved cut. The thrust and rip skills must be integrated into one smooth movement (figs. 4-1-17 and 4-1-18).

Fig. 4-1-17

Fig. 4-1-18

The Edge of the Sword

Daoren (刀刃)—the sword edge: The edge of the sword is the part most often used. In Taiji Dao, *daoren* generally refers to the middle section of the edge, although the reference sometimes also includes the front edge. Usually, the edge of the sword is sharpest at the tip and least sharp near the handle. The skills that use daoren are described below.

Pi (劈)—split, chop: *Pi* is a large powerful chop that uses your whole arm. It is usually directed downward (figs. 4-1-19 and 4-1-20).

Fig. 4-1-19   Fig. 4-1-20

Kan (砍)—chop: Like pi, *kan* is a powerful, downward chopping skill that uses your forearm. Kan usually follows a diagonal rather than a straight path toward the target (figs. 4-1-21 and 4-1-22).

Fig. 4-1-21   Fig. 4-1-22

Duo (剁)—cut, chop, mince: *Duo* most commonly means to cut off a small piece of something. It is a chopping skill used for short-distance strikes and is accomplished by a quick, powerful movement of your wrist (figs. 4-1-23 and 4-1-24).

Fig. 4-1-23   Fig. 4-1-24

Zhan (斩)—sideways chop, behead: *Zhan* is typically a horizontal chop that moves the sword across a long edge of the target. The zhan movement can be either big or small, and either quick or powerful (figs. 4-1-25 and 4-1-26).

Fig. 4-1-25   Fig. 4-1-26

Pi, kan, duo, and zhan are the main chopping skills and comprise the most important category of daoren skills. The distinctions between the main chopping skills are only relative: many applications involve blendings or combinations of pi, kan, duo, and zhan.

Mo (抹)—wipe: *Mo* is a cutting skill in which the edge of the sword touches the target first and then is pulled to make a cut (figs. 4-1-27 and 4-1-28).

Fig. 4-1-27   Fig. 4-1-28

Xiao (削)—scooping slice or scooping chop: *Xiao* is a slice or light chopping skill that uses a scooping motion. When executing xiao, the angle between the blade and the target should be very small, and the edge of the sword should travel in a curved path as if to scoop up a portion of the target (figs. 4-1-29, 4-1-30, and 4-1-31).

Fig. 4-1-29   Fig. 4-1-30

Fig. 4-1-31

Jian (剪)—shear off: *Jian* is a very quick scissoring motion in which the edge of the sword is moved against the target as though to cut or shear off a piece of it (figs. 4-1-32 and 4-1-33).

Fig. 4-1-32

Fig. 4-1-33

Lan (拦)—parry: *Lan* is a parry skill that can originate from any direction. In lan, the edge of the sword blocks or knocks away an opponent's weapon. This skill is often used against a wooden staff or a wooden shaft spear (fig. 4-1-34). Because lan involves a strike to an opponent's weapon with the edge of your sword, it is usually not advisable to use this skill to block a hard or heavy weapon directly. A direct block is likely to damage your sword and also violates the Taiji Quan principle that cautions against *ding*—force used directly against force.

Fig. 4-1-34

Jie (截)—intersect: *Jie* is a block to the middle of an opponent's weapon or to his or her arm. It is a commonly used skill because blocking the front of your opponent's weapon is usually difficult or impossible, especially when the attack is strong and his or her weapon is heavy (figs. 4-1-35 and 4-1-36).

Fig. 4-1-35

Fig. 4-1-36

Gua (刮)—scrape, shave: *Gua* is a cutting skill in which the edge of the sword is used to scrape an opponent's arm. This skill results in a cut that is long but not deep (figs. 4-1-37 and 4-1-38).

Fig. 4-1-37

Fig. 4-1-38

Hua (滑)—sliding: *Hua* is a cutting skill commonly used to defend against long weapons when it is not possible to reach an opponent's body directly. Initially, it involves touching the opponent's weapon with your sword, then using hua to stick your sword on your opponent's weapon and slide it quickly toward him or her. The final goal is usually to cut your opponent's hand or some other part of his or her body. Keeping your sword inside your opponent's weapon will increase your ability to control any changes your opponent might make. Figures 4-1-39 and 4-1-40 show a hua skill used to move an opponent's spear to the right, while figures 4-1-41 and 4-1-42 show a hua skill used to move it to the left.

Fig. 4-1-39

Fig. 4-1-40

Fig. 4-1-41

Fig. 4-1-42

Fangua (反挂)—hang back: *Fangua* is a parry skill in which the sword moves upward from a low position and then blocks the opponent's weapon, moving it to the left and back along a curving path. The key point in this skill is to move forward toward your opponent while sticking and parrying his or her weapon as it moves past your body (figs. 4-1-43 and 4-1-44).

Fig. 4-1-43

Fig. 4-1-44

Yun (云)—circle: *Yun* means "cloud," and this skill involves waving the sword in many different, random circles as though creating clouds rolling in ahead of a storm. These circles can be used at any moment for either attack or defense because they encompass every kind of change (figs. 4-1-45 to 4-1-49).

Fig. 4-1-45

Fig. 4-1-46

Fig. 4-1-47

Fig. 4-1-48

Fig. 4-1-49

Sao (扫)—sweep: In *sao*, the sword is swept around your body in a large circle. Sao can be used as a blocking skill or as an attack skill (figs. 4-1-50 and 4-1-51).

Fig. 4-1-50

Fig. 4-1-51

Jia (架)—upward block: *Jia* is an upward block that is both powerful and quick and usually requires the use of both hands. It is typically used when two weapons collide as a result of your using excessive force directly against your opponent's weapon. This direct use of force-against-force is not in accordance with Taiji Quan principles, so jia is only rarely used in Taiji Dao (fig. 4-1-52).

Fig. 4-1-52

Tui (推)—push: *Tui* is a blocking skill used when weapons have already made contact with each other. In tui, while contact with an opponent or his or her weapon is maintained, you push your sword forward with both hands. Using two hands allows you to gain control more easily and also increases the power of your push. The key to the successful application of this skill is finding the optimal angle for the push (fig. 4-1-53).

Fig. 4-1-53

Shangtuo (上托)—hold or push up: Like tui, *shangtuo* is a two-handed blocking skill used when weapons have already made contact and when that contact is sustained. Unlike tui, however, shangtuo involves an upward push rather than a forward push (fig. 4-1-54).

Fig. 4-1-54

Xiaan (下按)—pressing down: *Xiaan* is a two-handed blocking skill used, like tui and shangtuo, when weapons are already in contact. In xiaan, the sustained contact is followed by a downward press on the opponent or his or her weapon (fig. 4-1-55).

Fig. 4-1-55

Many push-hand skills, such as sticking and following, can be applied when tui, shangtuo, and xiaan are used. Without a thorough knowledge of push-hand techniques, effective application of tui, shangtou, and xiaan skills will be difficult to achieve.

Chantou guonao (缠头裹脑)—wind-up block and wrap-around head: *Chantou guonao* is a block-and-parry skill in which the sword moves around your head and body. In this skill, your body and sword are like two points along the rim of a wheel. If one point moves forward, the other moves back.

In chantou guonao, the sword blocks an oncoming weapon frontally and then parries it to the left. At the same time, you should move back and then forward toward your opponent. This back-and-forth movement is called *gun jin* (滚进)—rolling in.

Chantou guonao starts with the sword held vertically, the tip pointing to the ground, and the palm of your sword hand facing down and away from your body. Then, in one large, continuous, smooth motion, you raise your sword on the left side of your head and move it in a circular path around the back of your head to the right side of your body and finally forward toward your opponent.

The back of the blade should face your body throughout the circle. The plane of the circular movement should be high as it passes the left side of your head and tilt slightly down as it reaches the right side (figs. 4-1-56 to 4-1-59).

Fig. 4-1-56

Fig. 4-1-57

Fig. 4-1-58

Fig. 4-1-59

Guonao chantou (过脑缠头)—passing overhead block and wind-down: *Guonao chantou* is a block-and-parry skill in which the sword is moved around your head and body from right to left. The sword is used to block the opponent's weapon from the front and then to parry it to the right. Your body and sword wind down together in a movement called *xuan rao*—rotation and winding.

Guonao chantou starts with the sword held vertically, the tip pointing to the ground, and the palm of your sword hand facing up and toward your body. Then, the sword is raised above the right side of your head and moved to the left behind your head in a large, continuous, smooth movement. The circular movement continues past the left side of your head and tilts slightly down as it ends in front of your body, which should be facing to the right. The back of the blade should face your body throughout the entire movement (figs. 4-1-60 to 4-1-63).

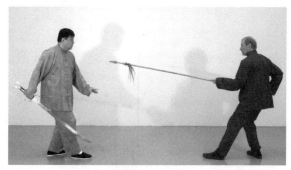
Fig. 4-1-60

Fig. 4-1-61

Fig. 4-1-62

Fig. 4-1-63

Chantou guonao and guonao chantou are two of the most common regular *dao* skills. Although very useful for defending against a spear, they are not often used in Taiji Dao because both upper edges of a *dao* are very sharp and the back edge that faces your body throughout the circular movements of these two skills is always very close to your body. If the sharpened upper edge area is less than one foot long, these skills can be safely used, but if the length of the sharpened edges is about two feet, these skills should not be used because the greater length of the sharp upper edges makes it easy for you to cut yourself. Great care must be taken if these skills are attempted with a sword that has a long upper edge.

The Back of the Sword

Daobei (刀背): The back of the sword is thick and strong and, as a result, commonly used for blocks or hard knocks to an opponent or his or her weapon. When you use the edge of the sword, your empty hand or arm can be placed on the back of the sword to add extra force. The skills using daobei are below.

Shan (扇)—knock away: *Shan* is a defense skill in which the sword is moved upward and to the right in a large diagonal motion as if you were waving a giant fan. In shan, the back of the sword is used to knock away the opponent's weapon with a powerful movement (figs. 4-1-64 to 4-1-66).

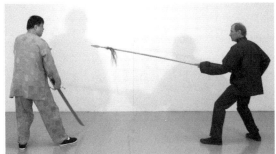

Fig. 4-1-64

Fig. 4-1-65

Fig. 4-1-66

Ke (磕)—jab: *Ke* is a defense skill in which the back of the sword is used to knock away an opponent's weapon in a smaller, quicker, and more sudden version of shan. It is used when the opponent is close (figs. 4-1-67 and 4-1-68).

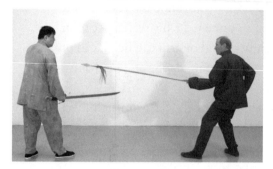

Fig. 4-1-67

Fig. 4-1-68

Dai (带)—bring along, drag: In *dai,* contact with an opponent's weapon is made and maintained, and then, following the opponent's weapon, the movement of the sword is accelerated in the same direction as the incoming weapon. This allows you to gain control of the opponent's weapon and bring it along in the wake of your own. Dai is much easier to use when the opponent's attack involves side-to-side force (figs. 4-1-69 and 4-1-70).

Fig. 4-1-69

Fig. 4-1-70

Lü (捋)—deflect: *Lü* is a skill in which the back of the sword sticks on an opponent's weapon, follows its force, and finally changes the direction of that force. *Lü* can be applied more easily when the opponent's attack is quick and powerful (figs. 4-1-71 and 4-1-72).

Fig. 4-1-71

Fig. 4-1-72

Gou (勾)—hook: *Gou* starts with contact between an opponent's weapon and your sword held vertically with the tip pointing to the ground and the back facing your body. It continues as you move your sword down and back in a circular motion on one side of your body. If done correctly, the movement gives the impression that you are trying to hook something on the ground and lift it up. *Gou* ends with the tip of the sword pointing diagonally up and forward (figs. 4-1-73, 4-1-74, and 4-1-75).

Fig. 4-1-73

Fig. 4-1-74

Fig. 4-1-75

Gua (挂)—hang: *Gua* starts with the tip of the sword pointing upward. After making contact with an opponent's weapon, the blade of the sword remains in a vertical position and is used to draw a half-circle backward alongside your body. A gua movement should create the impression that you are hanging the opponent's weapon on a hook behind him or her (figs. 4-1-76, 4-1-77, and 4-1-78).

Fig. 4-1-76

Fig. 4-1-77

Fig. 4-1-78

Za (砸)—reverse hammer block: In *za,* a blocking skill, the blade is turned over so that its back faces the ground and then is used like a hammer to strike down on an opponent's weapon. The movement can be small and quick like a sharp tap or big and powerful like the blow of a sledgehammer (figs. 4-1-79, 4-1-80, and 4-1-81).

Fig. 4-1-79

Fig. 4-1-80

Fig. 4-1-81

The Flat of the Blade

Daomian (刀面): The flat surface or side of the sword blade is used for blocks or parries that require a light, soft touch. Typical applications include adhering, sticking, linking, and following. The daomian is used very frequently in Taiji Dao, because the manner of its use accords well with Taiji Quan principles. The skills using daomian are below.

Lan (拦)—parry: *Lan* uses the flat of the blade to make contact with an opponent's weapon, usually from the side, and then to push the attacking weapon aside. Figure 4-1-82 shows a lan to the left, and figure 4-1-83 shows a lan to the right.

Fig. 4-1-82

Fig. 4-1-83

Ge (格)—follow and softly parry: *Ge* uses the flat of the blade to make contact with an opponent's weapon, usually from the side, and then to follow the movement of the opponent's weapon with a soft parry as you approach him or her. Figures 4-1-84 and 4-1-85 show a left ge, and figures 4-1-86 and 4-1-87 show a right ge.

Fig. 4-1-84

Fig. 4-1-85

Fig. 4-1-86

Fig. 4-1-87

Ya (压)—press down: In *ya*, the flat of the blade is used to touch an opponent's weapon and then to gain control of his or her weapon by pressing down on it. Figures 4-1-88 and 4-1-89 show a left block followed by a left ya, and figures 4-1-90 and 4-1-91 show a right block followed by a right ya.

Fig. 4-1-88

Fig. 4-1-89

Fig. 4-1-90

Fig. 4-1-91

Quan (圈)—circling parry: *Quan* uses the flat of the blade to make contact with an opponent's weapon and then to change the direction of his or her weapon by moving the sword in a vertical circle in front of your body while maintaining contact with the attacking weapon. Figures 4-1-92 through 4-1-95 show a clockwise circular parry.

Fig. 4-1-92

Fig. 4-1-93

Fig. 4-1-94

Fig. 4-1-95

Chan (缠)—spiral: *Chan* uses the flat of the blade to make contact with an opponent's weapon and then to gain control of his or her weapon by spiraling your sword inward or outward in front of your body. The direction of the spiral can be to the right or left, and the control achieved can be used for either attack or defense. Figures 4-1-96 and 4-1-97 show a counterclockwise spiral.

Fig. 4-1-96   Fig. 4-1-97

Jiao (搅)—stir up, flip: *Jiao* starts with the sword in front of your body, with the blade facing in and the tip pointing toward the ground. After making contact with the opponent's weapon in that position, your sword is used to follow the incoming attack by drawing a large circle on one side of your body, moving first downward and to the back, then upward and to the front. This circular movement causes the opponent's weapon to flip out of his or her grip. Figures 4-1-98 through 4-1-101 show a jiao on the left side of the body.

Fig. 4-1-98   Fig. 4-1-99

Fig. 4-1-100

Fig. 4-1-101

Gun (滚)—roll: *Gun* begins with the edge of the sword facing your body and the flat of the blade making contact with an opponent's weapon. Then, you roll your sword along the opponent's weapon by turning the wrist of your sword hand so that the edge of your sword faces your opponent and is positioned for an attack. Because rolling your sword can generate force to control your opponent's weapon and also allows you to move closer to him or her, *gun* is commonly used to defend against long weapons. Figures 4-1-102 through 4-1-105 show a *gun* skill.

Fig. 4-1-102

Fig. 4-1-103

Fig. 4-1-104

Fig. 4-1-105

The Root (Ricasso) of the Blade

Daogen (刀根): The root of the blade is the strongest part of the sword, and because it is the part closest to your hand, it can be used for hard, powerful blocks. When using daogen, your empty hand can always be placed on the sword to add control and power. The skills using daogen are described below.

Ke (磕)—knock away, jab: *Ke* is a small and quick, yet powerful, defense skill used when an opponent's weapon is already very close. If the opponent's weapon is a sword, a hard ke can be used to damage the edge of his or her sword as well as to gain control of his or her weapon (fig. 4-1-106).

Fig. 4-1-106

Ya (压)—press down: *Ya* skill uses the root of the blade to press down on an opponent's weapon in order to control it. Daogen provides the strongest leverage for such control because it is the part of the sword closest to your hands (fig. 4-1-107).

Fig. 4-1-107

Tui (推)—pushing: *Tui* uses the root of the blade to gain control of an opponent's weapon by pushing it. Again, for this skill, daogen provides the strongest leverage (fig. 4-1-108). Your empty hand can be added to the push in order to strengthen the application of tui.

Fig. 4-1-108

Guard Skills

Hushou (护手): The guard of a sword is always designed to protect the hand that holds it. The Taiji *dao* guard is unique in that its special design provides not only protection but also the means to catch and trap an opponent's weapon. The skills using hushou are described below.

Dang (挡)—block: *Dang* means to use the guard to block a weapon, usually a short, light weapon like a jian. If an opponent attacks with a hard, heavy weapon, a direct dang block is risky and usually not effective. Figure 4-2-1 shows a common dang skill.

Fig. 4-2-1

Na (拿)—catch and twist: *Na* means to hold something and take control. Here, the guard is used to catch an opponent's weapon and is then twisted to control the attacking weapon. Figures 4-2-2 and 4-2-3 show a dang used to block an opponent's weapon and then a na used immediately afterward to control it.

Fig. 4-2-2

Fig. 4-2-3

Na can be applied in many different ways. Figures 4-2-4 and 4-2-5 show the use of na against a sword, while figures 4-2-6 and 4-2-7 show the use of na against a spear. Figure 4-2-8 illustrates na used against a spear with the sword held in a fanwo position. Great care is required in this position. To avoid injury, it is important to move your index finger to the bottom of the sword handle (fig. 4-2-9). In a common and effective maneuver, your index finger can also be used to grab the opponent's spear and thereby increase your control over it (fig. 4-2-10).

Fig. 4-2-4

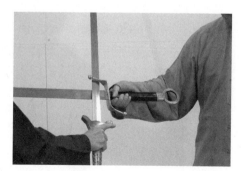

Fig. 4-2-5

Fig. 4-2-6

Fig. 4-2-7

Fig. 4-2-8

Fig. 4-2-9

Fig. 4-2-10

Handle Skills

Daobing (刀柄) or *daoba* (刀把): The handle of the sword is used for holding and controlling the weapon. Because the handle of a Taiji *dao* is long, it can also be used for blocking. Handle skills are most often used when the sword is held in fanwo, the reversed-holding position in which the edge of the sword faces up and the handle points forward. The skills using daobing are described below.

Jia (架)—block up: Because the sword is held in a fanwo position in *jia,* the block is actually delivered by the bottom side of the handle when the sword is raised to defend against an attack. To avoid being injured when using a jia skill, your index finger should move to the part of the handle that faces the ground (fig. 4-3-1).

Fig. 4-3-1

Ya (压)—block and press down: In *ya,* the sword is held in a fanwo position and controls the opponent's weapon by blocking and pressing down with what is normally the bottom left side of the handle. When applying this skill, the edge of the blade faces the opponent, and, again, your index finger must be moved to the side of the handle away from the opponent's weapon to avoid injury (fig. 4-3-2).

Fig. 4-3-2

Lan (拦)—block side-to-side: *Lan* is a horizontal block that uses the handle of the sword (fig. 4-3-3).

Fig. 4-3-3

Hengguo (橫裹)—block and inward rolling: *Hengguo* is an inward block that has a rolling component used for control. In skills involving rolling, there is a good chance that the contact point may shift, so you must be careful to avoid the opponent's weapon hitting your sword hand (figs. 4-3-4 and 4-3-5).

Fig. 4-3-4

Fig. 4-3-5

Ring Skills

Daohuan (刀环): The ring at the end of a Taiji *dao* can be grasped and manipulated by your empty hand to assist your sword hand. Although both hands are used in these circumstances, ring skills are distinguished from regular two-handed grips. Usually, a two-handed grip adds power at the expense of liveliness and agility. Using the ring adds less power but retains more nimbleness and control. As opposed to the typically large movements of both hands in a two-handed grip, ring skills involve small, quick movements by your rear hand holding the ring, while your front hand, on the handle, remains relatively still.

Compared to one-handed grips, holding the ring with your empty hand in Taiji Dao yields greater power. Compared to regular two-handed grips, holding the ring with your empty hand in Taiji Dao yields greater liveliness and agility. Overall, ring grips balance the relative advantages and disadvantages of other kinds of grips.

There are several different ways to grip the ring with your empty hand. The most common ways are to use your palm or fingers to grip the ring (figs. 4-4-1 and 4-4-2); to use your index finger, middle finger, and thumb for the grip (figs. 4-4-3 and 4-4-4); and to use your index finger, middle finger, ring finger, and thumb (figs. 4-4-5 and 4-4-6). For increased nimbleness, the grip of your thumb can be loosened or eliminated so that only two or three fingers are on the sword. Figures 4-4-7 through 4-4-10 show several of these positions. The skills using daohuan are described below.

Fig. 4-4-1

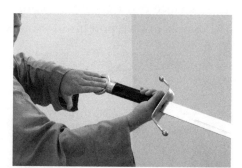
Fig. 4-4-2

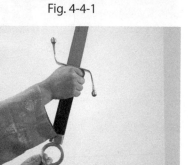
Fig. 4-4-3

Fig. 4-4-4

Fig. 4-4-5

Fig. 4-4-6

Fig. 4-4-7

Fig. 4-4-8

Fig. 4-4-9

Fig. 4-4-10

Tui (推)—pushing: With the tip of the sword facing directly away from your body, *tui* uses either the center of your palm (fig. 4-4-11) or the fingers (fig. 4-4-12) to push forward on the ring.

Fig. 4-4-11   Fig. 4-4-12

La (拉)—pulling: The opposite of tui, *la* is a pull using your thumb and two or three fingers that are hooked through the ring (fig. 4-4-13).

Fig. 4-4-13

Ti (提)—lifting up: In *ti,* your sword hand remains relatively still, while your thumb and two or three fingers are hooked through the ring and pull up on it, causing the front of the sword to move downward (fig. 4-4-14).

Fig. 4-4-14

Ya (压)—pressing down: The opposite of ti, *ya* involves hooking your thumb and two or three fingers through the ring of the sword and pushing down on it, while your sword hand remains relatively still. Your downward push on the ring causes the front of the sword to move upward (fig. 4-4-15).

Fig. 4-4-15

Yao (摇)—waving:

• *Zheng yao* (正摇)—waving in front: In *zheng yao,* your fingers are hooked through the ring and you move the ring in circles in front of your body. Similar to chan, zheng yao causes the tip of the sword to circle through an ever-enlarging spiral (figs. 4-4-16 to 4-4-19).

Fig. 4-4-16

Fig. 4-4-17

Fig. 4-4-18

Fig. 4-4-19

- *Ce yao* (侧摇)—waving to side: In *ce yao,* your fingers are hooked through the ring and you move the sword so that it traces a very large circle along the side of your body. This is similar to jiao (figs. 4-4-20 to 4-4-23).

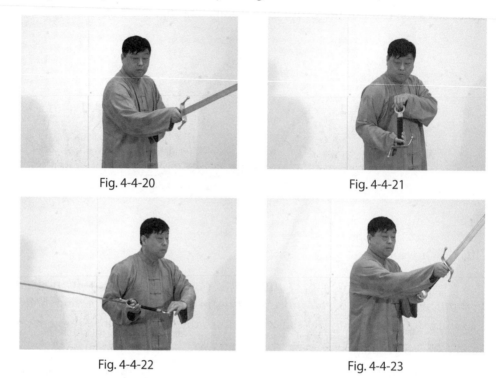

Fig. 4-4-20

Fig. 4-4-21

Fig. 4-4-22

Fig. 4-4-23

The ring can also be used for direct strikes:

Ji (击)—strike: Used in extremely close proximity to an opponent, *ji* uses the ring of the sword to strike the opponent or his or her weapon (figs. 4-4-24 and 4-4-25).

Fig. 4-4-24

Fig. 4-4-25

Different Taiji Dao skills are used to defend against different types of weapons. The way different parts of the sword are used can also vary widely depending on the opponent's weapon. Even when the same skill and part of the sword are used, your internal feelings may differ from one situation to another. Because of these complexities, you should not limit your sword practice to the study of the sword alone. You should also research the skills required for the proper use of other weapons.

Empty-Hand Skills

Dao practice is not only about how to use your sword but also about how to deliver punches, palm strikes, and kicks, as well as how to throw hidden weapons. Correct practice will increase the coordination among all parts of your body. So empty-hand skills, those performed with the hand that is not holding the sword, have a special importance in Taiji Dao. It is said that "in single *dao* practice, watch the empty hand" (单刀看手). This means that your overall single-*dao* skill level is revealed to others and can be evaluated by them when they observe how well you use your empty hand. The empty hand can refer to either hand because the sword is often transferred from one hand to the other in the execution of Taiji Dao skills.

It should be noted that sword practice can involve the use of weapons other than swords, and that the use of such weapons, known as throwing darts or *biao,* is an important, though traditionally secret, aspect of empty-hand skills. Descriptions of these weapons and the hand skills needed to throw them will be included in this section.

Hand Skills

Hand skills are those that use the empty hand directly to attack or defend against an opponent.

Qie zhang (切掌)—cutting palm strike: In this skill, the edge of your standing palm strikes forward as if to cut the opponent (figs. 4-5-1 and 4-5-2).

Fig. 4-5-1

Fig. 4-5-2

Pai zhang (拍掌)—clapping palm strike: In this skill, the flat of your palm faces the ground and strikes forward and/or down (figs. 4-5-3 and 4-5-4).

Fig. 4-5-3   Fig. 4-5-4

Tui zhang (推掌)—pushing palm strike: This skill involves using your standing palm to push and/or strike forward (fig. 4-5-5).

Fig. 4-5-5

Ya zhang (压掌)—pressing-down palm strike: In this skill, your flat palm presses downward (fig. 4-5-6).

Fig. 4-5-6

Quan zhang (圈掌)—circling palm strike: *Quan zhang* uses a tile palm to parry an attack by encircling the opponent's arm or weapon. A tile palm is an open palm with your fingers extended and a rounded tiger mouth (figs. 4-5-7, 4-5-8, and 4-5-9).

Fig. 4-5-7

Fig. 4-5-8

Fig. 4-5-9

Cheng zhang (撑掌)—parrying and pushing-upward palm strike: A tile palm is used to parry and push upward. The palm of your empty hand should face outward (figs. 4-5-10 and 4-5-11).

Fig. 4-5-10

Fig. 4-5-11

Zhua (抓)—grabbing, catching: In *zhua,* your empty hand grabs an opponent's arm or weapon in order to control it (figs. 4-5-12 and 4-5-13).

| Fig. 4-5-12 | Fig. 4-5-13 |

Diaoluo zhang (叼捋掌)—gripping and pulling palm strike: Here, an open palm is used to capture and then pull on your opponent's arm or weapon. *Diao* means "capture like an eagle sinking its beak into a prey." *Luo* refers to a very hard and quick pull, as if against the other's will. In luo, your hand does not have to stay in one spot but can instead slide along the length of your opponent's arm (figs. 4-5-14 and 4-5-15). When your empty hand forms a hook in the Taiji Dao form described in the next chapter, it is usually done to execute a diaoluo skill.

| Fig. 4-5-14 | Fig. 4-5-15 |

Dabiao zhang (打镖掌)—throwing dart palm: *Dabiao zhang* describes how to throw *biao* or hidden weapons. These weapons are small and easily concealed, and the keys to their effective use are surprise and speed. All elements comprising biao-throwing skills, including drawing the weapons out, aiming them, and throwing them, must be done in one smooth, economic motion. The method for drawing, aiming, and throwing a particular type of biao determines where the weapon should be carried on your body. Illustrations of how to hold biao were provided in the previous chapter (see figs. 3-2-7, 3-2-8, and 3-2-9).

- *Fei biao* (飞镖)—flying dart: A flying dart with a tassel should fly straight when thrown and strike the target with its sharp tip. To achieve this result, the dart should lie flat in your hand and be thrown straight ahead. These darts are usually carried at your waist, either on a belt or in a special pouch with a strap *(biao nang)*. There are two common ways to throw a flying dart. In the first method, called a lower-hand throw, the dart is thrown forward at waist level with the palm of the hand that holds the dart facing up (figs. 4-5-16, 4-5-17, and 4-5-18). In the second method, called an upper-hand throw, the dart hand is raised diagonally up across the body to head level, with the palm facing inward toward the body, and then the dart is thrown forward (figs. 4-5-19, 4-5-20, and 4-5-21). The use of flying darts in the Taiji Dao form will be described in the next chapter.

Fig. 4-5-16

Fig. 4-5-17

Fig. 4-5-18

Fig. 4-5-19

Fig. 4-5-20

Fig. 4-5-21

- *Fei dao* (飞刀)—flying dagger: A flying dagger or knife that has a handle and is slightly longer than a flying dart will flip end-over-end when thrown. It is usually gripped by the handle or tip and thrown out in an arc. Since knives are thrown using an overhand motion, they are usually carried on the upper part of your back where grasping, aiming, and throwing them can be done in one simple motion. When carried on the back, knives can be drawn over your shoulder and thrown forward in one uninterrupted movement (figs. 4-5-22 and 4-5-23).

Fig. 4-5-22   Fig. 4-5-23

- *Jin qian biao* (金钱镖)—golden coin dart: A golden coin dart resembling a coin with sharp edges is small and light, so it cannot be thrown very far or with great force. Usually, several coins are thrown at once. Because at least three coins are usually thrown together, special skill must be taken to ensure that the edges do not cut your throwing hand. It is said that three golden coins can hit a target in several different configurations: an upward triangle, a downward triangle, a vertical line, a horizontal line, or successively to one point. Although some Taiji Dao practitioners use this weapon today, the details of golden coin dart skills have been lost over time.

- *Shihui bao* (石灰包)—lime powder packet: Lime is historically one of the most basic and commonly used building materials. A corrosive, powdered alkaline compound, it is mixed with water to make mortar. During the mixing process, it reacts vigorously, giving off tremendous heat before hardening to a paste-like substance. When thrown into your opponent's eyes, it has a similar effect. Your opponent immediately experiences an intense burning sensation and quickly becomes blinded. To avoid permanent blindness, the affected areas must be thoroughly and quickly washed to remove the lime. When used as a weapon, lime powder is carried in small square packets made of very low-quality paper that readily breaks apart, releasing a cloud of powder when thrown against an opponent's face.

Hidden weapons can be thrown with either hand, but throwing with the dominant hand will always be preferable to throwing with the nondominant hand. As a result, the sword should usually be transferred to your nondominant hand in preparation for using darts. This transfer occurs in the Taiji Dao form that will be introduced in Chapter Five, but to retain an element of surprise, sometimes the nondominant hand is used to throw the darts in real fighting situations.

The hand used depends on the habits and abilities of the practitioner. Because hidden weapons are small and light, they are not effective when used across long distances. Some types of biao can be used in such situations, but the chances of success are minimal. The small size and weight of hidden weapons also make them less fatal than other weapons. It is unlikely that you will be able to dispatch your enemy using only these weapons.

Taking into account all these considerations, the greatest value of hidden weapons is the distraction they provide. If, for example, your opponent has managed to lock your weapon in an awkward outside position and is about to strike a finishing blow, a well-applied hidden weapon can force him or her to release your weapon. Regardless of whether a hidden weapon has caused serious damage or even hit its target, if it has startled or momentarily paralyzed your opponent, made him or her flinch, turn away, or close his or her eyes, you will have earned at least a brief chance to approach and attack your opponent with your main weapon.

There are no rules or etiquette governing the use of hidden weapons in real life-and-death struggles. In contests of skill, however, hidden weapons are rarely used. If you do have them on your body and plan to use them, an informal rule of martial arts challenge fighting requires that you either warn your opponent about them before the match or call out a warning right before you release them.

By tradition, martial arts challenge fighting involves different levels of contact, from light touches to strong attacks that can result in serious injury or death. Regardless of level, these matches are meant to provide pure measures of martial arts skill. In such circumstances, the use of certain types of hidden weapons, like lime powder, is generally considered very low level, almost criminal. Masters with good reputations do not resort to such tactics even when their lives are in danger. In the tradition of martial arts instruction, discussion of such tactics has been provided here not to encourage you to use these weapons, but only to alert you to the possibility that such weapons may be used against you in situations of real combat.

Supplemental Hand Skills

Any skill can be enhanced if your empty hand is placed on the sword. This hand provides additional control and power to the movements of the sword.

On the Back of the Sword

Tui (推)—pushing:

* *Hengtui* (横推)—horizontal pushing: When the sword is horizontal, and the edge faces away from your body, your empty hand is held vertically, and the center of your palm is used to push the sword (fig. 4-5-24).

Fig. 4-5-24

* *Litui* (立推)—vertical pushing: When the sword is vertical, with the edge facing away from your body and the tip pointing either down or up, the web of your hand is used to push the sword. To avoid injury when contact with an opponent or his or her weapon occurs, it is important to make sure that the fingers of your empty hand do not go past the edge of your blade (fig. 4-5-25).

Fig. 4-5-25

Shangtuo (上托)—holding up: When the edge of the blade is facing up, and the palm of your empty hand is facing away from your body, the web of your empty hand can be used to push the sword. To avoid injury when making contact with an opponent, make sure the fingers of your empty hand do not extend forward above the edge of your blade (fig. 4-5-26).

Fig. 4-5-26

Xiaya (下压)—pressing down: When the edge of the blade faces down, and the palm of your empty hand faces away from your body, the web of your empty hand can be used to press down on the sword. To avoid injury when making contact with an opponent, make sure the fingers of your empty hand do not extend down along the side of your blade (fig. 4-5-27).

Fig. 4-5-27

On the Sword Hand

Cheng (撑)—outward pushing: Your empty hand is placed on top of or inside your sword hand and wrist. The web of your empty hand faces the wrist of your sword hand, and the edge of the sword faces away from your body (fig. 4-5-28).

Fig. 4-5-28

Ya (压)—pressing down: The edge of the sword faces the ground, and your empty hand is placed on top of your sword hand and the sword guard. The web of your empty hand faces the wrist of your sword hand (fig. 4-5-29).

Fig. 4-5-29

On the Handle of the Sword

Wo (握)—gripping: Your left hand grips your sword, usually very loosely, behind your right hand and pushes down or forward (figs. 4-5-30 and 4-5-31).

There is also a special *wo* skill in which the arm of your empty hand helps push against the back of the sword for extra power. In this variation, it is important to bend your arms so that they form an expanding circle.

Fig. 4-5-30

Fig. 4-5-31

Cheng (撑)—expanding push, brace: The front upper part of your empty-hand arm, near the elbow, is used to push against the top portion of the back of the sword. This push gives the sword extra power (fig. 4-5-32).

Fig. 4-5-32

Transferring *Dao* from One Hand to the Other

Sometimes it is necessary to transfer the Taiji *dao* from one hand to the other. The most common example of such a transfer occurs when the *dao* is originally held in one hand with a zhengwo grip and is moved to the other hand to be held in a fanwo grip. Usually, the transfer is from your dominant hand, which is the right hand for most people, to your nondominant hand, and it is done to free your dominant hand for some other purpose, such as throwing a biao, after which the sword is transferred back to your dominant hand. Although a biao can be thrown with either hand, throwing with your dominant hand will always be more effective.

Transfer from the Right Hand to the Left

With your right hand holding the sword in a zhengwo position (fig. 4-6-1), open your right hand and grip the guard and handle of the sword from the other side with your left hand (fig. 4-6-2). Your left hand will be gripping the sword in a fanwo position (fig. 4-6-3).

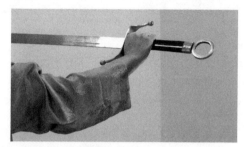

Fig. 4-6-1

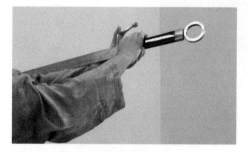

Fig. 4-6-2

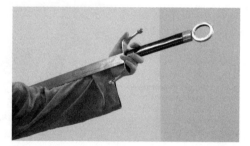

Fig. 4-6-3

Transfer from the Left Hand to the Right

Holding the sword in a fanwo position with your left hand (fig. 4-6-4), open that hand and grip the guard and handle of the sword from the other side with your right hand (fig. 4-6-5). Your right hand will be gripping the sword in a zhengwo position (fig. 4-6-6).

Transfer from One Hand to the Other without Changing the Grip

Transfers are often done to extend the reach of the sword. Suppose, for example, that the sword is sticking to an opponent's spear on your left side with your left foot in front and that the opponent tries to pull his or her spear back. Because the opponent's maneuver takes very little time, it is unlikely that you will be able to step forward with your right foot quickly enough to maintain contact

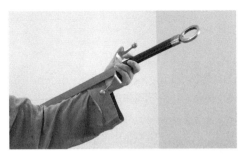

Fig. 4-6-4

Fig. 4-6-5

Fig. 4-6-6

with your opponent's spear. If, however, you transfer the sword from your right hand to your left, you will be able to continue sticking your opponent's spear as you pursue him or her because transferring your sword to your left hand, which is closer to your opponent, makes it easier for you to reach him or her. Figures 4-6-7 through 4-6-9 illustrate this sequence.

Fig. 4-6-7

Fig. 4-6-8

Fig. 4-6-9

Kicks

Taiji Dao practice includes some simple but useful kicking skills. When defending against a spear, it is always important to be close to the opponent. This can be more easily accomplished if, while holding the sword with one hand, you can use the other hand to grip and control the incoming spear. In such circumstances, a well-placed kick is a useful method of attack.

Qian ti (前踢)—front kick: In this kick, you use either your toes to kick your opponent's knee or the upper surface of your foot to kick the groin or lower abdomen. The placement of this kick is usually no higher than stomach level (fig. 4-7-1).

Fig. 4-7-1

Qiance ti (前側踢)—front oblique kick upward: Using your toes or the sole of your foot, you kick forward and obliquely up. *Qiance ti* can be directed to the opponent's knee (fig. 4-7-2), groin (fig. 4-7-3), or lower abdomen (fig. 4-7-4).

Fig. 4-7-2

Fig. 4-7-3

Fig. 4-7-4

Ce chuai (侧踹)—side kick: This is a powerful kick that uses your whole foot. It is usually necessary to turn your body sideways and to bring your knee up before delivering a side kick. The placement of the kick can be at knee level or head level, but most commonly *ce chui* is directed at the opponent's ribs (fig. 4-7-5).

Fig. 4-7-5

Qianshang ti (前上踢)—front high kick: This is a high kick using either your toes or the upper surface of your foot. Usually directed above shoulder level, it can be used to kick the opponent's head (fig. 4-7-6) or the wrist of the hand with which your opponent holds his or her weapon (fig. 4-7-7).

Fig. 4-7-6

Fig. 4-7-7

Basic Combination Skills

Basic combination skills refer to either a sequence or to a mixture of skills. An example of a sequential-combination skill is *pi liao,* which involves the chopping down skill, *pi,* followed by the cutting up skill, *liao.* The skills must be smoothly connected so that they form one continuous movement.

Dian pi is an example of a mixture-combination skill. Here, the pointing skill of *dian,* which is small and quick, is added to the larger and more powerful chopping skill of *pi.* The resulting dian pi skill combines the features of both components, making it quicker and smaller than pi but more powerful and larger than dian.

Most skills used in real fighting are combination skills. Only rarely is a skill used in its pure form. Depending on your ability and body conditioning, you can always create your own combination skills. Below are some examples of combination skills that are commonly used. The key points to remember when practicing combination skills are to relax your whole body, connect all your movements smoothly, and maintain a state of mental concentration.

Basic combination skill practice is a very important aspect of training. Not only are basic combination skills useful, but they also help develop internal feelings. Concentrating on one skill is not extremely difficult, but coordinating the internal components of shen, yi, qi, and jin with external movements along with combining several skills continuously and smoothly is far from easy. Because your steps must be quick and nimble when practicing basic combination skills, you should not use low stances. It is also important to coordinate the movements of your sword, body, and feet.

Under conditions of combat or competition, it is often difficult to perform well after executing your first few skills. In addition to nervousness, the problem derives from an inability to maintain shen concentration and yi focus and to keep qi stable and quiet while also relaxing and moving jin force smoothly throughout your body. Combination-skill practice can improve all of these key capacities.

A very important principle to remember is that there are no pre-designed skills in Taiji Quan. It is always necessary to follow your opponent and the changes he or she makes and to combine this awareness with your own sensitivity and ability to remain relaxed so that you can determine when to change your skills in a timely manner. This principle applies not only to empty-hand skills but also to weapons skills. When you practice combination skills, remember that the goal is not to use these skills directly but rather to increase your understanding of basic Taiji Quan principles. Ultimately, the particular skills will not be important; you will be able to do whatever a given situation requires in an effortless and natural way.

As you study the skill descriptions for two-person applications in this and subsequent chapters, it is important to note that the directions of right and left, whether referring to the fighters or to the relative positions of their weapons, are defined from the point of view of the person wielding the sword.

Simple Combinations

Zuo You Shang Liao Xia Pi (左右上撩下劈) —Left and Right Upward Cut and Chop Down

This combination of *liao,* an upward cut, and *pi,* a chop, helps develop the ability to attack in a continuous vertical circle. In liao, the edge of the sword faces up to make an upward cut, while in pi, the edge faces down to execute a chop. In both skills, your body should turn from one side to the other so that the sword appears to wave back and forth in front of you. If you alternate sides as you perform each skill, your sword will always be moving in the same direction.

It is also possible to interchange the two skills. When the sword is over your head, you can change liao to pi, and when the sword is in a lower position, you can change pi to liao. Each time you change one skill to the other, you can step either forward or backward.

This combination skill can be practiced using either a one-handed or a two-handed grip. Both practice routines described in this section use a two-handed grip. The first combination is for a liao from the right and left sides with a step forward followed by one pi with a step backward. The second combination is for two liao and one pi without an accompanying step.

Movements: Using both hands, hold your sword in front of your body. Turn your body slightly to the right, and, putting most of your weight on your right leg, take a half-step forward with your left foot to form a left insubstantial stance. Look straight ahead and imagine that your opponent is holding a spear in front of you (fig. 4-8-1).

Next, imagine that the opponent thrusts his or her spear at your chest. Step forward with your right foot. At the same time, move your sword up and back on the right side of your body and then down and forward in a circle

Fig. 4-8-1

until the edge of the sword faces up at shoulder level. Imagine cutting the shaft of your opponent's spear from underneath. This is *you liao*—a right upward cut (fig. 4-8-2).

Fig. 4-8-2

Shift your weight forward and move your sword up and back on the left side of your body (fig. 4-8-3) and then down, forward, and up in a circle until once again the edge of the sword faces up at shoulder level. Again, imagine cutting the shaft of your opponent's spear from underneath. This is *zuo liao*—a left upward cut (fig. 4-8-4).

Fig. 4-8-3

Fig. 4-8-4

If your opponent were to pull his or her spear back, causing you to miss your upward cut, and then immediately thrust toward you again, turn your hands over so that the edge of your sword faces down, and raise your hands until they are level with the top of your head. Let the tip of your sword point up and the edge face forward (fig. 4-8-5). Without interruption, step back with your left foot and simultaneously chop forward and down in a curving path until your sword points slightly down at an oblique angle. Imagine chopping the shaft of your opponent's spear from above. This is a left side chop, *zuo pi* (fig. 4-8-6).

Your backward step and your forward chop must be seamlessly coordinated to form a single movement.

Fig. 4-8-5

Fig. 4-8-6

In the second combination of liao and pi, begin by turning your hands over and cutting upward in a left zuo liao (fig. 4-8-7). Without interruption, step forward with your left foot and move your sword backward (fig. 4-8-8). Shift your weight forward and cut upward in a right-side you liao (fig. 4-8-9). Then, turn your hands over, raise your sword (fig. 4-8-10), and deliver a right-side forward chop *(you pi)* while letting your body sink slightly down (fig. 4-8-11).

Fig. 4-8-7

Fig. 4-8-8

Fig. 4-8-9

Fig. 4-8-10

Fig. 4-8-11

Zuo You Shang Jia Xie Kan (左右上架斜砍)
—Upward Block and Diagonal Chop from Left and Right

This combination includes two skills, *shang jia*—upward block—and *xie kan*—diagonally downward chop. The key point is that the component skills should be smoothly linked and continuous. The combination of shang jia and xie kan is commonly used to defend against a spear. It is important to move close to the opponent quickly in order to make sure that the head of his or her spear goes past your body and cannot cause you difficulty when you execute your chop.

Movements: Use both hands to hold your sword in front and to the right of your body. Turn your body to the right slightly and put most of your weight on your right leg. Move your left foot a half-step forward to form a left insubstantial stance. Look straight ahead and imagine that your opponent is holding a spear in front of you (fig. 4-8-12).

Fig. 4-8-12

Imagine next that your opponent uses his or her spear to thrust toward your face. Step forward with your left foot and simultaneously move your sword forward and up to head level. Imagine using your sword to block up by striking the shaft of your opponent's spear from underneath. Your sword will be oriented horizontally in front of your head with the tip pointing forward and to the right and the edge facing up. This is *zuo shang jia,* a left upward block (fig. 4-8-13).

Fig. 4-8-13

Step forward with your right foot, and at the same time, turn your hands counterclockwise and move your sword down and around in a counterclockwise circle. When your sword starts to move down, add extra power to the downward chop by accelerating the downward movement and slightly dropping and turning your wrist to the right as it slants from upper left to lower right. This is *you xie kan*—a right diagonal downward chop (fig. 4-8-14). Imagine that your sword remains in contact with your opponent's spear as it moves through its circular path.

Fig. 4-8-14

Follow the right xie kan movement with a right upward block (fig. 4-8-15), and then follow the upward block with a left downward-slanting chop (fig. 4-8-16).

Fig. 4-8-15

Fig. 4-8-16

Jin Bu San Dian Pi (进步三点劈)—Three Snap-Down Chops with Forward Steps

This is a combination of the basic skills of *dian*—snap down or peck—and *pi*—chop. In *dian,* a small and not very hard movement, you use your wrist to move the tip of your sword quickly downward in a pecking or snapping motion. The chopping skill *pi,* on the other hand, is a large and very powerful but slower movement. Dian and pi together create a movement that looks similar to pi, but because the pi in the combination skill is smaller than a single pi, it can be delivered more quickly. Likewise, the dian in the dian pi combination becomes more powerful than it is in a single dian because it has been smoothly integrated with the preceding pi. The dian pi combination skill illustrated in this section is comprised of three continuous repetitions with steps moving forward. The footwork in this combination skill must be quick.

Movements: Use both hands to hold your sword in front of your body. Put most of your weight on your left leg and move your right foot a half-step forward to form a right insubstantial stance. Look straight ahead and imagine that your opponent is holding a spear in front of you (fig. 4-8-17).

Fig. 4-8-17

Imagine next that your opponent thrusts his or her spear toward your face or chest. Withdraw your stomach and hollow your chest. These movements will make you feel as though your body has moved slightly back. At the same time, drag your right foot slightly back and raise your sword. You will feel as though the back of your sword has acquired additional power for an upward strike (fig. 4-8-18). Continuing without interruption, lunge forward with your right foot to form a right bow stance and chop forward at head level. At the end of the chop, drop your wrist slightly so that your sword gains extra downward power. Imagine using the tip or front edge of your sword to chop or strike your opponent's head (fig. 4-8-19). This completes the first dian pi.

Fig. 4-8-18

Fig. 4-8-19

Continuing without interruption, withdraw your stomach, drag your right foot back, and pull your sword back as quickly as possible. These movements restore full power to your right leg so that you can immediately lunge forward again (fig. 4-8-20). Follow this with a second dian pi (fig. 4-8-21). Then repeat the process to execute a third dian pi (figs. 4-8-22 and 4-8-23).

Fig. 4-8-20

Fig. 4-8-21

Fig. 4-8-22

Fig. 4-8-23

Quan Lan Zhi Ci (圈拦直刺)—Circling Parry and Straight Thrust

This combination links the basic skill of *quan lan*—circling parry—with that of *zhi ci*—straight thrust. As a highly flexible and changeable skill that is not very hard, a circling parry exemplifies a sword skill imbued with a fundamental Taiji Quan principle. Many other skills can be generated from it.

Straight thrusts are used often in Taiji Dao primarily because a *dao* is long and has only a gentle curve. Given that circling parries and straight thrusts are core spear skills, including them in your sword practice will enhance your basic understanding of all Taiji Dao skills, especially the ability to move with agility and to make changes quickly and flexibly.

This combination skill can be done very quickly if you hold the sword with only one hand or very powerfully if you hold it with both hands. It is common to start with a one-handed grip and then to add the second hand to offer extra power to the sword.

Movements: Using your right hand, hold your sword in front of your body and parallel to the ground with the tip pointing forward. Put most of your weight on your right leg and take a half-step forward with your left foot to form a left insubstantial stance. Look straight ahead and imagine that your opponent is holding a sword in front of you (fig. 4-8-24).

Fig. 4-8-24

Imagine next that your opponent uses his or her sword to attack your chest. Step forward with your right foot and, putting most of your weight on your left leg, lift your right heel so that only the toes of your right foot touch the ground. At the same time, smoothly draw a clockwise circle with the tip of your sword so that the right flat side can be used for a soft parry (fig. 4-8-25).

Fig. 4-8-25

Imagine that your sword sticks on your opponent's sword as your sword moves through the circle. When the circle is complete, withdraw your stomach and hollow your chest. Your body will seem to move slightly back. Simultaneously, drag your right foot back a few inches and pull your sword back slightly while also letting it sink down slightly. This will store power in your left leg (fig. 4-8-26). Continuing without interruption, lunge forward with your right foot to form a right bow stance and thrust your sword straight ahead at chest level. Imagine holding your sword with both hands like a spear (fig. 4-8-27). In this skill, the circling parry can be done in any direction and at any time.

Fig. 4-8-26

Fig. 4-8-27

Zuo You Ce Ya Qian Xiao (左右侧压前削)
—Sideways Press-Down and Forward Scooping Slice from Left and Right

This combination skill is comprised of *ce ya*—sideways press-down—and *qian xiao*—forward scooping slice. In ce ya, you press your opponent's weapon sideways to the left or right after following and redirecting the movement of his or her weapon. Your body should sink down so that your press feels very heavy to your opponent and leads him or her to believe that it would be difficult to pull his or her weapon back. In a forward scooping slice, which is a quick and agile movement rather than a forceful one, the sword should move in a curving path as though to scoop something up. The key point is to connect the two separate skills very smoothly so that they become one movement. As a whole, this combination involves drawing a vertical circle backward and then a horizontal circle forward.

Movements: Look straight ahead and imagine your opponent holding a sword in front of you. Hold your sword vertically with the tip pointing up in front of your body. Put most of your weight on your right leg and take a half-step forward with your left foot to form a left insubstantial stance. Imagine next that your opponent uses his or her sword to thrust toward your chest. Turn your wrist slightly inward so that the edge of your sword faces forward and to the left. Imagine parrying your opponent's sword to the left (fig. 4-8-28).

Fig. 4-8-28

Shift your weight forward to form a left bow stance. At the same time, move your sword backward in a circle and then press it down in front of your left side. Imagine that your sword is on top of your opponent's sword and press down. The tip of your sword should point to the left. Simultaneously, turn your right hand to make the edge of your sword face forward. Imagine your sword sticking to and rolling on your opponent's sword. Put your left hand on your right wrist to increase the force of your press (fig. 4-8-29).

Fig. 4-8-29

Continuing without interruption, move your sword forward and up to make a scooping slice from left to right until your sword is in the front of your body. When moving your sword forward, imagine pushing slightly down first and then quickly upward so that contact between the two weapons is suddenly broken. The tip of your sword should point forward, and the edge should face to the right (fig. 4-8-30). Continue the movement with a right-side downward press and a forward scooping slice from right to left (figs. 4-8-31, 4-8-32, and 4-8-33).

Fig. 4-8-30

Fig. 4-8-31

Fig. 4-8-32

Fig. 4-8-33

You Heng Shan Zhi Kan (右横扇直砍) —Right Knock-Away and Straight Chop Forward

This basic skill combines *shan*—knock away—with *kan*—chop. Shan, the most common sword defense skill, uses the back of the sword to knock away an opponent's weapon. Since the sword is held in your right hand, this skill always moves it from a left low position to a right high position. The movement always follows a curvilinear path, and the name *shan* is derived from the fact that the sword appears to wave to the right like a traditional folding fan. The force in shan, called *kai*—open—is a storing or defense force and is achieved by separating your arms and expanding and rounding your chest.

Shan is followed by a straight chop forward, the force of which is called *he*—close. *He* is a release or attack force and is accomplished by rounding your back and pushing your arms forward together. The force in each arm supplements or supports the force in the other.

Movements: Hold your sword in front of your right hip in a relaxed, natural way and let the tip of the sword point forward. Stand with your right foot in front of your left to form a right high bow stance. Look straight ahead and imagine an opponent holding a sword in front of you (fig. 4-8-34).

Fig. 4-8-34

Then, imagine that your opponent uses his or her sword to attack your chest. Move your sword up and slightly to the right and back in a curving path, as though waving a fan upward. Think about using the back of your sword to knock your opponent's sword away to the right from underneath. The tip of your sword should point up and the edge should face forward. At the same time, push your left hand to the left and a little bit back. Separate your hands outward to the sides of your body to create an expansive feeling, and simultaneously shift your weight back to your left leg and drag your right foot a half-step back. This will create a rounded feeling in your chest, stomach and arms (fig. 4-8-35).

Fig. 4-8-35

Stomp forward with your right foot and shift your weight to your right leg to form a right bow stance. At the same time, chop forward quickly and push your left hand forward. Make sure that your foot stomp occurs at the same time as the extension of your hands so that your force is released suddenly and fully. Imagine chopping your opponent's neck from the right (fig. 4-8-36).

Fig. 4-8-36

Zuo Heng Ke Zhi Kan (左橫磕直砍)—Left Jab and Straight Forward Chop

In this combination of *zuo heng ke*—a left jab—and *zhi kan*—a chop straight ahead—*ke* uses the root of the sword to knock an opponent's weapon aside to the left. The opposite of shan, *ke* is a small movement that is quick and sudden like a jab. As you move the sword to the left with your right hand, your left hand should move to the right and touch your right wrist in a *he*—a coming-together move that is used defensively in this combination skill. As you chop forward with your right hand, push your left hand back in a *kai*—an open or separating move that, here, is used for attack. The force in each arm supplements or supports the force in the other.

Movements: Hold your sword in front of your right hip with the tip pointing forward. Stand in a relaxed manner with your right foot forward to form a right high bow stance. Look straight ahead and imagine that your opponent is holding a spear in front of you (fig. 4-8-37).

Fig. 4-8-37

Then, imagine that your opponent uses his or her sword to attack your chest. Move your sword up and slightly to the right and back with the tip pointing up and the edge facing forward. Push your sword quickly and suddenly to the left until it is in front of your left hip, and simultaneously turn your right wrist slightly inward. At the same time, move your left hand to your right wrist and position your arms so that they form a circle. This will cause an expansive feeling in your chest, stomach, and arms. Simultaneously, step forward with your left foot and shift your weight to it to form a left high bow stance. Imagine using the root of your sword suddenly to jab your opponent's sword (fig. 4-8-38).

Fig. 4-8-38

Stomp forward with your right foot and shift your weight forward to form a right bow stance while simultaneously chopping quickly forward and pushing your left hand backward. In order to ensure that your force will be suddenly and fully released, you must push forward with your right hand and back with your left hand at the same moment. Imagine chopping toward your opponent's neck from the left (fig. 4-8-39).

Fig. 4-8-39

Zuo You Ti Lan Qian Liao (左右提拦前撩)
—Left and Right Parry with the Tip of the Sword
Pointing Down and a Forward Upward Cut

This combination includes *ti lan* and *qian liao*. *Ti* means to hold the sword with the tip pointing down and *lan* is a parry, so *ti lan* is a parry skill that can be effectively used to defend against attacks below the level of your stomach. This defensive skill is seamlessly combined with *qian liao,* a common attack skill. *Qian* means to go forward and *liao* is an upward cut.

Opponents using long weapons, like spears, very often aim their attacks at the legs of sword-wielding fighters. The *zuo you ti lan qian liao* combination is well suited to defending against such attacks and to counterattacking with a forward upward cut. This combination requires very quick and nimble footwork, usually including a toe-hop step.

Movements: Imagine that your opponent uses his or her spear to thrust toward your knees or feet. Hold your sword in a relaxed manner in front of your right hip with the tip pointing down. Put almost all your weight on your right foot. Look straight ahead and down, and ready your sword for a left parry. Turn your right hand up so that the edge of your sword faces to the left. Imagine parrying your opponent's spear to the left. At the same time, step forward with your left foot letting only the toes of that foot touch the ground (fig. 4-8-40).

Fig. 4-8-40

Then, turn your right hand outward to the right, so that the edge of your sword faces to the right. At the same time, step forward with your right foot letting only the toes of that foot touch the ground. Imagine parrying your opponent's spear to the right (fig. 4-8-41).

Fig. 4-8-41

Continue to turn your right hand over so that the edge of your sword faces forward. Simultaneously, step forward with your left foot and immediately make an upward cut. Imagine cutting your opponent's front hand if he or she does not pull it away. If you imagine that your opponent does pull it away, just keep going forward to cut his or her body directly (fig. 4-8-42).

Fig. 4-8-42

You can continue by stepping forward with your right foot to make another right parry (fig. 4-8-43). Then, step forward with your left foot to make a left parry (fig. 4-8-44) and follow it by stepping forward with your right foot to deliver another upward cut (fig. 4-8-45).

Fig. 4-8-43

Fig. 4-8-44

Fig. 4-8-45

Four-Basic-Skills Routine

The four-basic-skills routine is a short form, the main section of which consists of the two most important regular broadsword skills. These two, the details of which have already been described, are *chantou guonao*—a wind-up and wrap-around head block—and *guonao chantou*—a passing-overhead block and wind-down. Both skills need to be practiced thoroughly so that they can be applied very quickly and smoothly, and the four-basic-skills routine provides a very suitable opportunity for such training. The routine can be repeated many times.

You must be very careful to avoid injury when using these two skills because your Taiji *dao* is sharp on both upper edges. If the length of the upper edge is less than one foot, the danger is somewhat reduced. Nevertheless, you should always remain alert to the possibility of injury in this training.

Gong Bu Qian Ci (弓步前刺)—Forward Thrust with a Bow Stance

Stand straight and hold your sword in your right hand in a zhengwo position (fig. 4-8-46). Step forward with your left foot and shift your weight to your left leg to form a left bow stance. At the same time, thrust your sword forward and diagonally down in a quick, powerful movement. Put your left hand on the side of the handle of your sword to ensure that the sword's movement will be strong and stable (fig. 4-8-47).

Fig. 4-8-46   Fig. 4-8-47

Chan Tou Guo Nao (缠头裹脑)—Wind-Up Block and Wrap-Around Head

Shift your weight back to your right leg and straighten your body. At the same time, push your left hand to the right until it is under your right arm. Raise your right hand and turn it outward in front of your chest. The tip of your sword should point down, and the edge should face forward and to the left. Your arms should feel as though they are holding something (fig. 4-8-48).

Fig. 4-8-48

Continuously shift your weight back and drag your left foot slightly backward, letting only the toes of your left foot touch the ground. At the same time, keep pushing your left hand to the right and slightly back, and continue to raise your right hand until your sword is higher than your head in a wind-up motion. The tip of your sword should point down and to the left, and the edge should face up and to the left. During this wind-up, your arms will cross and create a twisting feeling in your body (fig. 4-8-49). Continue to hold your right hand higher than the top of your head and then drop it slightly as it moves past your left shoulder.

Fig. 4-8-49

Continue to move your right hand so that it passes over your head from the left to the right. When your sword is behind your body with the tip down, push your left hand further to the right and then forward. This moves your sword first forward and then backward around your body from the left side. It should appear as though your sword is being wrapped around your head. When this movement is complete, push your left hand forward and withdraw your body slightly, keeping a distance of about six inches between your sword and your right shoulder (fig. 4-8-50).

Fig. 4-8-50

Continue without interruption to move your right hand forward on the right side of your body and simultaneously push your left hand to the left. At the same time, shift your weight forward to form a left bow stance (fig. 4-8-51) and move your sword forward in a side chop at chest level. The palm of your right hand should face up, the tip of your sword should point forward, and the edge should face to the left. While chopping to the side, continue to push your left hand slightly to the left and then turn your left hand so that your left palm faces up. Your left arm should form a semicircle over your left shoulder (fig. 4-8-52).

In the first part of this skill, your sword winds around the front of your body

Fig. 4-8-51   Fig. 4-8-52

from right to left, and, during this wind-up, your body should move slightly backward to create a circular feeling that encompasses your sword, your right arm, and your back. You should feel as though this circle is expanding and rising.

The second part of this skill involves wrapping your sword around your head and moving it behind your body. When your sword moves backward, your body should move slightly forward to create a feeling that there is a circle that encompasses your chest, your right arm, and your sword. The circle should feel as though it is expanding and moving slightly downward. The two parts of this skill must be very smoothly coordinated to form one continuous sequence.

Ti Xi Xia Lan (提膝下拦)—Raising Knee and Low Parry

Continuing without interruption from the end of the chan tou guo nao combination skill, turn your right hand over so that your right palm faces downward. Keep moving your sword to the left and back. Your right arm should encircle your body until your right hand is under your left shoulder, and your sword is behind your body with the tip pointing to the right and the edge facing back. At the same time, push your left palm slightly up to create a twist in your torso (fig. 4-8-53).

Fig. 4-8-53

Push your left hand forward and down in front of your right shoulder and move your right hand slightly to the left so that your arms are crossed and can generate force in opposite directions. Raise your body slightly (fig. 4-8-54).

Fig. 4-8-54

Straighten your left leg and raise your right knee toward the left. Simultaneously, separate your arms and move your right hand holding your sword forward, down, and to the left to make a low parry. At the same time, push your left hand to the left and then up and back. Your hands and your sword should form an oblique line from the left upper corner behind you to the right lower corner in front. Look forward along an imaginary line extending along the tip of your sword (fig. 4-8-55)

Fig. 4-8-55

Guo Nao Chan Tou (过脑缠头)—Passing Overhead Block and Wind-Down

Maintain the *ti xi xia lan*—single-leg stance—and look forward and to the left. Turn your right hand, holding your sword inward in front of your head so that the tip of your sword points down and the edge faces forward and to the right. At the same time, move your left hand over your head and place it on the inside of the handle of your sword (fig. 4-8-56).

Fig. 4-8-56

Put your right foot down behind your left foot and shift your weight onto your right leg. This will cause your body to sink down. Relax your left leg and raise your left heel. At the same time, raise your right hand over your head and slightly to the left and back, so that your sword is on the right side of your body with the tip pointing down and the edge facing outward. Simultaneously, push your left hand down until it is under your right shoulder and slightly to the right. This will cause your body to turn slightly to the right and sink further down (fig. 4-8-57).

Fig. 4-8-57

Continue without interruption to wind your sword around your body from your right side to behind your back, then to your left side, and finally back to your right side. Then, pull your sword down until it is beside your right hip with the tip pointing forward and down. At the same time, push your left hand forward in a cutting-palm strike and sink your body down slightly to form a left insubstantial stance (fig. 4-8-58).

Fig. 4-8-58

The first part of this skill involves raising your sword and passing it over your head while letting your body sink down. The movements of your arms inward should produce a rising feeling in your right hand and a sinking feeling in your left hand. At the same time, these movements should create a sense of winding down in your right hand and of rotation in your left hand.

In the second part of this skill, the movements of your arms should result in a feeling that your right hand is pulling back and your left hand is moving forward. Your arms should feel as though they are expanding and opening out.

Straighten your right leg and move your left foot back beside your right foot. Move your left hand back to your left side and drop your right hand down in a natural way. Stand straight and look forward. Your sword should point diagonally down and forward in this, the ending posture of the routine (fig. 4-8-59).

Fig. 4-8-59

Often in practice, this routine is performed several times without interruption. To repeat the routine, do not assume the ending posture shown in figure 4-8-59 but proceed from the stance shown in figure 4-8-58 by stepping forward with your left foot and thrusting your sword forward and down, as shown in figure 4-8-47. Then, repeat the entire routine. Be sure to perform all movements of the routine smoothly, nimbly, and as quickly as possible.

Chapter Five

Thirteen-Posture Form

Taiji Dao Form Practice

Form practice is one of the most important aspects of Taiji Dao training. Today, in Yang and Wu style Taiji Quan groups, a thirteen-posture Taiji Dao form is popularly practiced. The origin of this form has not been definitively determined, but it is known that the form was first practiced in Beijing when Master Yang Luchan (杨露禅, 1799–1872) was teaching there in the mid-nineteenth century. By the end of the century, the form had spread to other areas of China and in the twentieth century was widely promulgated to areas outside of China as well. Neither this form nor any similar form has been traced to Chen Village—where he learned Taiji Quan—or to Master Yang's hometown in Yong Nian County—where he taught Taiji Quan before moving to Beijing—so it is thought that Yang created the form while he was teaching Taiji Quan in Beijing from the 1850s to the 1870s. It is also possible that the form originated later in classes taught by Yang's sons or by his students.

Two name lists for Taiji Dao can be found in the writings of Master Wu Yuxiang (武禹襄, 1812–1880) and his nephew Master Li Yiyu (李亦畬, 1832–1892). Master Wu studied Taiji Quan with Master Yang Luchan and Master Chen Qingping. Although not the same as the thirteen-posture form described here, one of these lists is called *Shi San Dao* (十三刀), or the "Thirteen Sword Skills," and the other list is called *Si Dao Fa* (四刀法), or the "Four Sword Skills." As can be seen, both lists may refer to a sequence of basic skills rather than to a complete form. The thirteen-posture form presented in this book is the most popular Taiji Dao form practiced today.

Because this form has been taught for more than one hundred years and also because different approaches, understandings, and methods of training characterize different groups of practitioners, it is not surprising that many variations have emerged. Although the movements of the form may differ from one group to another, all variations derive from the same fundamental Taiji Dao principles.

As mentioned in Chapter Two, a specially designed Taiji *dao* should be used when practicing the Taiji Dao form. The Taiji *dao* in use today retain the same special shape as the nineteenth-century Taiji *dao* used in Beijing.

The form described in this book was taught by Grandmaster Wang Peisheng (王培生, 1919–2004), the president of the Beijing Wu Style Taiji Quan Association. He was instructed in this form by his grandmaster, Wang Maozhai (王茂斋, 1862–1940), and his master, Yang Yuting (杨禹廷, 1887–1982). Wang Maozhai had learned it from Quan You (全佑, 1834–1902), a student of Yang Luchan and the founder of Wu Style Taiji Quan.

Before studying the Taiji Dao form, you should practice both the empty-hand Taiji Quan form and also push hands. The better your understanding and execution of these skills, the more easily you will be able to understand and master the Taiji Dao form. Diligent practice of basic Taiji Dao skills is, of course, also necessary.

When practicing the Taiji Dao form, you should strive for a thorough understanding of at least one application for each movement. Give careful attention to Taiji Quan principles in your sword practice and do not confuse Taiji Dao skills with regular sword skills. Always remember that the goal of skill practice is to understand Taiji principles and to develop broad abilities rather than just a talent for performing particular sword skills. This is one of the most important concepts in Taiji Quan, and it distinguishes Taiji Quan from other martial arts styles.

Although the skills that comprise the form can be applied in many different ways, they should be modified when they are used in actual fighting. When practiced in the form, all movements should be large and performed slowly so that every detail can be correctly executed. Large, slow movements will also promote the development of the internal components and increase your physical strength. When the movements from the form are applied against a real opponent, however, they should usually be as small and quick as possible. It is important that you pay attention to these differences and understand how the movements of the form must be changed when they are used in real combat or competitions.

How Taiji *Dao* Use Differs from Regular *Dao* Use in Form Practice

As was made clear in Chapter One, *dao* date from ancient times and, during their long history, were produced in many different shapes, sizes, and designs. While it is not known exactly when the unique shape of the Taiji *dao* was designed nor who designed it, records indicate that the special features of Taiji *dao* were developed exclusively within the Taiji Quan group more than one hundred years ago in order to foster improvements in sword skill practice.

Because the shape of a high-quality Taiji *dao* is difficult to produce, this sword is neither widely used nor easily available. It can be special ordered from factories that produce customized weapons, but such a sword will be very expensive. For these reasons, form practice with Taiji *dao* is relatively uncommon, and the full complement of Taiji Dao skills practiced with Taiji *dao* has been passed to only a few disciples in each generation. The great majority of students continued to train with regular single *dao.*

Today, it is common to find that many groups and individual practitioners of Taiji Dao use regular *dao* to practice the Taiji Dao form. Beginning in the nineteenth century, the most prevalent regular *dao* found in most martial arts schools were *nu wei dao,* or oxtail swords; *yan ling dao,* or goose-feather swords; and *liu ye dao,* or willow-leaf swords. Most of these swords have much shorter blades and handles than Taiji *dao,* and, unlike Taiji *dao,* they do not always have an upper edge.

Because the shape of a Taiji *dao* differs from that of a regular *dao,* the practice of some sword skills will vary depending on which *dao* is used. The details of such differences will be fully considered in the form description section of this chapter, but some of the major features of Taiji Dao skills and the principles on which these skills are based will be described here.

1. A Taiji *dao* is narrower than a regular *dao.* Because of its slender shape, a Taiji *dao* should not be used with great force.

2. A Taiji *dao* is longer than a regular *dao,* so extra care is needed when executing skills that require low stances. It is important not to let the tip of your *dao* touch the ground.

3. Unlike a regular *dao,* Taiji *dao* has an upper edge. As a result, the Taiji Dao form, unlike the form for a regular *dao,* includes skills for this sharp part of the sword.

4. Having an upper edge, a Taiji *dao* is more dangerous than a regular *dao* if you swing it close to your body. As a result, there are fewer sword skills that require raising a Taiji *dao* over your head or moving it around your body than there are for a regular *dao.*

5. The handle of a Taiji *dao* is longer than that of a regular *dao,* so there are more sword skills that require two-handed grips for a Taiji *dao* than for a regular *dao.* The Taiji Dao form includes some hidden two-handed gripping skills.

6. The special design of the hand guard of a Taiji *dao* allows for some special skills that are not possible with a regular *dao*.

7. The ring of a Taiji *dao* allows for easier control of the sword than is available with a regular *dao*.

Although there are many differences between Taiji *dao* practice and regular *dao* practice, if you cannot find a Taiji *dao,* you can still benefit from using a regular broadsword. Just remember that when you use a regular broadsword to practice Taiji Dao skills, some details will be different and some may disappear altogether.

Description and Illustrations of Taiji Dao Form

The Taiji Dao form we introduce here is commonly called *Taiji Shisan Dao* (太极十三刀), or Thirteen Postures of Taiji Dao. The name list of the thirteen postures in this form was composed as part of a traditional Chinese poem in which the postures are described in terms of beautiful imagery that makes them easier to learn and remember. When translated into English, however, some of the loveliness may be lost. The name list of the thirteen postures that comprise the Taiji Dao form is presented here.

Tai Ji Qi Shi (太极起式)—The Beginning Posture of Taiji Dao

1. *Qi Xing Kua Hu Jiao Dao Shi* (七星跨虎交刀势)—Seven Stars, Ride Tiger, and Hand over *Dao*

2. *Shan Zhan Teng Nuo Yi Qi Yang* (闪战腾挪意气扬)—Dodge and Focus, Jump and Move, Excite Mind and Qi

3. *Zuo Gu You Pan Liang Fen Zhang* (左顾右盼两分张)—Guard Left and Right, Opening and Extending Two Times

4. *Bai He Liang Chi Wu Xing Zhang* (白鹤亮翅五行掌)—White Crane Spreads Its Wings and *Wuxing* Palm

5. *Feng Juan He Hua Yie Di Cang* (风卷荷花叶底藏)—Wind-Swept Lotus Flower Hidden beneath Leaves

6. *Yu Nü Chuan Suo Ba Fang Shi* (玉女穿梭八方式)—Fair Lady Passes the Shuttle in Eight Directions

7. *San Xing Kai He Zi Zhu Zhang* (三星开合自主张)—Three Stars Open and Close Freely and Naturally

8. *Er Qi Jiao Lai Da Hu Shi* (二起脚来打虎势)—Double Kick and Strike Tiger

9. *Pi Shen Xie Gua Yuan Yang Jiao* (披身斜挂鸳鸯脚)—Slant and Twist Body Sideways, Diagonal Block, and Mandarin Duck Kick

10. *Shun Shui Tui Zhou Bian Zao Gao* (顺水推舟鞭造篙)—Push a Boat along with the Tide, Raise the Sword Like a Whip, and Use It like a Punt-Pole

11. *Zuo You Fen Shui Long Men Tiao* (左右分水龙门跳)—Swim and Leap over the Dragon Gate

12. *Xia Shi San He Zi You Zhao* (下势三合自由招)—Assume a Low Position with Three Integrations and with Free and Natural Changes

13. *Bian He Xie Shi Fang Huan Chao* (卞和携石凤还巢)—Bian He Carries Jade Like a Phoenix Returning to Its Nest

Tai Ji Shou Shi (太极收式)—The Ending Form of Taiji *Dao*

All the movements of the form and some of the applications associated with each will be described in this section. Form practice requires that all movements be fluidly connected and rhythmic. In application practice, these requirements are less stringent and often the movements comprising the applications are smaller than those practiced in the form. Some of the steps, empty-hand movements, and movements used with single-leg stances in the form may be omitted or changed in application practice.

For each movement description, there is a Key Points section that focuses on internal components, feelings, and how to apply *jin*—trained force. This information will become more relevant once you have thoroughly learned all the physical movements of the form.

In the traditional Chinese writing style, historical stories and evocative imagery rather than direct descriptions are used to name actions or events. This style has come to typify much of martial arts writing, and we have adopted it here in using traditional poetic nomenclature to identify each posture. Some of the posture names may be difficult to understand or may seem odd when translated into English because they reflect a different cultural heritage and because there may not be words in English that exactly convey the meanings expressed by the Chinese characters. Rather than trying to understand each posture name literally, you should focus on the feeling that each name evokes.

Tai Ji Qi Shi (太极起式)—**The Beginning Posture of Taiji Dao**

Posture Name Explanation

This is a preparatory posture that adjusts your body, inside and out. It is important for increasing the efficiency of the subsequent postures of the form. When done well, this posture allows you to feel the effects of proper practice in greater detail. The beginning posture is not counted as one of the thirteen postures of the form.

The preparatory posture has two parts. The first concerns how to hold your sword and how to move it from your right hand to your left. The movements of this posture are very simple but must be done carefully in order to create feelings of excitement and concentration. The second part prepares you for practice by readying the internal components of jin, qi, yi, and shen. This part does not involve overt movements but, rather, requires that you assume a post-position and mentally move your attention from one acupoint to another.

The preparatory posture embodies the Taiji concept of wuji, the state of the universe at the beginning of time. In wuji, all skills are potential, but none have yet been individually realized. When wuji state changes to the state of taiji, yin and yang are differentiated, and all skills are generated. Like all skills, Taiji Dao skills originate from this posture that signifies the wuji state.

Zuo Shou Ti Dao (右手提刀)—Hold Sword in Right Hand

Movements: Walk naturally to the place you plan to practice and face any direction. The direction you choose is designated as south. This is a convention in Taiji Quan practice and is simply a way of orienting your movements with respect to a mental compass. Hold your sword in your right hand with the blade in front of you and the tiger mouth of your right hand touching the guard. Let the tip of your sword point forward and down. The blade should slant down naturally, and the back of your sword should face up (figs. 5-0-1a, b). Be careful not to let the tip of your sword touch the ground.

Key Points: Your internal feeling should be one of quiet alertness, as though you are in a dangerous place, preparing to defend yourself against an attack from any direction. You should be focused, calm, and alert but not nervous, and you should experience an internal sense of quickly flowing motion while maintaining an external appearance of great stillness.

Fig. 5-0-1a

Fig. 5-0-1b

You Shou Fan Ti (右手反提)—Reverse Sword Grip in Right Hand

Movements: Turn your right hand over and let your right palm face up so that your *daxi* acupoint faces up. Let your sword drop down vertically on your right side and in front of your body. The tip of your sword should point to the ground and the edge should face forward (fig. 5-0-2).

Fig. 5-0-2

Key Points: Maintain a feeling of quiet alertness as though danger is close, and you may need to move quickly. It is said of this state that "from quiet, motion arises."

Tui Shen Huan Shou (退身换手)—Withdraw Body and Change Sword Hand

Movements: First, look forward and to the right; then, look forward and to the left. Turn your right hand inward so that your sword traces a circular path upward and then from right to left. At the end of this circular movement, the tip of your sword should be pointing to the left of your body, and the blade should be horizontal to the ground with the edge facing forward. At the same time, take a step back with your right foot and let your left foot just follow. Only the toes of your left foot should touch the ground (fig. 5-0-3). Bend your left elbow and put your left hand under the handle of your sword. Grip your sword with your left hand, and, opening your right hand, let your right palm rest on the handle of your sword (fig. 5-0-4).

Fig. 5-0-3

Fig. 5-0-4

Key Points: Continue to maintain a feeling of quiet alertness. Imagine an attack coming from your left. With a modest and courteous feeling, step back and turn to the left to dodge the attack. Imagine that you still need to see what is going on before mounting a counterattack. Remain internally calm and quiet. A traditional adage used to characterize this state is "in motion, quiet remains."

Bao Dao Tiao Xi (抱刀调息)—Hold Dao in Left Hand and Adjust Qi

Movements: Step forward with your right foot and turn your body so that you face to the south. Drop both arms. Hold your sword in your left hand with the tip pointing up, the back of your blade touching the front of your left arm, and the edge facing forward. Your right arm should rest naturally along the right side of your body with your right palm flat against the side of your right leg and the middle finger of your right hand touching the outside of your right leg. Look forward and stand erect, keeping your body relaxed. This position is called *bao dao shi*—hold sword posture (fig. 5-0-5). Breathe deeply until your whole body feels comfortable and until your breathing is smooth and your mind quiet and clear.

Fig. 5-0-5

Key Points: Having completed the preparatory posture, your body should be excited and eager to move. Your mind should be relaxed yet vigilant. Imagine that your qi is sinking down and let this feeling cause your body to become very stable. At the same time, imagine that the baihui point at the top of your head is suspended from above. Imagine, too, that you have become a powerful and fleet-footed giant whose movements are quick and light.

Adjust your breath and qi as you would in empty-hand form practice and alternate your mental focus between the shenque point on your navel and the mingmen point on the center of your lower back in order naturally to establish reverse breathing. Imagine that qi is drawn into your whole body with each inspiration, and let this feeling of the intake and flow of qi animate all your movements.

1. *Qi Xing Kua Hu Jiao Dao Shi* (七星跨虎交刀势) —**Seven Stars, Ride Tiger, and Hand over *Dao***

Posture Name Explanation

This posture has three parts. Parts one and two are identical respectively to "step forward to form seven stars" and "step back to ride a tiger" in the empty-hand form. Part three involves transferring the *dao* from your left hand to your right hand.

The term "seven stars" refers to the parts of your body that are considered to be the most important. These are: the *baihui* acupoint on the top of your head, the *jianjing* acupoint on your shoulders, the *quchi* acupoint on your elbows, the *laogong* acupoint on the palm of your hands, the *huantiao* acupoint on your hips, the *yanglingquan* acupoint on your knees, and the *yongquan* acupoint on the soles of your feet. Paying attention to these "seven stars" will improve the integration of movements throughout your body.

1.1. *Ri Yue Sheng Hui* (日月生辉)—The Sun and Moon Are Bright

Movements: The sun represents your left eye and is yang; the moon represents your right eye and is yin. The term "bright" signifies a state of concentrated excitement that indicates your readiness to practice.

Turn your head to the left and look to the east (fig. 5-1-1). Following your gaze, your body should turn to the left as you step forward with your right foot. Touch the ground with the heel of your right foot and turn your right foot to the left until your toes point to the east. Shift your weight onto your right foot and move your left foot alongside your right foot. You will now be facing toward the east (fig. 5-1-2).

Fig. 5-1-1

Fig. 5-1-2

Application: Feel alert as you hold your sword. Imagine that your opponent is on your left side and keep your mind quiet and focused on him or her (fig. 5-1-3).

Fig. 5-1-3

Key Points: Direct your shen to the left. Put your *yi,* mind, on the *yuzhen* point at the back of your head. This will cause you to lean back slightly and to feel as though your body is dodging to the right and away from your opponent. Qi should be flowing throughout your body and reaching the baihui point on the uppermost part of your head. You should feel as though you are powerful, big, nimble though stable, and excitedly focused on engaging an opponent who might approach from any direction.

1.2. *Qu Xi Xu Shi* (曲膝蓄势)—Bend Knees to Prepare for Practice

Movements: Look straight ahead to the east. Relax your body and bend your knees. With your right palm facing the ground, push downward with your right hand. This will cause you to shift your weight onto your right leg. At the same time, move your left foot forward about one foot and let only the toes of your left foot touch the ground. You will now be in a left insubstantial stance (fig. 5-1-4).

Fig. 5-1-4

Application: Look to the left and turn your body to the left as you concentrate on your opponent and prepare to defend yourself (fig. 5-1-5).

Fig. 5-1-5

Key Points: Let your qi and your whole body sink down to create a sense of increased stability. As energy is stored in your right leg, your right knee can act as a spring and cause your body to bounce upward in any direction at any time.

Put your mind on the right laogong point at the center of your right palm and imagine pressing this palm downward. Look straight ahead and feel as though your whole body is chasing an imaginary spot along your line of vision.

1.3. *Gong Bu Heng Lan* (弓步横拦)—Block to the Left in Left Bow Stance

Movements: Look straight ahead to the east. Raise your sword with your left hand until your left thumb is opposite your nose. Step forward with your left foot, letting only your left heel touch the ground, and then shift your weight onto your left leg. You will now be in a left bow stance (fig. 5-1-6).

Fig. 5-1-6

Application: If your opponent attacks your face with a spear, step forward and use the handle of your sword to block the attack by making light contact with the shaft of the spear (fig. 5-1-7a). Move quickly toward your opponent as you block the spear and move your left index finger away from the left side of the handle of your sword in order to avoid injury to it when the two weapons make contact (fig. 5-1-7b).

Fig. 5-1-7a

Fig. 5-1-7b

Key Points: While using the handle of your sword to block left, upward, and forward, focus your mind on your right hand and, without actually moving it, think about pushing it down, back, and to the right. The trained force in both hands should be integrated, and your mind should be focused on your right laogong point. This will ensure that the downward force of your right hand supports the blocking force of your left hand.

1.4. *Shang Bu Qi Xing* (上步七星)
—Step Forward and Assume Seven-Star Posture

Movements: Thrust your right hand forward with the right palm facing to the left until your hands cross each other with your right wrist underneath your left wrist. Then, immediately push both hands forward and, at the same time, step forward with your right foot, letting your right heel touch the ground and your right toes point up. You will now be in a left sitting stance (fig. 5-1-8).

Fig. 5-1-8

Application: Without interruption from the last movement, continue to block your opponent's spear with the handle of your sword. Step forward with your right foot and quickly slide your sword down along your opponent's spear toward his or her left hand. At the same time, grip your opponent's right hand with your right hand and use your right foot to kick his or her left knee (fig. 5-1-9). If you are successful in sliding your sword along your opponent's spear, your opponent will open his or her left hand and lose control of his or her weapon. You can also use your right hand to strike your opponent directly.

Fig. 5-1-9

Key Points: With both hands in front of your body, feel as though your chest and arms enclose a ball and then sink your shoulders and drop your elbows to make the circle expand. This will cause a slight rounding of your back so that power gathers in your hands without your directly using the force in them. Relax your left leg and keep it very stable by putting your mind on the left *yinqiaomei* acupoint channel on the inside of your left leg. This will cause your right leg to be very light and flexible.

1.5. *Che Bu Xia Jie* (撤步下截)—Step Back and Block Down

Movements: Look forward and down. Push both hands directly down until they are at waist level. At the same time, lean forward a little bit and step back with your right foot. You will be in a left bow stance (fig. 5-1-10).

Fig. 5-1-10

Application: If your opponent attacks your right knee with his or her spear, step back with your right foot and push the handle of your sword down to block your opponent's spear lightly (fig. 5-1-11).

Fig. 5-1-11

Key Points: When you push down, you should feel as though you are stretching forward. Step back with your right foot and imagine that your abdomen is withdrawing. Relax your waist and put your mind on the left huantiao point on your left hip to create the sense that this point is sinking down to the ground.

1.6. *Tui Shen Xiao Lan* (退身下拦)—Move Body Back and Make a Low Block

Movements: Keep looking forward and down. Turn your body to the right. Separate your hands and move your left hand, holding your sword, down slightly and to the left. Rotate your left hand slightly to the left. Swing your right hand back to waist level with your palm facing up and straighten your back slightly so that your body rises. At the same time, turn on the ball of your right foot so that the toes of that foot point to the south. Shift your weight to your right leg to form a right half horse-riding stance (fig. 5-1-12). Keep swinging your right hand up to head level and shift your weight onto your right leg to form a right side-bow stance (fig. 5-1-13). Continue to look forward and down.

Fig. 5-1-12   Fig. 5-1-13

Application: The swing of your right hand back and up will generate power in your left hand that can then be used to pull your opponent's spear to your left side and back (fig. 5-1-14). This will make your opponent lean forward and lose his or her balance.

Fig. 5-1-14

Key Points: Think about your right hand's rising up. Put your mind on your right laogong point to create the sense that it is pushing outward. The higher your hand is raised, the more downward power the handle of your sword will acquire.

1.7. *Li Shen Cheng Zhang* (立身撑掌)—Stand Up and Push Palm Up

Movements: Raise your head slightly to look straight ahead to the east. Push your right palm up and raise your body until you are standing straight up with your weight on your right leg. At the same time, move your left foot back beside your right foot. Move your left hand, holding your sword, to the left side of your left leg (fig. 5-1-15).

Fig. 5-1-15

Application: Continuing the last movement, swing your right hand up and raise your body. This will generate additional downward pressure on your opponent's spear and will cause your opponent to lose balance.

Key Points: Keep your mind on your right laogong point to increase the feeling that your right palm is pushing up. Imagine that you are so huge that your hand can reach the sky even while your feet are deeply planted in the ground.

1.8. *Dun Shen Hui Bao* (蹲身回抱)—Squat Down and Hold *Dao* Back

Movements: Keep looking to the east. Raise your left hand, holding your sword, back to the right side of your body at the level of your lower ribs. Your left forearm should be horizontal, and your sword should be positioned horizontally along your left arm with its tip pointing to the east and its edge facing to the south. Your left palm should face up, and both feet should point to the south as should your body. Look to the east. Bend both legs to assume a squatting position. At the same time, continue pushing up with your right palm until your right hand is over your head, and your right palm faces up (fig. 5-1-16).

Fig. 5-1-16

Application: Continue the last movement. If your opponent leans toward you, plunge the tip of your sword into his or her chest or ribs. This is the thrust skill called *zha* (fig. 5-1-17).

Fig. 5-1-17

If your opponent's spear is in front of your body, use the handle of your sword to block it (fig. 5-1-18). Then, grip your opponent's spear with your right hand, pull it to the right, and deliver the zha thrust (fig. 5-1-19).

Fig. 5-1-18

Fig. 5-1-19

Key Points: When the tip of your sword points to your opponent, imagine stepping back from him or her. The orientation of your sword will convey to your opponent that you are ready to lunge toward him or her at any moment and that you are confident in your ability to attack at will. The sense that you are about to step back from your opponent will cause him or her to worry about exactly when your attack might come. Focus intently on your opponent to increase his or her fear. Keep your mind on your right laogong point as you imagine pushing your right hand outward.

1.9. *Kai Bu Shang Lan* (开步上拦)—Step Forward and Block Up

Movements: Look to the east. Turn your body to the left and step to the left with your left foot so that the toes of your left foot point to the east. Sweep upward with your left hand and, at the same time, sweep your right palm down in front of your body. Both palms should face each other and cross in front of your body (fig. 5-1-20).

Fig. 5-1-20

Keep sweeping your left hand up until it is level with your eyebrow while also continuing to push your right hand down and back until it is alongside your right hip. Turn on the ball of your right foot until the toes of your right foot point to the east. As you turn, shift your weight onto your left leg to assume a left bow stance (fig. 5-1-21).

Fig. 5-1-21

Application: If your opponent attacks your face with a spear, step forward and use the handle of your sword to block the spear along its shaft (fig. 5-1-22). Move quickly toward your opponent and lightly block his or her thrust. Move your left index finger away from the left side of the handle of your sword to avoid having your finger hit by the shaft of your opponent's spear (fig. 5-1-7b).

Fig. 5-1-22

Key Points: When you block to the left, forward, and up, put your mind on your right laogong point and think about pushing your right hand to the right, back, and down. This mental focus will balance the force of your block. Also, think about relaxing your left leg.

1.10. *Jiao Dao Hu Wan* (交刀护腕)
—Change Dao to Right Hand and Push Right Wrist Out

Movements: Look straight ahead. Raise your right hand to the left until it reaches the upper side of the handle of your sword. As soon as your right hand touches the handle of your sword, release the handle with your left hand and grip it with your right hand (fig. 5-1-23). After changing your grip from your left hand to your right, turn your left hand over and move it to the inner edge of your right wrist. Then, push your hands slightly up and to the left while turning your body slightly to the left. Drop your right elbow to protect your chest. Look to the right and down (fig. 5-1-24).

Fig. 5-1-23

Fig. 5-1-24

Application: As soon as the handle of your sword touches your opponent's spear, grip the handle of your sword with your right hand and transfer your sword to this hand. At the same time, push the handle of your sword to the left and slightly upward to gain better control. Immediately after transferring your sword to your right hand, use your left hand either to push on your right wrist or to grip your opponent's spear (fig. 5-1-25).

Fig. 5-1-25

Key Points: Think about the circle formed by your arms and imagine that it is expanding. Straighten your right leg and put your mind on the right *cheng-shan* point on your right ankle to create a feeling that your right foot is being inserted into the ground. Feel that the force from your right foot is flowing to your left hand as it pushes outward. Imagine that you can dodge quickly and nimbly to the left.

2. *Shan Zhan Teng Nuo Yi Qi Yang* (闪战腾挪意气扬) —Dodge and Focus, Jump and Move, Excite Mind and Qi

Posture Name Explanation

Shan means to dodge and *zhan* refers to a state of concentration with a tinge of fear and a gingerly attitude. *Teng* means to jump up easily and lightly, and *nuo* means to move sideways. *Yi* (mind) *qi yang* means that all your internal feelings are heightened and activated.

The main goal of this posture is to excite shen, yi, and qi and to make them expansive and highly focused. Your internal feelings and external sensations should be characterized by nimbleness and a readiness to fight. Your movements should be quick and agile, ideal for jumping and dodging.

It is important to note that in this second posture some of the movements in the Taiji Dao form are different from the movements that should be used if a regular *dao* is used. These differences occur after movement 2.3, *ce shen quan zha* (側身圈扎)—dodge body and thrust *dao* forward in a curve. In the discussion of the second posture, all the movements in the Taiji Dao form will be described first; those for a regular *dao* variation of the form will be presented second.

2.1. *Ti Xi Xia Jie* (提膝下截)—Raise Right Knee and Block Down

Movements: Look down and to the right. Separate your hands and move your right hand, holding your sword, forward and to the right in a downward chop or block. Make a hook with your left hand and move that hand back and up so that your arms form a straight diagonal line from the upper left behind you to the lower right in front of you. At the same time, raise your body by straightening your left leg. Raise your right knee to the left as though to evade a strike at your right leg (fig. 5-2-1).

Fig. 5-2-1

Application: Continue the previous movement without interruption. If you can grip your opponent's spear with your left hand, pull it behind you to the upper left. At the same time, use your sword to chop your opponent's leg. Your raised knee can be used to initiate a large step (fig. 5-2-2), or, if you imagine that your opponent is about to attack your right knee with his or her spear, you can dodge the attack by pulling your right knee up and away from the point of attack while using your sword to block your opponent's spear (fig. 5-2-3).

Fig. 5-2-2   Fig. 5-2-3

Key Points: Raise your body and turn your torso slightly to the left while using your sword to chop or block to the right and down with quick and nimble movements. Think about lifting your right knee higher. Focus your mind on your left laogong point to create a feeling that your left hand is pushing outward. This feeling will generate power in the front edge of your sword. Feel your body move to the left and upward as you chop to the right and downward.

2.2. *Gong Bu Shan Shen* (弓步闪身)—Dodge to the Right in a Bow Stance

Movements: Look forward. Drop your right knee and step forward with your right foot to form a right wide bow stance. At the same time, drop both arms down to hip level. Push down with your left palm and hold your sword in your right hand so that the blade is horizontal and the tip points to the east (fig. 5-2-4).

Fig. 5-2-4

Application: Imagine that your opponent pulls his or her spear back and then attacks your chest or face. Lower your body and dodge to the right (fig. 5-2-5).

Fig. 5-2-5

Key Points: Relax your waist and let your body sink down. Feel as though your right leg is very agile and can quickly and nimbly step aside to dodge an attack. Put your mind on the mingmen point on your waist and turn to the right. Feel as though you are dodging to the right while focusing on your opponent's left side.

2.3. *Ce Shen Quan Zha* (侧身圈扎)
—Dodge Body and Thrust *Dao* Forward in a Curve

Movements: Continuing without interruption, move your body slightly to the right and forward. Look forward and to the left. Raise your right hand and thrust your sword forward and to the left in a curving path at shoulder or rib level. Move your left hand around to the right side of your body until your left palm reaches the inner side of your right wrist (fig. 5-2-6).

Fig. 5-2-6

Application: Continue to dodge your opponent's attack and use the tip of your sword to thrust at your opponent's left arm or ribs. Usually this thrust is called *quan ci,* or circling thrust (fig. 5-2-7).

Fig. 5-2-7

Key Points: The movement of your body and the motion of your sword should be curvilinear. Your dodge to the right and downward must be coordinated with the thrust of your sword to the left and upward. Your left palm should touch the inside of your right wrist in order to help control your sword. If necessary, your left hand can grip the handle of your sword underneath your right forearm to give your thrust extra power. Put your mind on your mingmen point and turn slightly to the left.

2.4. *Ti Xi Quan Bi* (提膝圈臂)—Raise Right Knee and Move Arms in a Circle

Movements: Look forward. Shift your weight back onto your left leg and raise your right knee so that your right foot leaves the ground. At the same time, move your right hand slightly to the left and your left hand slightly to the right to form a circle. Both arms should move up slightly as you begin these movements (fig. 5-2-8).

Fig. 5-2-8

Application: If your opponent uses his or her spear to attack your chest or face, move your body back slightly and move your sword forward to block your opponent's spear lightly (fig. 5-2-9).

Fig. 5-2-9

Key Points: Form a circle with your arms and imagine that the circle is expanding. Put your mind on the tanzhong point on the center of your chest to create a hollow feeling in your chest.

2.5. *Bai Kou Xuan Dao* (摆扣旋刀)
—Sweep the Sword around with Baibu and Koubu

Movements: Look around toward the right side of your body. Step forward with your right foot and turn your toes to the south in a *baibu*—swing step. At the same time, separate your arms as though to enlarge the circle they form. Keep the blade of your sword flat and the edge facing outward along the perimeter of the circle (fig. 5-2-10).

Fig. 5-2-10

Continue turning your body to the right. At the same time, make a left *koubu* —buckle step—by placing your left foot in front of your right foot at a right angle (fig. 5-2-11). Keep turning your body to the right until you face to the northwest. Let your gaze sweep to the right as you turn. At the same time, shift your weight onto your left leg. Keep moving your sword along the perimeter of the circle created by the turn of your body (fig. 5-2-12).

Fig. 5-2-11   Fig. 5-2-12

Application: Continuing from the previous movement, as soon as your sword touches your opponent's spear, use your left hand to grip his or her weapon. At the same time, step with your right foot in a baibu and then with your left foot in a koubu to turn your body to the right. This is called "rolling one's body toward the opponent" (fig. 5-2-13).

Fig. 5-2-13

Key Points: Keep your mind on your tanzhong point and feel as though the circle formed by your arms is expanding and moving in a spiral. Move your feet nimbly and quickly to follow the spirited movement of your body. Your shen should be located in your back, and your mind should chase your shen. The feeling associated with this configuration is called "a cat chases its tail."

2.6. *Hui Shen Heng Sao* (回身横扫)—Turn Body Back with a Sweep of the Sword

Movements: Continue turning your body to the right until you are facing to the east. Look to the east. At the same time, make a right baibu by moving your right foot to the right and back until your toes point to the east. Shift your weight onto your right foot and turn on the ball of your left foot until it also points to the east. This results in a right bow stance. As your body turns, sweep your sword to the right (fig. 5-2-14).

Fig. 5-2-14

Application: Continuing the previous rolling movement, turn your body to the right. At the same time, sweep your sword to the right to chop horizontally at your opponent (fig. 5-2-15).

Fig. 5-2-15

Key Points: Follow the feeling of expansion in your arm circle by looking suddenly backward and separating your arms to your sides. Focus your mind on the *xuanguan* point midway between your eyebrows to create a feeling that your body is moving forward. The movement of your sword should chase the path of your gaze.

2.7. *Tui Shen Shang Peng* (退身上掤)
—Withdraw Body, Expand Arms, and Move Sword Upward

Movements: Look straight ahead. Shift your weight back and move your right foot back slightly, letting only the toes of that foot touch the ground so that you assume a right insubstantial stance. At the same time, move your left arm forward and slightly up in a counterclockwise semicircle and move your right arm, holding your sword, horizontally forward and upward in a clockwise semicircle. Your sword should be in front of your body (fig. 5-2-16). Continue the circling movements by bringing your arms back toward the center of your chest and, as you do, expand the circle and drop your arms slightly (fig. 5-2-17).

Fig. 5-2-16

Fig. 5-2-17

Application: If your opponent attacks your face with a spear, move your body back slightly and block your opponent's thrust lightly by letting your sword cross the shaft of his or her spear. Follow your opponent's force by moving your sword back and slightly to the right in a circular path. This will move the tip of your opponent's spear away from the front of your face (fig. 5-2-18).

Fig. 5-2-18

Key Points: Keep your mind on your xuanguan point and move your body slightly back. When your arms have once again formed a circle, put your mind on the laogong point on your left palm and imagine pushing it forward. Relax your waist and imagine that your left leg is a spring ready to propel your body upward. The springy feeling in your left leg should be coordinated with the feeling of expansion in your arm circle.

2.8. *Quan Dai Heng Zhan* (圈带横斩)—Circle Sword and Chop Horizontally

Movements: Look forward and slightly up. Shift your weight forward to form a right bow stance and continue to let your arms and your sword form a circle (fig. 5-2-19). Then, immediately step back with your right foot (fig. 5-2-20), shift your weight onto it and take a small step back with your left foot while leaning back. At the same time, draw a clockwise circle in front of your face with your sword. Move your left hand forward slightly as though to grab something (fig. 5-2-21).

Fig. 5-2-19   Fig. 5-2-20   Fig. 5-2-21

Continue to move your left hand to the left and then back. Form a hook with the fingers of your left hand and point them upward as you move your left hand back. Chop horizontally from right to left with your right hand until your sword is in front of your body. Your right palm should face up. Keep the blade of your sword flat. The tip of your sword should point to the east and the edge should face to the north. At the same time, step forward with your left foot to form a left bow stance. This step can be bigger than a regular step and can draw your right foot somewhat forward (fig. 5-2-22).

Fig. 5-2-22

Application: If you succeed in crossing your opponent's spear with your sword, continue the previous application by stepping forward and using your left hand to grip his or her spear. At the same time, swing your sword in a circle from your right side (fig. 5-2-23). Continue to pull your opponent's spear to the left and back with your left hand while chopping horizontally at his or her body from right to left (fig. 5-2-24).

Fig. 5-2-23

Fig. 5-2-24

If your sword crosses your opponent's spear (fig. 5-2-25), you can also stick your sword on his or her spear and turn your sword over on top of and inside your opponent's weapon. This will move your opponent's spear to the right and allow you to move forward and chop at him or her horizontally (fig. 5-2-26).

Fig. 5-2-25

Fig. 5-2-26

Key Points: Keep your mind on your left laogong point and imagine pulling it backward. Feel your hands separating in opposite directions as your waist turns. The force in your left hand, as you think about pulling it back, and the force of your side chop should be coordinated.

Note: The movement descriptions just presented for the second posture are applicable if you are using a Taiji *dao*. If you are using a regular *dao*, there is a commonly practiced and shorter variation of the form that has simpler movements. This variation has three movements following those delineated in section 2.3, rather than the five just described. The three alternate movements are presented next.

2.4. *Zuo Chan Tou* (左缠头)—Wind Sword Up to the Left around Head

Movements: Continue from figure 5-2-6 by raising your right hand, holding your sword. Rotate your right arm by moving it first forward and then winding it up and to the left until it is on the left side of your head. Your right arm should be rising throughout this arc so that when your sword reaches the left side of your body, your right elbow is level with the top of your head. Your sword should be held vertically on the left side of your body, and the tip should point to the ground. The edge should face outward, away from your body. During the rotation of your right arm, turn your body slightly to the right and push your left palm to the right and back. Form a right bow stance (fig. 5-2-27).

Fig. 5-2-27

Application: When your opponent thrusts at your chest (fig. 5-2-28), move forward and raise your sword vertically to parry his or her spear to the left (fig. 5-2-29).

Fig. 5-2-28

Fig. 5-2-29

Key Points: Put your mind on the right *jiquan* point under your armpit and feel as though this area is opening up. Feel the force in your right hand pushing to the left and the force in your left hand pushing to the right. These feelings should create a sensation that your upper body is spiraling upward and that your lower body is turning downward.

2.5. *Guo Nao Qian Lu* (裹脑前捋)
—Wrap Sword around Head and Reach Hand Forward

Movements: Continue the previous movement without interruption by moving your right hand around and over your head until it is over your right shoulder. Begin to step forward with your left foot while keeping your weight on your right leg (fig. 5-2-30). As you step forward with your left foot, move your left hand forward and hold your sword on the right side of your body (fig. 5-2-31).

Fig. 5-2-30   Fig. 5-2-31

Application: Continue moving your right arm from the previous movement so that your sword appears to wrap around your head to keep parrying your opponent's spear to the left until your sword is over your right shoulder. At the same time, step forward with your left foot toward your opponent. The backward movement of your sword will direct your opponent's spear behind and to the left of your body as you step toward him or her. Use your left hand to grip your opponent's spear (fig. 5-2-32).

Fig. 5-2-32

Key Points: Put your mind on your left laogong point and push it to the right. Imagine using your stomach to touch your right leg. This will create a sinking feeling in your body. The backward movement of your sword and the forward movement of your left hand should be integrated.

2.6. *Gong Bu Heng Zhan* (弓步横斩)—Horizontal Chop in Bow Stance

Movements: Without interruption, continue to shift your weight onto your left foot and turn your right foot to form a left bow stance. At the same time, move your left palm forward, then to the left and finally behind your back. While moving your left hand back in a horizontal circle, make a hook with the fingers of your left hand as though you were about to grab something. Simultaneously, chop down with your sword in a horizontal curve from right to left until the tip points to the east. The blade of your sword should be flat and the edge should face to the north (fig. 5-2-33).

Fig. 5-2-33

Application: When your left hand grips your opponent's spear, pull it to your left and then behind your body. At the same time, swing your sword from right to left in a horizontal chop at your opponent's body (fig. 5-2-34).

Fig. 5-2-34

Key Points: Keep your mind on your left laogong point as you pull your left hand, holding your opponent's spear, back and as you swing your sword forward with your right hand to chop at your opponent. The backward pull of your left hand and the swing forward of your right hand should be coordinated in an uninterrupted flow so that the two movements form a single unit. When you swing your sword forward, imagine that you are wielding a large, long-handled sword held in a two-handed grip.

3. *Zuo Gu You Pan Liang Fen Zhang* (左顾右盼两分张) —Guard Left and Right, Opening and Extending Two Times

Posture Name Explanation

Zuogu means "looking after the left," and *youpan* means "watching the right." These are commonly used terms in Taiji Quan practice, and their meanings are essentially equal, although *zuogu* is sometimes used to describe turning to the side and going forward, while *youpan* is used to describe turning to the side and going backward. Both terms advise you to be watchful in order to protect or defend yourself from an attack that may come from any direction at any moment.

Liang fen zhang means to "open and extend your palms twice" as if you were swimming and reaching out to part the water ahead of you. The movements of both zuogu and youpan involve separating your hands, and each is done twice in this posture.

The main idea of this posture is to be vigilant at all times, ready to defend against attacks from any direction. The movements are designed to protect against attacks from the left and right, the front and back, and from high and low. In most of the movements of this posture, your sword should stick on your opponent's spear and follow it. Embodying Taiji Quan principles, this is a typical Taiji Dao skill.

3.1. *Li Dao Zuo Gu* (立刀左顾)—Block Vertically and Look to the Left

Movements: Turn your right hand inward toward your body and move it to the left and back until your right forearm is close to your stomach and your sword is on the left side of your body at rib level. Rotate your sword vertically on the left side of your body so that the tip points up and the edge faces back. This position is called "looking after the left" (fig. 5-3-1).

Application: If your opponent attacks your chest with a spear, raise your sword to touch the left

Fig. 5-3-1

side of the spear lightly. Your sword should point up in front of your chest, and the blade should cross your opponent's spear. As soon as you make contact with his or her spear, turn your right wrist inward. This will cause your sword to turn so that the edge faces backward. The turn of your sword should follow the motion of your opponent's spear and parry it to the left (fig. 5-3-2).

Fig. 5-3-2

Key Points: Maintain a circling feeling in your right arm. Let the handle of your sword sink slightly so that the blade gains vertical power. When your sword parries or blocks to the left and back, you should feel as though you can move your body forward from the right. Relax your left leg and put your mind on your baihui point to create a feeling that your body is suspended from above.

3.2. *Ti Xi Lan Gua* (提膝拦挂)—Raise Left Knee, Block, and Let Sword Hang

Movements: Shift your weight back onto your right leg. Raise your left knee and point it to the southeast. At the same time, turn your body slightly to the right and move your right hand, holding your sword, down and forward to the southeast. Your sword should move in a curved path on the left side of your body. At the end of the movement, your right hand should be over your left knee, and your sword should be oriented vertically beside your left knee with the tip pointing down and the edge facing to the southeast. This is called "watching the right." Keep your left hand in a hook behind your body (figs. 5-3-3a, b).

Fig. 5-3-3a   Fig. 5-3-3b

Application: If your opponent turns his or her spear down to attack your left knee, withdraw your body and raise your left knee to the right. At the same time, move your sword to follow your opponent's spear to the left and down and then diagonally forward and to the right. Your sword should be held vertically in front of your left knee. The tip of your sword should point down with the edge facing forward. Keep your sword sticking to your opponent's spear and parry it to the right (fig. 5-3-4).

Fig. 5-3-4

Key Points: Relax your waist to turn to the right and lift your left knee to the right and upward. Feel as though you can jump lightly away from your opponent's attack with your sword providing protection in front of you. Put your mind on your xuanguan point. Feel as though your arms are stretching out and extending force in opposite directions.

3.3. *Gong Bu Tui Hua* (弓步滑推)
—Smoothly Push Sword Forward in Left Bow Stance

Movements: Step forward toward the southeast with your left foot to form a left bow stance. At the same time, put your left hand on the back of your sword and push it forward and slightly down. Keep your sword oriented vertically and lean slightly forward (fig. 5-3-5).

Fig. 5-3-5

Application: As soon as your opponent's spear is parried and passes over your left knee to the right, continue without interruption from the previous movement by stepping forward with your left foot to form a left bow stance. At the same time, stick your sword on your opponent's spear, put your left hand on the back of your sword and push it forward along his or her spear. Your footwork must be quick and nimble. However quickly your opponent steps back or retracts his or her spear, you must keep your sword sticking on your opponent's weapon and slide it smoothly and quickly toward his or her front hand (fig. 5-3-6).

Fig. 5-3-6

Key Points: Stretch your left leg out as though you were getting ready to jump very far forward. Relax your waist so that you feel as though your body is sinking down. This will add power to the movement of your sword. Keep your sword sticking on your opponent's spear and following it continuously. Put your mind on the right yongquan point on the sole of your right foot, and imagine that it can continuously push your body forward. Feel a bounce in your left foot so that you can continue to step forward without interruption.

3.4. *Dao Cha You Ge* (倒插右格)—Block Right in Back Insert Step

Movements: The three connected lower parry movements that follow form a sequence called "a lion shakes its head three times." In the first of these movements, step back with your left foot to form a back insert step. At the same time, pull your sword to the right and slightly back with both hands. Keep your sword oriented vertically in front of your body and a little to the right of your right knee with the tip pointing down (fig. 5-3-7).

Fig. 5-3-7

Application: If your opponent steps quickly and can adjust his or her spear to attack your right knee with considerable force, maintain contact between your sword and your opponent's spear and follow his or her spear toward your right knee. While following the spear, push your sword slightly to the right to parry attack (fig. 5-3-8). If the attack is very hard, step back with your left foot to follow your opponent's thrust and simultaneously parry the spear further to the right (fig. 5-3-9).

Fig. 5-3-8

Fig. 5-3-9

Key Points: Continue to stick and follow your opponent's spear. Put your mind on your tanzhong point and feel your chest hollowing as you step back with your left foot. This will create a sense that your sword is moving forward. Feel springiness in your right foot. This will help you step backward smoothly without interruption.

3.5. *Che Bu Zou Lan* (撤步左拦)—Step Back and Block Left

Movements: Step back with your right foot to form a left bow stance. Use both hands to push your sword to the left until it is in front and a little to the left of your left knee. Your sword should remain vertical with the tip pointing down (fig. 5-3-10).

Fig. 5-3-10

Application: If your opponent pulls his or her spear back and again attacks your left leg quickly and forcefully, step back with your right foot and move your sword to the left to touch his or her spear (fig. 5-3-11). Push your sword slightly to the left and forward while continuing to stick your opponent's spear with your sword. Make sure the tip of your opponent's spear is not far from your left leg so that if he or she keeps moving forward, you will be close enough to cut his or her front hand with your sword (fig. 5-3-12).

Fig. 5-3-11   Fig. 5-3-12

Key Points: Relax your waist and sink your body. Continue to stick and follow your opponent's spear. Put your mind on your left laogong point to push your sword forward. Feel a bounce in your left foot so that your backward steps will be smooth and continuous.

3.6. *Xu Bu Hui Dai* (虚步回带)—Pull Sword Back in Insubstantial Stance

Movements: Take a half-step back with your left foot. Touch the toes of your left foot to the ground in front of your right foot to form a left insubstantial stance. At the same time, use both hands to pull your sword back until it is in front of your left knee. Keep your sword vertical with the tip pointing down (fig. 5-3-13).

Fig. 5-3-13

Application: If your opponent pulls his or her spear back and then attacks your right leg again, shift your weight back and withdraw your body. At the same time, pull your sword back to parry your opponent's spear to the right (fig. 5-3-14).

Fig. 5-3-14

Key Points: Relax your waist and let the weight of your body sink down onto your right leg. Continue to stick and follow your opponent's spear. Put your mind on the left yanglingquan point on the outside of your left knee. Feel as though your left knee can move upward in order to create a sense of lightness in your left leg.

3.7. *Jin Bu Hua Tui* (进步滑推)
—Step Forward and Smoothly Push Sword Forward

Movements: Step forward with your left foot to form a left bow stance. At the same time, push your sword forward with both hands in a smooth sliding motion. Your sword should remain vertical with the tip pointing down (fig. 5-3-15).

Fig. 5-3-15

Application: Continue the previous movement without interruption by maintaining contact between your sword and your opponent's spear. Parry your opponent's spear slightly to the right. As soon as his or her spear moves to the right, step forward quickly with your left foot and push your sword forward, sliding it along your opponent's spear toward his or her front hand (fig. 5-3-16).

Fig. 5-3-16

Key Points: Continue to stick and follow your opponent's spear. Put your mind on your right yongquan point to push your body forward. Your left leg should feel nimble so that you can quickly take a long step forward.

3.8. *Fan Shen Pi Dao* (翻身劈刀)—Turn Body and Chop Back

Movements: Turn your head to the right and look back to the west. Turn your body to follow your gaze. At the same time, shift your weight slightly onto your right leg and turn on the ball of your right foot until your right toes point to the southwest. As you begin to pivot on your right foot, move your left palm close to your right wrist and raise both hands upward. Then, separate your hands and use your right hand to chop to the right with your sword. Push to the east with your left palm. At the same time, continually shift your weight onto your right leg and turn on the ball of your left foot until the toes of your left foot point to the southwest. You will be in a right high side-bow stance (fig. 5-3-17).

Fig. 5-3-17

Application: If your opponent attacks you from behind, turn your body back and use your sword to parry his or her spear lightly to the left. Continue to stick your sword on your opponent's spear. At the same time, move your left hand underneath your right hand to grip his or her spear (fig. 5-3-18) and immediately pull it backward. Simultaneously, move your sword up and then forward to deliver a powerful chop to your opponent's head (fig. 5-3-19a).

This skill can also be used when your opponent attacks you from the front. In this case, instead of turning your body back, turn to the left and step forward with your right foot to execute your chop (fig. 5-3-19b).

Fig. 5-3-18

Fig. 5-3-19a

Fig. 5-3-19b

Key Points: Relax your waist. When you look back and turn your body to chop at your opponent approaching from behind, imagine that your sword is chasing the path of your gaze. Put your mind on your left laogong point and imagine using your left hand to push your body to the east. The forces in your right and left hands should extend in opposite directions.

3.9. *Hui Shen Fan Liao* (回身反撩)—Turn Body Back and Make a Reverse Cut

Movements: Turn your head back to look to the east. Then, turn to the left by swiveling on the ball of your left foot until your toes point to the east. Shift your weight slightly onto your left leg. At the same time, push your left palm to the left and slightly down. Drop your right hand with your sword, bend your right elbow and move your right hand along the right side of your body. Hold your sword in your right hand in a relaxed manner with the tip pointing toward the ground and the edge facing to the east (fig. 5-3-20).

Fig. 5-3-20

Continue the previous movement without interruption by shifting your weight forward onto your left foot and turning on the ball of your right foot until your right toes point to the east. You will now be in a standard left bow stance. At the same time, move your left palm down and back and let your fingers form a hook. Push your right hand forward and turn your right wrist outward so that your right palm faces to the south. The tip of your sword should move in an upward arc until it is at chest level, parallel to the ground, and pointing to the east. The edge of your sword should face up (fig. 5-3-21).

Fig. 5-3-21

Application: If your opponent attacks your right leg with a spear, let the tip of your sword drop down and turn your wrist outward. Holding your sword vertically, stick it to your opponent's spear with the edge facing out (fig. 5-3-22). Parry your opponent's spear slightly to the right to move it away from your right leg. Then, step forward with your right foot.

While maintaining contact between your sword and your opponent's spear, slide your sword along the shaft of your opponent's spear to cut his or her front hand (fig. 5-3-23). Your footwork should be quick and nimble so that your opponent has no chance to step away from you. If your opponent opens his or her hand to avoid injury when you slide your sword toward him or her, keep moving your sword forward to attack your opponent's body directly (fig. 5-3-24).

Fig. 5-3-22

Fig. 5-3-23

Fig. 5-3-24

Key Points: Keep your mind on your left laogong point and imagine pulling it back. Follow this feeling by turning your waist to the left and imagine that you are throwing your sword forward. Feel as though the forces in your hands are extending in opposite directions. The force on your sword, rather than being circular (as is often the case), should be more like a push followed by a forward throw.

It is important to stick and follow your opponent's spear. Also, because your Taiji *dao* is long, you must hold it high when it passes the right side of your body so that the tip does not touch the ground.

3.10. *Li Dao Zuo Gu* (立刀左顾)—Block Vertically and Look Left

Movements: Move your right hand, holding your sword, to the left and then back to the left side of your body at rib level. Your sword should be held vertically on the left side of your body with the tip pointing up and the edge facing the back of your body (fig. 5-3-25).

Fig. 5-3-25

Application: If your opponent attacks your chest with a spear again, raise your sword to touch the left side of his or her weapon lightly. Your sword should point upward in front of your chest with the blade crossing the shaft of your opponent's spear. As soon as you make contact with his or her spear, turn your right wrist inward so that the edge of your sword faces backward. The turn of your sword should follow the motion of your opponent's spear and parry it to the left (fig. 5-3-26).

Fig. 5-3-26

Key Points: Imagine inserting the handle of your sword into the ground. This will increase the vertical power in the blade of your sword. When you parry or block to the left and backward with your sword, you should feel as though you can move your body forward from the right. Relax your left leg and put your mind on your baihui point to create a feeling of being suspended from above.

3.11. *Ti Xi Lan Gua* (提膝拦挂)—Raise Left Knee, Block, and Let Sword Hang

Fig. 5-3-27

Movements: Shift your weight back onto your right leg. Raise your left knee and point it to the southeast. At the same time, turn your body slightly to the right and move your right hand, holding your sword, down and then forward to the southeast. Your sword should move in a downward arc along the left side of your body, and this movement should end with your right hand over your left knee and your sword oriented vertically beside your left knee with the tip pointing down and the edge facing to the southeast (fig. 5-3-27).

Application: If your opponent turns his or her spear down to attack your left knee, withdraw your body and raise your left knee to the right. At the same time, move your sword to follow the movement of your opponent's spear to the left and downward and then diagonally forward and to the right. Hold your sword vertically in front of your left knee with the tip pointing down and the edge facing forward. Keep your sword sticking to your opponent's spear and parry it to the right (fig. 5-3-28).

Fig. 5-3-28

Key Points: Relax your waist as you turn to the right and feel as though you can jump up lightly behind the protection of your sword. Put your mind on your xuanguan point and imagine your arms stretched outward and extending force in opposite directions.

3.12. *Zuo Gong Tui Zha* (左弓推扎)
—Push Sword to Thrust Forward in Left Bow Stance

Movements: Turn your body slightly to the right. Put your left hand on the back of your sword (fig. 5-3-29). Step forward to the southeast with your left foot to form a left bow stance. At the same time, push your sword forward and upward. Keep your sword horizontal with the tip pointing forward and the edge facing up. Lean slightly forward (fig. 5-3-30).

Fig. 5-3-29

Fig. 5-3-30

Application: Continue the previous movement without interruption. Keep sticking your opponent's spear and put your left hand on the back of your sword to push it forward and up. At the same time, step forward with your left foot (fig. 5-3-31) and keep pushing your sword forward and up in a circle until it is at head level. This movement will "roll up" your opponent's spear so that your sword is underneath his or her spear and the tip of your sword points to his or her face (fig. 5-3-32). Keeping your sword on your opponent's spear, slide your sword forward and thrust toward his or her face. If you can grip your opponent's spear with your left hand as your sword slides along the shaft, you will gain additional control (fig. 5-3-33).

Fig. 5-3-31

Fig. 5-3-32

Fig. 5-3-33

Key Points: Continue to stick and follow your opponent's spear. When stretching your right leg out and pushing your sword forward and up, put your mind on your right yongquan point. Feel force originating in your right foot and flowing directly to your left hand.

4. *Bai He Liang Chi Wu Xing Zhang* (白鹤亮翅五行掌) —White Crane Spreads Its Wings and Wuxing Palm

Posture Name Explanation

The external movements of this posture mimic those of a white crane spreading and flapping its wings. The first part of the posture involves raising your arms as you would in the White Crane Spreads Its Wings posture of the empty-hand form. Internally, the core idea of this posture is the five elements principle, a traditional Chinese concept dating from ancient times.

According to this principle, the world is composed of five basic elements: metal, water, wood, fire, and earth. The elements do not refer to the actual objects named but are, rather, metaphors for qualities or attributes. They are said to interact by either promoting or inhibiting each other's qualities depending on the situation. These relationships have traditionally been expressed as two circles, one of which describes the productive relationships among the set of elements and the other describes the inhibitory relationships among them.

The central feature of this posture is *wu xing zhang*—wuxing palm. *Wuxing* refers to the five-elements principle and the term "five-element palm" indicates that the attack or defense skill used here is not fixed. In this posture, the specific skill chosen depends on what is appropriate to a particular situation at a given moment.

4.1. *Ma Bu Dai Dao* (马步带刀)—Pull *Dao* Back in Horse-Riding Stance

Movements: Look to the east. Shift half of your weight back onto your right leg and turn both feet so that they point to the south. You will be in a horse-riding stance. At the same time, use both hands to move your sword up and back until it is above and slightly in front of your head. Keep your arms almost straight. Your sword should be parallel to the ground, the tip should point to the east, and the edge should face up. Your body should face to the south and your head should be held high as though lightly suspended from above (fig. 5-4-1).

Fig. 5-4-1

Application: If your opponent pushes his or her spear downward and forward for a hard strike to your head, you can either strike him or her directly or continue the previous movement by using your sword to block your opponent's spear in front of your head. If you choose to block the attack, stick your sword on your opponent's spear and follow his or her force to draw a small circle. At the same time, shift your weight back slightly and pull your sword back with the motion of your opponent's spear (fig. 5-4-2). Do not block his or her spear directly or forcefully. Instead, use soft power to block and redirect your opponent's force.

Fig. 5-4-2

Key Points: Relax your waist and feel as though your body is sinking down to create stability as you push your sword up. Put your mind on the right yinlingquan point on the inside of your right knee. Imagine that raising your right knee causes your left hand to push forward. When you hold your sword over your head, keep it sticking on your opponent's spear and feel as though your sword can move forward and slightly backward to follow the motion of the spear.

4.2. *Du Li Jü Dao* (独立举刀)—Hold Sword Up in Single Leg Stance

Fig. 5-4-3

Movements: Shift your weight onto your left leg. Straighten your left knee to make your body erect. Simultaneously, raise your right knee to assume a single-leg stance. Push your sword upward with both hands as you straighten your body and raise your right knee (fig. 5-4-3).

Application: Continue the previous movement without interruption. Raise your body slightly to follow the small circular motion of your sword and then push your sword up and forward. This will move your opponent's spear upward.

At the same time, shift your weight onto your left leg and feel as though you might raise your right knee (fig. 5-4-4). This will create a sense of wariness in your opponent. He or she will not want to move his or her spear away from your sword. If the downward force of your opponent's spear is reduced even for a moment, you will be able to slide your sword down the shaft of your opponent's spear to cut his or her hand.

Although your right knee should actually be raised when you practice the Taiji Dao form, this is not always the case when you apply this skill in fighting. In application, it is necessary only to feel as though your knee is raised. This feeling will generate additional power in your sword while allowing you to maintain the stability gained by keeping both feet on the ground.

Key Points: Imagine that you can touch your left elbow with your right knee. Put your mind on the huiyin point on the bottom of your torso and feel as though it is lifting up. When you push your sword up, keep it sticking on your opponent's spear and feel as though it can be moved slightly forward and back just far enough to follow the motion of your opponent's spear.

Fig. 5-4-4

5. *Feng Juan He Hua Yie Di Cang* (风卷荷花叶底藏)
—Wind-Swept Lotus Flower Hidden beneath Leaves

Posture Name Explanation

The main idea of this posture is to hide your sword underneath your opponent's weapon as though it were a beautiful lotus flower hiding beneath its leaves and swaying in the breeze. This signifies that while things might seem superficially quiet and peaceful, a powerful attack is hidden beneath appearances. All the movements of this posture are done from a low position.

5.1. *Bei Bu Cang Dao* (背步藏刀)—Take Back Insert Step and Hide Sword

Movements: Bend your left knee and lower your body. At the same time, step sideways to the left with your right foot by placing it behind your left leg. This is a back insert step. Keep your body straight. As you make the back insert step with your right foot, bend both elbows and move your sword horizontally down behind your head. Continue to face to the east (fig. 5-5-1).

Fig. 5-5-1

Application: Continue the previous movement without interruption. If your opponent pushes his or her spear forward and presses down hard against your force as you push up, follow your opponent's force by moving your sword slightly back until it passes over your head. At the same time, lower your body slightly and take a back insert step with your right foot. As your sword moves back, your body should simultaneously move forward (fig. 5-5-2).

Fig. 5-5-2

Key Points: Put your mind on the jiaji point at the center of your upper back. Think about the stability of your body and about the agility and freedom of movement of your arms and legs. When your sword moves down, feel as though your body is pushing up. This feeling will help you avoid collapsing under the weight of your opponent's downward force.

5.2. *Zhuan Shen Tui Zha* (转身推扎)
—Turn Body Back and Push Sword to Thrust Forward

Movements: Turn your body to the right and touch the ring of your sword with your left hand. Keep looking to the east (fig. 5-5-3). Continue to turn clockwise on the balls of both feet until you face to the east and have assumed a right standard bow stance. You may need to adjust your left foot to get comfortable at the end of this turn.

As you complete the turn, push your sword forward with both hands in a forward thrust. Your right hand should be holding the handle of your sword to control the direction of thrust, and your left palm should push on the ring of your sword. Thrust your sword forward in a straight line parallel to the ground. The edge of your sword should continue to face up (fig. 5-5-4).

Fig. 5-5-3

Fig. 5-5-4

Application: Continuing the previous movement without interruption, follow your opponent's pressing force and turn your body clockwise around from the right until you are facing your opponent. At the same time, use both hands to thrust your sword toward your opponent's chest (fig. 5-5-5).

You can also use the back of your sword to press directly down on your opponent's spear (fig. 5-5-6) and then push your sword forward in a thrust (fig. 5-5-7). This is a commonly used move.

Fig. 5-5-5

Fig. 5-5-6

Fig. 5-5-7

Key Points: Your turn back should be quick and smooth. Put your mind on your right yongquan point. Straighten your right leg so that the power from your right foot can extend directly to the tip of your sword.

6. *Yu Nü Chuan Suo Ba Fang Shi* (玉女穿梭八方式) —Fair Lady Passes the Shuttle in Eight Directions

Posture Name Explanation

In this posture, your sword is thrust through a narrow space to attack your opponent, much the way a fair lady might quickly and skillfully pass her shuttle back and forth on a loom to weave a piece of cloth. In Chinese, the reference to *ba fang,* or eight directions, actually refers to all directions, not just eight. Here, the important implication is that although fighting takes place in three-dimensional space and in all directions, one's attack should nevertheless be very clear and never executed in a haphazard manner.

This posture is also called *ye zhan ba fang. Ye zhan* refers to fighting at night in total darkness. In such a circumstance, you need to be very alert and ready to defend an attack from any direction. The movements of this posture are performed in multiple directions.

6.1. *Tui Shen Chen Cai* (退身沉采)—Shift Weight Back and Sink Sword

Movements: Remove your left palm from the ring of your sword and push it back toward the west at head level. At the same time, take a small step (about half the distance of a usual step) with your left foot and turn your foot outward until your toes point to the northwest. Then, shift your weight onto your left leg and turn on the ball of your right foot so that the toes of that foot also point to the north or northwest. While shifting your weight to form a left high side-bow stance, drop your right hand, holding your sword, and pull it back until it is close to your body in front of your right hip. Keep your sword parallel to the ground and turn it until the edge faces to the north and the blade is horizontal (figs. 5-6-1a, b).

Fig. 5-6-1a   Fig. 5-6-1b

Application: If your opponent attacks your abdomen with a spear, step back with your left foot and turn your body slightly to the left. At the same time, turn your right wrist outward and pull your sword back. As soon as your sword touches your opponent's spear, relax and sink your body to exert a downward force on your sword as you parry your opponent's spear. Simultaneously, swing your left hand back to enhance your pull and to increase the downward pressure of your sword on your opponent's spear (fig. 5-6-2).

Fig. 5-6-2

Key Points: Straighten your right leg and move your body to the left. Imagine that you are using your left hand as well as your right hand to hold your sword and to pull it to the left. Your right hand must also exert downward pressure on your sword. Put your mind on your left *qichong* point, which is slightly above your left inguinal groove, and imagine that your abdomen is touching your left leg.

6.2. *Hui Shen Bai Bu* (回身摆步)—Turn Body Back with a Baibu

Movements: Push your left palm horizontally to the left and turn your body to the left and back until you are facing to the southwest. At the same time, shift your weight slightly back onto your right leg and turn your left foot outward with your heel touching the ground until your left foot points to the south. Relax your right hand and let your sword drop down along your right hip so that the tip points to the ground (fig. 5-6-3).

Fig. 5-6-3

Application: Imagine that your opponent is attacking you from behind. Turn your body counterclockwise from the left and use your left hand to block his or her spear (fig. 5-6-4).

Fig. 5-6-4

Key Points: Turn your head to the left and use your shen to lead your body in the turn back toward your opponent. Put your mind on your left laogong point and push it to the left. Feel as though your left hand is chasing your gaze.

6.3. *Gai Bu Jian Wan* (盖步剪腕)—Make Cover Step and Cut Wrist

Movements: Step forward with your right foot and, as this foot moves, turn your right toes outward to form a right covering step. Keep your weight on your left leg. At the same time, move your right hand forward in front of your body at chest level. Your sword should slant slightly upward so that the tip is at head level. The blade of your sword should be horizontal, and the edge should face to the left. Move your left palm down and put it on the top surface of the handle of your sword (fig. 5-6-5).

Fig. 5-6-5

Application: If your opponent attacks your head with a spear, step forward and sink down slightly. At the same time, using the front edge of your sword, move your sword forward and upward to cut your opponent's front hand. As soon as your sword nears his or her hand, turn your right wrist outward quickly and push your sword vigorously forward. At the same time, pull your abdomen slightly back (fig. 5-6-6).

Fig. 5-6-6

Key Points: Move your sword forward to follow the line of your gaze. When your sword cuts forward, hollow your chest and sit back slightly on your left leg to balance the forward force. Put your mind on your left yinlingquan point so that your leg will feel stable.

6.4. *Zhuan Shen Quan Dai* (转身圈带)
—Turn Body Back and Move Sword in a Circle

Movements: Continuing the last movement without interruption, shift your weight forward and move your sword up (fig. 5-6-7) and then back, as though tracing a circle, until the tip points to the northeast. At the same time, turn your body slightly to the right and turn your head back to look at the tip of your sword. Your right hand, holding your sword, should turn slightly inward, and your weight should shift completely onto your right leg. Lean slightly forward (fig. 5-6-8).

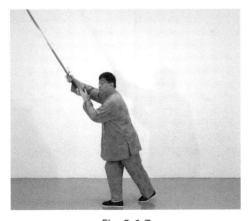

Fig. 5-6-7

Fig. 5-6-8

Application: Continue the previous movement without interruption. If your opponent moves his or her chest back or rises up slightly to avoid your cut, your opponent will be able to use his or her spear again to attack your head. If you raise your sword and push it forward in a circle as soon as you feel that your attack has failed, you can use the back of your sword to block the second attack (fig. 5-6-9).

Fig. 5-6-9

Key Points: Wave your sword to the right and back and make your shen chase the tip. Look far ahead. Put your mind on your left laogong point to gain a feeling of pushing back. Feel as though your body is dodging slightly to the left.

6.5. *Xie Bu Cang Dao* (歇步藏刀)—Hide Sword in Resting Stance

Movements: Continuing without a break, turn your right hand inward until your sword is almost vertical and the tip points to the ground. Turn your head to the southwest and continue to lean slightly forward. Remain in a right covering stance and move your left hand back until your left palm is in front of your right hip (figs. 5-6-10a, b).

Fig. 5-6-10a

Fig. 5-6-10b

Application: Continue the previous movement without interruption by sticking your sword on your opponent's spear and moving it down and back toward you in a circular path. When your sword moves his or her spear back, stretch your left hand forward to grip your opponent's spear and then push it to the right and downward (fig. 5-6-11).

Fig. 5-6-11

Key Points: As soon as your gaze reaches the tip of your sword, turn your head around so that you are looking forward. Relax your right arm and put your mind on the right *hegu* point on the tiger mouth of your right hand. Feel as though your legs have stored enough power to make possible a long step forward and as though your sword can immediately chase your gaze.

6.6 .*Tiao Zhang Qian Zha* (挑掌前扎)
—Punch Palm Up and Thrust Sword Forward

Movements: Move your left hand forward and up to shoulder level, with your left palm facing up and the fingers of your left hand pointing to the southwest (fig. 5-6-12). As you move your left hand up, turn your left palm outward, then to the left and up until your left hand is above and slightly in front of your forehead. The fingers of your left hand should point to the northwest, and the nail of your left index finger should be opposite the outer end of your left eyebrow.

At the same time, step forward with your left foot to form a left standard bow stance and move your right hand from the back of your body to the front as you

Fig. 5-6-12

thrust your sword forward. The tip of your sword should point to the southwest and slightly up, and the edge should face down (fig. 5-6-13).

Fig. 5-6-13

Application: Continue the previous movement without interruption by turning your left hand over and pushing your opponent's spear to the left and upward (fig. 5-6-14). As soon as you are able to move his or her spear out of the way, step forward with your left foot and thrust your sword toward him or her (fig. 5-6-15).

Fig. 5-6-14   Fig. 5-6-15

Key Points: First, swing your left hand forward to follow the line of your gaze. As soon as you feel that you have made contact with the target, put your mind on your left laogong point and feel as though it is pushing upward. Immediately, move your sword forward again to chase your gaze. Feel as though the forces in your hands unite in a single expression of power.

6.7. Pie Shen Dai Dao (撇身带刀)
—Turn Body Back and Carry Sword on Left Shoulder

Movements: Turn your body to the right by pivoting on the heel of your left foot. Move your right hand, holding your sword, to the right and slightly up. Put your left arm underneath your sword and let your left hand follow the turn of your body with your left palm facing out close to the inside of your right elbow. Keep the back of your sword in touch with the outside of your left arm and the edge facing out. Rotate your right hand counterclockwise and raise your sword slightly as you relax your grip just enough to let the tip drop down and point to the ground. Look to the left (fig. 5-6-16).

Continue turning your body to the right and look to the east over your right shoulder. Let your right hand, holding your sword, move toward the front of your left shoulder. The tip of your sword should continue to point down. Keep your weight fully on your left leg as you turn (fig. 5-6-17).

Fig. 5-6-16

Fig. 5-6-17

Application: If your opponent sweeps his or her spear toward you from your left side, move your right hand, holding your sword, in front of your left shoulder and keep the blade of your sword on the left side of your body pointing diagonally downward. Use the edge to block your opponent's spear. At the same time, put your left hand on your right hand and let your left arm touch the back of your sword. Your arms should form a circle, and you should feel as though the circle is expanding (fig. 5-6-18).

Fig. 5-6-18

Key Points: Put your mind on the yuzhen point at the back of your head. Use your shen to chase your mind as your body turns back. Imagine that the circle formed by your arms is continually expanding.

6.8. *You Gong Cang Dao* (右弓藏刀)—Hide Sword in Right Bow Stance

Movements: Step to the right with your right foot and turn on the ball of your left foot until both feet point to the east. Shift your weight onto your right leg to assume a right bow stance. At the same time, move your right hand forward, holding your sword, to bring your sword over your left shoulder and then down until it is beside your right thigh (fig. 5-6-19). Move your left hand forward along the back of your sword and then push it forward with your left palm facing to the south. Drop your left elbow and slightly push your left palm to the right until it is in front of your right shoulder. At the same time, pull your right hand, holding your sword, backward behind your right hip. The tip of your sword should point down (fig. 5-6-20).

Fig. 5-6-19

Fig. 5-6-20

Application: Continue the previous movement without interruption by sticking your sword on your opponent's spear and widening your arm circle. Then, turn your body suddenly to the right. The turn of your body will draw your sword in a vertical circle to the right and will cause your opponent's spear to pass over your head to the right side of your body. Initially underneath your opponent's spear, your sword will eventually be on top of it. At this moment, you should immediately use your left hand, left arm, or both to push down on the back of your sword, increasing the pressure on your opponent's spear (fig. 5-6-21).

Fig. 5-6-21

Maintain your pressure on the spear. If you can push your sword down to hip level, it will be easy to control your opponent (fig. 5-6-22). If, at this point, you put your left hand over your opponent's right hand, you will increase your control still further. Then, you can relax your right hand, remove your sword from the top of your opponent's spear (fig. 5-6-23), and mount an attack of your choice.

Fig. 5-6-22

Fig. 5-6-23

Key Points: Initially, your arms form a circle. The circle should sink down and expand until your arms separate. Put your mind on your right hegu point to create a feeling of holding your sword back. Press your left hand down on your sword and then push it forward to balance the pull-back force in your right hand.

6.9. *Gai Bu Jian Wan* (盖步剪腕)—Make Cover Step and Cut Wrist

Movements: Look to the northeast and push your left palm to the left. At the same time, step forward with your left foot to form a left insubstantial stance (fig. 5-6-24). Then, step forward with your right foot, turning the toes of your right foot outward to form a right cover step. Keep your weight on your left leg. At the same time, move your right hand forward, holding your sword, until it is in front of your body at chest level. Your sword should slant slightly upward, and the tip should be level with your head. The blade of your sword should be horizontal, and the edge should face to the left. Move your left palm down and put it on the top surface of the handle of your sword (fig. 5-6-25).

Fig. 5-6-24

Fig. 5-6-25

Fig. 5-6-26

Application: If your opponent attacks your face with a spear, use your left hand to parry and block the spear. At the same time, push your right hand, holding your sword, quickly forward and upward to cut your opponent's front hand (fig. 5-6-26).

Key Points: Move your sword forward to follow the line of your gaze. When your sword cuts forward, hollow your chest and sit slightly back on your left leg to balance your forward force. Put your mind on your left yinlingquan point to increase the feeling of stability in your left leg.

6.10. *Zhuan Shen Quan Dai* (转身圈带)
—Turn Body Back and Move Sword in a Circle

Movements: Continuing the last movement without interruption, turn your body slightly to the right and move your sword up and to the right. At the same time, shift your weight forward onto your right leg (fig. 5-6-27). Continue to move your sword back in a circular movement until the tip of your sword points to the southwest. At the same time, turn your body slightly to the right and turn your head back to look at the tip of your sword. Your right hand, holding your sword, should turn slightly inward, and your weight should shift completely onto your right leg. Push your left hand to the right and backward. Lean slightly forward (fig. 5-6-28).

Fig. 5-6-27

Fig. 5-6-28

Application: If your left hand cannot grip your opponent's spear, quickly and forcefully sweep your sword to the right and upward underneath his or her spear to knock it away (fig. 5-6-29).

Fig. 5-6-29

Key Points: Wave your sword to the right and backward, making your shen initially chase the tip of your sword and then extend far past it into the distance. Put your mind on your left laogong point to create a feeling that your left hand is pushing backward.

6.11. *Xie Bu Cang Dao* (歇步藏刀)—Hide Sword in Resting Stance

Movements: Continuing without a break, turn your right hand inward until your sword is almost vertical, and the tip points to the ground. Turn your head forward to face to the northeast and continue to lean slightly forward. Remain in a right covering stance and move your left hand back until your left palm is along the right side of your torso (fig. 5-6-30).

Fig. 5-6-30

Application: Continuing the previous movement without interruption, parry your opponent's spear lightly. To do this, first stick your sword on, and then wrap it around, your opponent's spear. This soft parry will allow you to control his or her spear effectively until it reaches the right side of your body. As soon as it does, you will have a chance to grab it again with your left hand (fig. 5-6-31).

Fig. 5-6-31

Key Points: When your gaze reaches behind you to the tip of your sword, immediately turn your head to look forward. Relax your right arm and put your mind on your right hegu point. Feel as though your legs have stored enough power to make possible a long step forward and as though your sword is ready to chase your gaze forward immediately.

6.12. *Tiao Zhang Qian Zha* (挑掌前扎)
—Punch Palm Up and Thrust Sword Forward

Movements: Continuing the last movement without interruption, move your left hand forward and up to shoulder level. Your left palm should face up, and the fingers of your left hand should point to the northeast (fig. 5-6-32). Continue moving your left arm up and let your left palm turn downward, then left and up until your left hand is above and slightly in front of your forehead. The fingers of your left hand should point to the northeast, and the nail of your left index finger should be opposite the outer end of your left eyebrow.

Fig. 5-6-32

At the same time, step forward with your left foot to form a left standard bow stance and move your right hand from the back of your body to the front as you thrust your sword forward. At the end of this move, the tip of your sword should point slightly up and to the northeast, and the blade should be vertical with the edge facing down (fig. 5-6-33).

Fig. 5-6-33

Application: Grip your opponent's spear with your left hand. Push it slightly to the left and then upward in a curving path (fig. 5-6-34). While pushing his or her spear to the left, you should also lightly pull it in the direction of his or her attack. Follow this pull by stepping forward with your left foot and thrusting your sword forward to attack your opponent (fig. 5-6-35).

Fig. 5-6-34

Fig. 5-6-35

Key Points: Swing your left hand forward to follow the line of your gaze. As soon as your left hand grips your opponent's spear, put your mind on your left laogong point and feel as though it is pushing up. Immediately use your sword to chase your gaze. Feel as though the forces in your hands are uniting to form one force.

6.13. *Pie Shen Ya Dao* (撇身压刀)—Turn Body Back and Press Dao Down

Movements: Turn your body to the right and, at the same time, bring your left hand toward the inside of your right wrist with your right palm facing out. Rotate your right hand counterclockwise and move it slightly forward and up. Let the tip of your sword drop down so that the tip points to the ground behind your left shoulder (fig. 5-6-36).

Continue your turn by stepping to the right with your right foot and shifting your weight onto your right leg. Simultaneously, move your right hand forward to pull your sword over your left shoulder. Your sword should be inclined slightly down behind the upper part of your left arm with the edge of your sword facing up (fig. 5-6-37). Place your left palm on the back of your sword as it moves forward and press down (fig. 5-6-38).

Fig. 5-6-36

Fig. 5-6-37

Fig. 5-6-38

Application: The application for this movement is the same as that for movement 6.7 (fig. 5-6-18) except that this application is performed in the opposite direction.

Key Points: Put your mind on the yuzhen point on the back of your head and use your shen to chase your mind as you turn around.

6.14. *You Gong Cang Dao* (右弓藏刀)—Hide Sword in Right Bow Stance

Movements: Continuing without interruption from the last movement, press your sword down until your right hand is alongside your right thigh and the edge of your sword points to the ground. At the same time, shift your weight fully onto your right leg to assume a right bow stance. Simultaneously, move your left hand forward and up until your left thumb is opposite your nose and your left palm faces to the north (fig. 5-6-39).

Fig. 5-6-39

Application: This application is the same as that described in movement 6.8 (figs. 5-6-21, 5-6-22, and 5-6-23) except that it is performed in the opposite direction.

Key Points: Your arms should form a circle that sinks down as you complete your turn. Let the circle expand until your arms separate in opposite directions. Put your mind on your right hegu point to feel a pull-back force in your right hand. Use your left hand to press down on your sword and then push your left hand forward to balance the feeling that your right hand is pulling back.

7. *San Xing Kai He Zi Zhu Zhang* (三星开合自主张) —Three Stars Open and Close Freely and Naturally

Posture Name Explanation

The "three stars" of this posture refer externally to the laogong point on your hand, the quchi point on your elbow, and the yongquan point on your foot; the terms "open" and "close" refer to the movements of these three parts of your body. The stars are considered open when your hands or arms are separated or spread apart and closed when they are drawn back together.

Internally, the three stars refer to the internal components of shen, yi, and qi. The stars are considered open when shen, yi, and qi extend outward to create an energetic expression of strong feeling and closed when shen, yi, and qi are quickly withdrawn. In general, the phrase "three stars open and close freely and naturally" means that external movements and internal components should be fully coordinated and integrated in a free and natural way. In this posture, the stars open and close several times.

7.1. *Ce Shen Qian Jie* (側身前截)—Turn Body and Block Forward

Movements: Look forward to the west. Move your right hand forward, holding your sword, until your right elbow is almost straight. Turn the palm of your right hand up so that the blade of your sword extends forward with the tip pointing to the west and the edge pointing to the south.

At the same time, push your left arm down and extend it back so that your left palm faces to the east. Also at the same time, turn your right foot on the heel until your right toes point to the south. Turn on the ball of your left foot so that your torso also faces to the south. Lean back slightly as though dodging your opponent's thrust (fig. 5-7-1).

Fig. 5-7-1

Application: If your opponent attacks your chest or face with a spear, step forward with your right foot to get close to him or her. At the same time, use your left hand to grip or parry the spear. As soon as your hand touches the spear, turn your body to the left and stretch your right hand directly out to cut your opponent's front hand, left arm, or head. As you move your sword forward, rotate your right arm so that your right palm faces upward, and simultaneously use your left hand to pull your opponent's spear backward (fig. 5-7-2).

Fig. 5-7-2

Key Points: Step forward and turn your body to the left simultaneously, but do not move your body away from your opponent. Rather, move toward your opponent on the right side of his or her spear, staying very close to it. Imagine that your opponent's weapon will just miss hitting you. Internal trained force will reach from your waist to your hands. Put your mind on your left laogong point and make sure that your right-handed forward cut is fully integrated with the backward pull of your left hand.

7.2. *Ti Xi Hui La* (提膝回拉)—Raise Knee and Pull *Dao* Back

Movements: Look to the west. Shift your weight back onto your left leg and pull your right leg back, bending your right knee slightly so that only the toes of your right foot touch the ground. At the same time, move your hands toward each other until your right hand, holding your sword, is in front of your face at about the level of your forehead. Bring your left palm close to the end of your sword's handle, and keep moving your hands toward each other until your left palm touches the ring of your sword. Immediately straighten your left knee and raise your right knee in front of your body and point it to the south. Your sword should be parallel to the ground with the tip pointing to the west and the edge pointing up (fig. 5-7-3).

Fig. 5-7-3

Application: Continue the previous movement without interruption. If your opponent shifts his or her weight back to avoid your attack and simultaneously pushes his or her spear to the left to attack your face, pull your right foot back, either raising your right knee or, less commonly, keeping your right foot on the ground. Pull your sword back until the handle is in front of your face to block your opponent's attack. Keep your sword underneath your opponent's spear and put your left hand on the ring of your sword to add extra power (fig. 5-7-4).

Fig. 5-7-4

Key Points: Put your mind on your baihui point and imagine that your body is suspended from above. This feeling should accompany the lifting of your right knee toward your left elbow. Your hands should feel as though they are charging toward each other to create a combined force.

7.3. *Zuo You Cheng Ci* (左右撑刺)
—Thrust *Dao* Forward and Push Palm Backward

Movements: With your right knee raised from the last movement and your left palm touching the ring of your sword, immediately thrust your sword forward to the west and push your left hand back to the east, turning your left palm first outward to the south and then back to the east. Both arms should extend outward, and your sword should be parallel to the ground with the tip pointing to the west, the blade held vertically and the edge facing up (fig. 5-7-5).

Fig. 5-7-5

Application: Continue the previous movement without interruption. If your opponent pulls his or her spear back, keep your sword sticking on your opponent's spear and follow the motion of his or her spear to thrust your sword toward him or her. At the same time, push your left hand to the left to balance your straight thrust forward (fig. 5-7-6).

Fig. 5-7-6

Key Points: Put your mind on your left laogong point. Separate your hands in opposite directions to make a two-part force in which your left hand pushes to the left and your right hand thrusts your sword to the right. At the same time, feel as though your head is suspended from above and lift your right knee up slightly to increase your feeling of stability.

7.4. *Ce Shen Zuo Lan* (侧身左拦)—Turn Body and Parry Left

Movements: Look back to the east. Turn your body slightly to the left to follow your gaze. At the same time, pull your sword back toward your body with your right hand and turn your wrist from right to left so that the blade of your sword moves in a vertical arc in front of your body until it is alongside and slightly in front of your left shoulder. The tip should point up and the edge should face to the east. At the same time, move your left hand down and toward the back of your body, letting the fingers of your left hand form a hook. The fingers in the hook should point up. Put your right foot down on the ground with your toes pointing to the west, but keep your weight on your left leg to assume a right insubstantial stance (fig. 5-7-7).

Fig. 5-7-7

Application: If your opponent attacks your chest with a spear, let your right hand sink down so that your vertically held sword points up. As soon as your sword touches your opponent's spear, turn your body to the left and parry his or her spear to the left (fig. 5-7-8).

Fig. 5-7-8

Key Points: Keep your mind on your left laogong point and feel ready to hook something behind you. Follow this feeling by looking backward and using your right hand, holding your sword, to track the path of your gaze. Slightly rotate your right wrist inward and imagine inserting the pommel of your sword into the ground. This will create a vertical force in your sword.

7.5. *Ce Shen Xia Jie* (侧身下截)—Turn Body and Block Down

Movements: Continue turning your body slightly to the left and simultaneously drop your body slightly. Drop your right wrist so that the tip of your sword moves back and down and then forward in a circular path until your right hand is in front of your left hip. Let your gaze follow the movement of the tip of your sword. Your sword should be parallel to the ground with the tip pointing to the north and the edge pointing down (fig. 5-7-9).

Fig. 5-7-9

Continue the previous movement without interruption by turning your body slightly to the right and shifting your weight onto your right leg. Let the turn of your body pull your sword forward. Keep your eyes focused on the tip of your sword (fig. 5-7-10).

Fig. 5-7-10

Application: Continue the previous movement without interruption by maintaining the contact between your sword and your opponent's spear and then dropping the tip of your sword down so that your sword crosses and is on top of your opponent's spear. Simultaneously, if you choose, you can put your left hand on the back of your sword to add extra power and to press it down on your opponent's spear (fig. 5-7-11).

Fig. 5-7-11

Key Points: Look to the left and move your body to the right. Pull your sword to the right with both hands. Imagine that your sword is very heavy and that you must put your mind on your left yongquan point in order to stretch your left leg out so that the force from your left foot can reach directly to your right hand and help you pull your heavy sword to the right.

7.6. *Yan Dao Qian Liao* (掩刀前撩)—Block Down Then Push Forward

Movements: Continue the previous movement without interruption by putting your left hand on the back of your sword and then using both hands to push your sword forward. Look forward and down. Your sword should be held vertically in front of your body with your right hand at chest level. The tip of your sword should point to the ground, and the edge should face to the west. Step forward with your left foot and shift your weight onto your left leg to form a left bow stance (fig. 5-7-12).

Fig. 5-7-12

Application: Continuing without interruption from the previous movement, keep your sword sticking on your opponent's spear and slide it forward along his or her spear to cut his or her front hand. If your opponent releases his or her left hand from the spear, you can direct your cut to his or her body (fig. 5-7-13).

Fig. 5-7-13

Key Points: Turn your head back to direct your shen forward. Put your mind on your right yongquan point to stretch out your right leg. Turn and move forward immediately so that your body follows your shen.

7.7. Pie Shen Dai Dao (撇身带刀)
—Turn Body Back and Carry Sword on Left Shoulder

Movements: Look back over your right shoulder. Following your gaze, turn to the right by pivoting on the heel of your left foot. Take your left palm off the back of your sword and place it inside your right forearm, letting it face outward as it follows the turn of your body to the north and then to the east.

At the same time, raise your right hand, holding your sword so that your right forearm is in front of your face. Let your sword hang down, its tip pointing to the ground, as your body turns under it until the sword is behind your left shoulder. Keep your weight fully on your left leg as you turn (fig. 5-7-14).

Fig. 5-7-14

Application: Continue the previous movement without interruption. If your opponent tries to push his or her spear up and forward to block your sword, relax your body and turn suddenly to the right. Simultaneously, pull your sword slightly upward so that it breaks contact with your opponent's spear and cuts directly at his or her neck (fig. 5-7-15).

Fig. 5-7-15

Key Points: Put your mind on the yuzhen point at the back of your head. Use your shen to chase your mind so that your body turns back. Relax your waist and hands and form a circle with your arms. Imagine that your body turns as though it were a big wheel.

7.8. *You Gong Cang Dao* (右弓藏刀)—Hide Sword in Right Bow Stance

Movements: Continuing without interruption, step to the right with your right foot, letting only the heel of that foot touch the ground. You will be in a left sitting stance facing to the east. Move your right hand forward to bring your sword over your left shoulder and then down until it is alongside your right hip. At the same time, shift your weight onto your right leg to assume a right bow stance (fig. 5-7-16). Then, push your left hand forward and slightly to the right so that your left palm faces to the south (fig. 5-7-17).

Fig. 5-7-16   Fig. 5-7-17

Application: Continue without interruption to turn your body to the right and pull your sword back to complete your cut. Put your mind on your left laogong point. Press the back of your sword down and then push it forward.

Key Points: Maintain the circle formed by your arms and sink down. Then, expand the circle until your arms separate in opposite directions. Put your mind on your right hegu point to pull your sword back. Feel as though your left hand is pushing to the right and your body is dodging to the left.

8. *Er Qi Jiao Lai Da Hu Shi* (二起脚来打虎势) —Double Kick and Strike Tiger

Posture Name Explanation

This posture has two parts: a double kick and a strike-tiger movement. Similar to the double-kick posture in the empty-hand form, this double kick involves kicking twice in quick succession to form one large movement. The first kick is a low kick and the second, a high kick. In modern-day practice, the lower kick is often omitted.

The strike-tiger portion of this posture is very similar to the posture of the same name in the empty-hand form. Practicing this movement, which mimics the nimble actions required to fight a tiger, will improve your ability to concentrate and your readiness to dodge.

8.1. *Shang Bu Qian Pi* (上步前劈)—Step Forward and Chop Forward

Movements: Look forward to the east. Holding your sword in a relaxed manner, move your right arm back and let the tip of your sword point to the ground.

Continue to move your right arm back and up behind your body, thus raising your sword in preparation for a forward chop. Rotate your right wrist clockwise in a half-circle as you move your sword back so that the sword's edge, which was initially facing the ground, faces to the south. At the same time, stretch your left arm forward and turn your left palm up (fig. 5-8-1).

Continue moving your arms so that your right hand moves up and then forward in an arc and chops straight ahead as far as possible and your left hand moves down and back. Form a hook with the fingers of your left hand with fingers pointing up as you extend the hook behind your back. Simultaneously, step forward with your left foot and shift your weight fully onto your left leg to form a left bow stance (fig. 5-8-2).

Fig. 5-8-1

Fig. 5-8-2

Application: If your opponent attacks your face or chest with a spear, dodge slightly to the right and use your left hand to parry the spear (fig. 5-8-3). As soon as your left hand touches the spear, turn your left hand outward to grip it and pull it backward and downward. At the same time, turn slightly to the left and raise your sword to chop at your opponent's head (fig. 5-8-4).

Fig. 5-8-3

Fig. 5-8-4

Key Points: Feel as though your waist is linked to your hands like an axle in which your arms are the wheels. Extend your shen straight ahead and far into the distance. Put your mind on your left laogong point and let your mind follow your shen. Then, pull your left hand suddenly backward. Simultaneously, follow the line of your gaze with your right hand holding your sword and chop forward powerfully and in complete coordination with the movement of your waist and body.

8.2. *Jiao Dao Qian Ti* (交刀前踢)
—Change the Sword Hand and Execute a Front Kick

Movements: Keep looking forward. Bring your left hand forward along the left side of your body and turn your left palm up. At the same time, turn your right hand to the left so that the tip of your sword points first to the north and then back toward the west. The blade of your sword should rest horizontally along your left forearm with the tip pointing to the west, the edge facing to the north, and the handle positioned just above your left palm.

Loosen the grip of your right hand on your sword, but do not move your right hand away from the handle. Let your sword's guard rest in the palm of your left hand with the index, middle, and ring fingers of your left hand lightly bracing your sword against your left palm in a fanwo position. Let the tip of your sword point slightly down behind you (fig. 5-8-5).

As soon as your sword hand has changed to the left, push your right hand slightly to the left and immediately raise your right knee to execute a front kick straight ahead. When you kick, let your left knee straighten slightly so that your body rises up (fig. 5-8-6).

Fig. 5-8-5　　　　　　　　　　　　　　　　Fig. 5-8-6

Application: If you dodge to the right and can move close to your opponent when he or she attacks you with a spear, change your sword to your left hand in a fanwo position so that you can use your blade to block your opponent's spear to the left. Put your right hand on the handle of your sword to support your block (fig. 5-8-7). Push your right hand to the left and backward and, if possible, grip your opponent's spear with either hand. At the same time, direct a low toe kick to your opponent's front knee (fig. 5-8-8).

Fig. 5-8-7   Fig. 5-8-8

Key Points: Relax your waist and slightly withdraw your abdomen. Keep your left leg bent and your hips level. Put your mind on the right huantiao point on your right hip and think about using your right thigh to bring your right leg forward as you kick. Feel that your left leg is very stable when you kick.

Note: The movement just described in section 8.2 often involves only the changing of your sword hand. The toe kick is usually omitted.

8.3. *Li Shen Qian Ti* (立身前踢)—Stand Erect and Kick Forward

Movements: Continue the previous movement without interruption. Swing your right leg back behind your left leg and complete the transfer of your sword to your left hand (fig. 5-8-9). Remove your right hand from the handle of your sword and move it to the right side of your head with your right palm facing in toward your ear (fig. 5-8-10). Straighten your left knee and kick to the east in a high front kick with your right foot. At the same time, extend your right palm forward to strike the upper surface of your right foot as you kick forward (fig. 5-8-11).

Fig. 5-8-9   Fig. 5-8-10   Fig. 5-8-11

Application: Continue the previous movement without interruption. If you have included the toe kick in movement 8.2, follow it immediately with a high kick. At the same time, make a clapping-palm strike forward to your opponent's face and simultaneously pull his or spear backward with your left hand. The high kick of your right leg should extend directly from your right hip to the ribs of your opponent or to his or her front arm or head (fig. 5-8-12).

Fig. 5-8-12

Key Points: Straighten your left leg, put your mind on your baihui point and feel as though your body is suspended from above. Feel very stable and then put your mind on your right laogong point to strike forward and simultaneously execute the high kick. Imagine that your right hand and right foot are striking the same target.

8.4. *You Gong Da Hu* (右弓打虎)—Strike Tiger in Right Bow Stance

Movements: After your forward kick, look to the northeast and move both hands together until they point to the northeast. At the same time, bring your right foot back but keep your right knee raised in front of your body (fig. 5-8-13). Continue to bend your left leg and step back with your right foot. Touch the ground with your right heel and let the toes of your right foot point to the south. Start to shift your weight onto your right leg, and simultaneously, extend both hands diagonally to the northeast. Then, push your hands down and turn your body slightly to the right so that the fingers of your right hand point to the inside of your left elbow. The handle of your sword, held in your left hand now, should point to the northeast, and your sword should continue to lay along your left forearm with the tip pointing diagonally up and back (fig. 5-8-14).

Bring both hands down and to the right in a sweeping diagonal curve to the southwest. Keep your hands close to your legs and let them pass over your knees while you continue to shift your weight onto your right leg (fig. 5-8-15). Let both feet point to the south. Form a fist with your right hand after it has

Fig. 5-8-13

Fig. 5-8-14

passed your right knee and swing both hands continually to the southwest in a curving path until they are level with your head. Your eyesight should follow the movement of your hands. Then, turn your head to the east and let your gaze lead the movement of your hands to the left.

Fig. 5-8-15

At the end of the movement, your weight should be fully shifted onto your right leg to form a right wide bow stance. The eye of your right fist should point to the east, and the ring of the handle of your sword should be under your right elbow. The tip of your sword should point slightly down behind your body. Your gaze should lead your hands to the left, and your body should follow your hands by turning slightly to the left at the end of this movement (figs. 5-8-16a, b).

Fig. 5-8-16a

Fig. 5-8-16b

Application: If you are holding your sword in your left hand in a fanwo position and have already gripped your opponent's spear in your right hand, put the handle of your sword on the right side (fig. 5-8-17) of the spear. Then push the handle of your sword down slightly so that the guard catches the shaft of your opponent's spear (fig. 5-8-18). Step to the right and use your right hand to pull the spear to the right, then back, and finally upward in a curving path.

At the same time, push the handle of your sword to the right and downward in a smaller curve. This will cause the root of your opponent's spear to move strongly down and to his or her right. If your opponent opens his or her hands, your opponent will drop the spear. If he or she tries to resist by holding the spear tightly, the force on it will unbalance and cause him or her to fall forward and down to his or her right (fig. 5-8-19).

Fig. 5-8-17

Fig. 5-8-18

Fig. 5-8-19

Key Points: Withdraw your abdomen and relax your waist. Put your mind on the right *houxi* point on the outer edge of your right hand. Think about your houxi point's passing sequentially over your left yanglingquan, left yinlingquan, right yinlingquan, and right yanglingquan points and then up and forward in a big circle.

8.5 . *Tui Bu Jü Quan* (退步举拳)—Step Back and Raise Fist

Movements: Look to the southeast and follow your gaze by pivoting on the heel of your right foot to turn to the left. Raise both hands up toward the southeast

Fig. 5-8-20

and let the handle of your sword point to this corner. The ring of your sword should be under your right elbow (fig. 5-8-20).

Application: Continue the previous movement by moving your hands up and then forward. This will cause your opponent to fall down.

Key Points: Hollow your chest and relax your waist. Keep your mind on your right houxi point as you continue to trace a circular path with your hands. Your body should follow the feeling of this turn.

8.6. *Zuo Gong Da Hu* (左弓打虎)—Strike Tiger in Left Bow Stance

Movements: Continuing without interruption, bend your right leg and step back to the northwest with your left foot, letting only the toes of this foot touch the ground. At the same time, move both hands down together (fig. 5-8-21). Look downward and to the southeast and swing both hands to the left, passing them over your knees, then up to the northwest (fig. 5-8-22), and finally toward the north.

Look to the east and turn slightly to the right. Form a fist with your right hand and place it under your left elbow with the eye of your fist pointing up as you finish the circuit. Shift your weight fully onto your left leg to form a left wide bow stance. The tip of your sword should point slightly down behind you (fig. 5-8-23).

Fig. 5-8-21

Fig. 5-8-22

Fig. 5-8-23

Application: If you hold your sword in your left hand in a fanwo position, having already used the handle of your sword to block your opponent's spear and gripped his or her spear in your right hand, step to the left and turn your body to the left. At the same time, pull your opponent's spear forward and to his or her right (fig. 5-8-24).

Keep pulling back and to your left with your left hand and push your opponent's spear to the left, forward, and slightly down with your right hand. This will cause the root of your opponent's spear to move strongly to his or her right, forward, and down. If your opponent opens his or her hands, he or she will drop the spear, but if your opponent tries to hold it too tightly in an effort to resist your push, the pressure on the spear will cause him or her to lose balance and fall down forward and to his or her right (fig. 5-8-25).

Fig. 5-8-24   Fig. 5-8-25

Key Points: Withdraw your abdomen and relax your waist. Keep your mind on the houxi point of your right hand. Think about its passing over your right yanglingquan, right yinlingquan, left yinlingquan, and left yanglingquan points, and then moving upward and forward in a big circle.

Note: Introduced here are some optional movements that can be used to hurl hidden weapons.

Historically, it was very common for swordsmen to surprise opponents by throwing out small, dart-like weapons concealed on their bodies. Because these weapons are rarely used today, many practitioners do not include throwing skills in their sword form practice. For those who are interested in developing such skills, however, three traditional right-handed throwing skills are described in this section.

While there are many different kinds of hidden weapons, the weapons used in the following descriptions and discussed in Chapter Three are *fei biao,* or flying darts. If you want to practice these throwing skills, imagine that you are carrying three darts in a bag hanging down along the left side of your waist.

Ce Shen Xia Shou Biao (側身下手鏢)
—Dodge Body and Throw *Fei Biao* (Flying Dart) with Lower Hand

Movements: Keeping your weight on your left leg, move your right hand to the left of your waist where a dart bag would be hanging. Imagine that you are holding a dart in your right hand, and extend your hand forward in a horizontal arc. Open your hand as though you are hurling the weapon toward an opponent approaching from the right. Your sword should remain resting along your left forearm with the tip pointing diagonally down and back (figs. 5-8-26a, b).

Fig. 5-8-26a

Fig. 5-8-26b

Application: If you dodge and block your opponent's spear to the left so that your opponent is on your right, take a flying dart out of your bag with your right hand and throw it to the right of your opponent. Your right hand should be at waist level. Imagine throwing your flying dart at your opponent's ribs or abdominal area (fig. 5-8-27).

Fig. 5-8-27

Key Points: Imagine that you are throwing a flying dart out as you dodge sideways. Look far into the distance and concentrate on your target. Then, let your right hand chase your gaze as you fling your dart forward.

Tui Bu Shang Shou Biao (退步上手鏢)
—Step Back and Throw Fei Biao with Upper Hand

Movements: Keep looking to the east. Turn on the heel of your left foot and on the ball of your right foot so that the toes of both feet point to the east. Step back with your right foot and shift your weight onto your right leg. Turn your body to the right. At the same time, move your left hand in front of your body and move your right hand back to the left side of your waist as though to remove a second dart from your bag (fig. 5-8-28).

Fig. 5-8-28

Move your right hand back and up behind your head. As you turn, move your left hand down in a clockwise circle until the handle of your sword points to the ground (fig. 5-8-29). Continue without interruption to move your right hand up behind your head and forward to release your dart with an overhead throw. Keep your weight on your right leg and move your left foot slightly back toward your body with only the toes of your left foot touching the ground. At the end of your throw, you will be in a left insubstantial stance facing east (fig. 5-8-30).

Fig. 5-8-29

Fig. 5-8-30

Application: When you face your opponent and can block his or her spear with your sword, step back and simultaneously take a flying dart from your bag with your right hand. Then, raise your right hand to shoulder level (fig. 5-8-31). Continue the previous movement without interruption by throwing the flying dart at your opponent. Imagine that your target is your opponent's face or chest area (fig. 5-8-32).

Fig. 5-8-31

Fig. 5-8-32

Key Points: The feeling is that your body is moving backward while you are throwing the flying dart forward. The forces on your body and your right hand should be coordinated and balanced, though in opposite directions. Look far ahead and concentrate on your target. Let your right hand chase your gaze as you throw the dart forward.

Hui Shen Fan Shen Biao (回身翻身镖)
—Turn Around and Throw Fei Biao from Behind Back

Movements: Make a left koubu by placing your left foot in front of your right foot at a right angle. Turn your body to the right by pivoting on the ball of your right foot. Move your left hand, holding your sword, up and to the right as you turn, and move your right hand down to the left side of your waist as though to take a third flying dart from your bag (fig. 5-8-33).

Continue the previous movement without interruption by turning to the right. Shift your weight onto your left leg, and step back with your right foot. You will be in a high left side-bow stance. The dart should already be in your right hand (fig. 5-8-34). Look to the east and continue turning to the right, following your gaze until you are once again facing to the east.

At the same time, shift your weight onto your right leg and fling your right arm forward and slightly up in a horizontal arc to propel the dart toward your opponent approaching from your right. You will be in a right bow stance with your torso facing to the northeast. At the same time, swing the handle of your sword downward in a clockwise circle until your left hand is by the left side of your left hip. The tip of your sword should be pointing up, and the edge should be facing to the east (fig. 5-8-35).

Fig. 5-8-33   Fig. 5-8-34   Fig. 5-8-35

Application: After using your sword to block your opponent's spear on the right side of your body, turn your body around from the right and release your grip on your opponent's spear (fig. 5-8-36). Take a flying dart from your bag with your right hand. Keep turning back until your opponent is on your right side again and immediately throw your flying dart at him or her. Keep your right hand at waist level and imagine that your flying dart will hit your opponent's ribs or abdominal area (fig. 5-8-37). Because the movement of this skill is big, your throwing force will be greater in this movement than in the previous two. As a result, your dart can be thrown further.

Fig. 5-8-36   Fig. 5-8-37

Key Points: Your flying dart should be released as soon as you turn back to your opponent. Look at the target and make your right hand chase your gaze. The turn of your body and the throwing of your dart should be done as one fluid motion. The force for your throw should originate in your left foot and be carried through the turn of your waist to your right arm as it propels your dart forward. To generate this force, all parts of your body should move in a wholly coordinated way.

9. *Pi Shen Xie Gua Yuan Yang Jiao* (披身斜挂鸳鸯脚)—**Slant and Twist Body Sideways, Diagonal Block, and Mandarin Duck Kick**

Posture Name Explanation

In this posture, you should bend at your waist to lean slightly to one side and, at the same time, twist your waist so that one shoulder is in front of the other. This position is called *pi shen*—slant and twist body sideways.

Xie gua means to hang something up diagonally. You should use the handle of your sword to block diagonally up to the left as though you were hanging something up diagonally.

A mandarin duck kick is a double kick. Mandarin ducks are famous for bonding in pairs. A male and female pair will always stay together, side-by-side, whether in water or on land. In Chinese, the term *yuanyang*—mandarin duck— always refers to a pair of things: one is yin and the other is yang. In a mandarin duck kick, the first kick—the yin kick—is a low side kick. The second—the yang kick—is a high straight kick. As in the previous posture, many people today include only the second kick in their form practice.

The main goal of this posture is to quickly and nimbly dodge attacks that are coming at you continuously from all sides. The movements consist of a series of jumps and kicks.

9.1. *Pi Shen You Zhuan* (披身右转)—Dodge and Turn Body to the Right

Movements: Keep looking forward to the east. Move your left hand, holding your sword, diagonally up in front of your body at chest level. Your left palm should be turned outward to face up. The ring of your sword should point to the east, and the edge should face to the north. At the same time, push your right palm to the left and downward and put it on the handle of your sword, slightly pushing your sword to the left. This will cause your body to turn slightly to the left. At the same time, step forward with your left foot and turn the toes of this foot outward to face to the north. Shift your weight forward and slightly sink your body to form a left covering stance (fig. 5-9-1).

Fig. 5-9-1

Application: If you hold your sword in your left hand in a fanwo position, block your opponent's spear to the left with the handle of your sword (fig. 5-9-2). As soon as your sword touches your opponent's spear, turn your body to the left and use your right hand immediately to grip his or her spear. Simultaneously, push the spear to the left and pull it backward (fig. 5-9-3).

| Fig. 5-9-2 | Fig. 5-9-3 |

Key Points: Put your mind on your right laogong point and think about pushing your right hand to the left. This thought will create a feeling that you are dodging to the left.

9.2. *Zuo Gua You Chuai* (左挂右踹)—Left Block with Right Side Kick

Movements: Look forward. Push your right hand to the left to move your left hand, holding your sword, toward the left side of your body. The tip of your sword should point diagonally down. Raise your right knee in front of your body and point it to the north. Then, immediately execute a side kick to the north with your right foot. Straighten your left leg slightly while delivering the side kick. You may lean slightly to the left (fig.5-9-4).

Fig. 5-9-4

Application: Continuing from the previous movement without interruption, keep pulling your opponent's spear backward. This will cause his or her body to lean forward, closer to you. As this occurs, aim a right side kick at either your opponent's knee or rib area (fig. 5-9-5).

Fig. 5-9-5

Key Points: Hollow your chest and form a circle with your arms. Feel stable and relax your right hip. Lift your right knee to the left toward your left elbow. Feel as though your limbs are gathering together to store force. Then, with a sudden explosive feeling, aim a side kick forward and simultaneously push your right hand to the left and backward.

Note: If you choose to include only one kick in your form practice, omit the two movements just described.

9.3. *Zhuan Shen Heng Lan* (转身横拦)—Turn Body Right and Side Parry

Movements: Look forward. Drop your right foot and turn the toes of this foot outward to point to the south. Let your body turn to the right as your toes point to the south. When your right foot touches the ground, shift your weight onto it to form a right high covering stance. At the same time, move your left hand with your sword to the left until it is in front of your body. Your left hand should turn inward slightly to face up. The ring of your sword should point up and forward, the tip should point down and diagonally back, and the edge should face to the north. Simultaneously, move your right hand down to the inside of your left elbow (fig. 5-9-6).

Fig. 5-9-6

Application: After executing the side kick in the previous movement, turn your body immediately to the right to face your opponent and move your sword to make a side parry from the left to the front of your body.

Key Points: Put your mind on your baihui point to create the sensation that your head is suspended from above. Stand erect and feel thoroughly relaxed.

9.4. *Shang Bu Qian Ti* (上步前踢)—Step Forward and Kick Forward

Movements: Step forward with your left foot. At the same time, raise your right hand up beside the right side of your head (fig. 5-9-7). Shift your weight forward onto your left leg and straighten your left knee. Then, kick your right foot forward in a front high kick, and while your right foot is extended in front of your body, hit the upper surface of this foot with your right palm (fig. 5-9-8).

Fig. 5-9-7   Fig. 5-9-8

Application: Continue the previous movement without interruption by aiming a front high kick at your opponent as soon as you face him or her. At the same time, keep pushing your opponent's spear to the left and backward with your left hand and make a clapping-palm strike to his or her face (fig. 5-9-9). Aim your front kick at your opponent's knee, ribs, front arm, or head.

Fig. 5-9-9

Key Points: Stretch your left leg out and withdraw your abdomen slightly. Put your mind on your right laogong point. Look forward toward your target and think that your right hand and right foot, together, are chasing the target quickly and powerfully.

9.5. *Jiao Dao Huan Shou* (交刀换手)—Change Sword to Right Hand

Movements: Immediately after hitting your right foot with your right hand, move your right hand back to your sword and grip the handle. Simultaneously, release the grip of your left hand on your sword and, as the sword is transferred from your left hand to your right, drop your right foot but keep your right knee raised. Put your left palm inside your right wrist and push slightly outward (fig. 5-9-10).

Fig. 5-9-10

Application: Immediately after your high kick from the previous movement, put your right hand on the handle of your sword and push your sword outward with both hands. At the same time, use your right hand to grip your sword. Release your left hand. These movements generate a circling power to block your opponent's spear (fig. 5-9-11).

Fig. 5-9-11

Key Points: Put your mind on your left laogong point. Think about pushing your left hand up and onto your right wrist and, simultaneously, feel your right knee moving upward.

9.6. *Ti Xi Xia Jie* (提膝下截)—Raise Right Knee and Block Down

Movements: Continue the previous movement without interruption. As your right leg swings back after the kick, bend your right knee so that your right foot stays suspended above the ground. Swing your right hand, holding your sword, in a chop down and forward so that the tip of your sword points diagonally to the southeast and the edge points to the right. Raise your left hand diagonally back and push it slightly up. Your arms should form a single diagonal line from your upward pointing left hand to the downward pointing tip of your sword.

Fig. 5-9-12

At the same time, lift your right knee up and slightly to the left. Look toward the tip of your sword (fig. 5-9-12).

Application: Continue the previous movement without interruption. If your opponent steps back, withdraws his or her spear to break contact with your sword, and then immediately attacks your leg, raise your right knee to avoid the attack. At the same time, use your sword to chop his or her spear from the upper left to the lower right (fig. 5-9-13).

Fig. 5-9-13

Key Points: Put your mind on your right laogong point to lift your sword. Withdraw your abdomen and pull your right knee back closer to your abdomen. Feel as though you can spring upward. Then, separate your hands and feel as though the force of your left hand pushing to the left and backward and the force of your sword chopping to the right and forward are balanced and coordinated. Also, imagine that the leftward movement of your right knee adds power to your rightward chop.

10. *Shun Shui Tui Zhou Bian Zao Gao* (順水推舟鞭造篙) —Push a Boat Along with the Tide, Raise the Sword like a Whip, and Use It like a Punt-Pole

Posture Name Explanation

"Push a boat along with the tide" is a common phrase in Chinese that means to make use of any opportunity to save your energy and gain your end. In martial arts, it always refers to using your opponent's force to beat him or her, as you might borrow the force of water to push a boat in the same direction as the tide. This is one of the most important principles in internal martial arts. It advises that you always follow your opponent's force rather than resist it directly.

"Raise the sword like a whip and use it like a punt-pole" means that when you raise your sword to create an upward force, it should look as though you are waving a horsewhip, and when you relax and let the sword sink to create a downward force, it should look as though you are pushing a boat with a punt-pole. The movements of this posture involve pushing your sword in a circle around your body, then raising it high, and finally relaxing and letting it sink as though you were pushing it down.

10.1. *Fan Shou Wai Jie* (翻手外截)—Turn Hand Over to Block Outside

Movements: Turn slightly to the left and look to the southeast. At the same time, raise your right hand to head level and turn it over clockwise so that your right palm faces your head, the edge of your sword faces forward and to the right, and the tip points down. Simultaneously, move your left hand toward the ring of your sword. Keep your right leg elevated with your right knee bent and your right foot suspended above the ground (fig. 5-10-1).

Fig. 5-10-1

Application: Continue the previous movement without interruption. If your opponent turns his or her spear up to attack your head from the right after you have blocked his or her low attack, raise your sword immediately to block the high attack (fig. 5-10-2).

Fig. 5-10-2

Key Points: Turn your right hand outward and lift your right knee to the left to create the feeling that your whole body is spiraling upward. Put your mind on the baihui point to create a feeling of suspension from above while also maintaining a feeling of stability.

10.2. *Ti Dao Guo Nou* (提刀过脑)—Raise Sword and Pass It over Head

Movements: Raise your right hand and then start to move it backward around your body. At the same time, turn your right wrist slightly counterclockwise and hold your sword loosely so that it drops into a vertical position with the edge facing out from your body. Drop your left hand under your right arm in front of your right ribs and push your left palm to the right (fig. 5-10-3).

Continue to turn your body to the right and to move your sword around your body. Bend your left knee and drop your right foot to the ground. Turn the toes of your right foot outward to point to the south. You will be in a covering stance (fig. 5-10-4).

Continue to turn your body to the right and step forward with your left foot to make a koubu. Turn your left foot to the right on your left heel. Your right hand, holding the sword, should be above your head and should move as though wrapping something around your body from your back to the front of your left shoulder. Keep pushing your left hand to the right (fig. 5-10-5).

Fig. 5-10-3

Fig. 5-10-4

Fig. 5-10-5

Application: Continue the previous movement without interruption by keeping your sword in contact with your opponent's spear and pushing it to the right and backward. At the same time, step forward to get close to your opponent and use your left hand to grip his or her spear (fig. 5-10-6). As soon as your left hand grips your opponent's spear, push it to the right and slightly backward. At the same time, remove your sword from the spear, raise it over your head, and circle it forward from behind your body. Because you are holding your opponent's spear in your left hand, your opponent's body will be open to your sword attack (fig. 5-10-7).

Fig. 5-10-6

Fig. 5-10-7

Key Points: Hollow your chest and withdraw your abdomen. Imagine that your qi is sinking down and that your body is dropping. Simultaneously, raise your right hand holding your sword. As your hand moves up, your body should be dropping down. Put your mind on your left laogong point to create a feeling of pushing your left hand to the right. Feel your body follow this push and turn to the right.

10.3. *Zhuan Shen Quan Lan* (转身圈拦)—Turn Body Back and Block Around

Movements: Continue without interruption to turn to the right. Begin by stepping with your right foot and pointing the toes of this foot to the northwest. At the same time, bend both knees so that your body assumes a squatting position. As your right hand passes around your head and to the left side of your body, place your left palm on the back of your sword.

Continue to move your right hand, holding your sword, around your body clockwise to your right until you face to the north. The tip of your sword should point to the ground and the edge should face to the north. As soon as the turn is complete, shift your weight onto your left foot and take a small step forward with your right foot letting only the toes of this foot touch the ground to form a right insubstantial stance (figs. 5-10-8a, b).

Fig. 5-10-8a

Fig. 5-10-8b

Application: After completing the turn in the previous movement, continue without interruption, using your sword to parry your opponent's spear to the right, or simply to maintain contact with his or her weapon (fig. 5-10-9).

If your opponent attacks your chest with a spear, keep the tip of your sword pointing vertically down and use the flat of your sword to parry the spear directly. Keep your sword positioned across the spear and sticking on it. At the same time, withdraw your abdomen and let your front foot touch the ground only lightly so that you can follow the motion of your opponent's spear and move smoothly and quickly either forward or backward as necessary (fig. 5-10-10).

| Fig. 5-10-9 | Fig. 5-10-10 |

Key Points: Hollow your chest and withdraw your abdomen. Relax your hips and lift your knees so that your feet feel very nimble. Put your mind on your left laogong point to increase the feeling of pushing your vertically held sword forward and slightly to the right. This will increase the strength of your side block. Imagine that you are chasing your tailbone as you turn into the side block.

10.4. *Gong Bu Ya Dao* (弓步压刀)—Press Sword Down in Right Bow Stance

Movements: Move your right hand to the right in a clockwise arc so that the tip of your sword points up. Keep the palm of your left hand on the back of your sword and press down slightly. Take a half-step forward with your right foot and then shift your weight onto your right leg so that you are in a right bow stance. At the same time, move your right hand back until the tip of your sword is beside your right knee. While pulling back your sword, push your left hand forward above the back of your sword until the fingers of your left hand point slightly up and the palm of your left hand faces to the east. At the same time, turn your head to the left and look to the west (figs. 5-10-11a, b).

| Fig. 5-10-11a | Fig. 5-10-11b |

Application: While continuing to stick your sword on your opponent's spear, turn your sword around the spear to control his or her movements. One common technique is to drop your right hand and pull it back while pushing your left hand forward on the back of your sword so that your sword moves over your opponent's spear. As soon as your sword is on the top of the spear, press down to control the weapon (fig. 5-10-12). As your sword sticks on the spear, you can follow the movement of the weapon and slide your sword along its shaft to cut his or her hands (fig. 5-10-13).

Fig. 5-10-12

Fig. 5-10-13

Key Points: Keep your mind on your left laogong point and feel it push downward. Imagine that your left palm can press against the ground. Then, feel your palm pushing forward. Turn your head to the left, but push your left hand slightly to the right. This will create a feeling that your body is twisting and dodging to the right.

Fig. 5-10-4a

10.5. *Ce Shen Jü Dao* (侧身举刀)
—Turn Body Left and Raise *Dao*

Movements: Look to the north. While turning your right wrist clockwise so that the edge of your sword faces west, push your right hand, holding your sword, forward and up until your right hand is at shoulder level. At the same time, move your left hand back until it touches the upper surface of the handle of your sword and turn your body to the left. Keeping your weight on your right leg, push your right hand slightly forward and push your left hand down slightly until your left hand is underneath your right elbow with your left palm facing down. Follow this small movement by letting your body sink down and lean slightly forward. Simultaneously, turn your head to the left and look to the west (figs. 5-10-14a, b).

Fig. 5-10-14b

Application: If your opponent attacks your abdomen with his or her spear, turn your right hand up and use the back of your sword to parry the spear slightly to the right (fig. 5-10-15). As soon as your sword touches your opponent's spear, follow the motion of the spear by pulling your sword back. You can use the guard of your sword to increase your control.

At the same time, step forward and use your left hand to grip your opponent's spear (fig. 5-10-16). As soon as your left hand grips the spear, step to the right and, with the spear in your grip, raise your right hand to the right and up and then slightly forward. Let your left hand follow the motion of your right hand. When your right hand is higher than your shoulder, pull your left hand slightly in toward your body and then press down on the spear with both hands. This will break your opponent's root, causing him or her to lean forward and fall to his or her right if he or she maintains a tight grip on the spear (fig. 5-10-17). If your opponent does not grip the spear tightly, he or she will lose it as it drops heavily to the left or behind your body.

This technique can be used directly to defend against your opponent's attack. If your opponent thrusts his or her spear at your chest, turn to the left and move forward. At the same time, use your left hand to grip the spear and pull it backward while stretching your sword forward to cut directly at his or her arm, neck, or head (fig. 5-10-18).

Fig. 5-10-15

Fig. 5-10-16

Fig. 5-10-17

Fig. 5-10-18

Key Points: Stretch your left leg out and let your body drop slightly down. Move your sword forward and up. Feel as though the force from your left foot can reach directly to the tip of your sword. There should be a bouncy feeling in your right leg that allows you to spring nimbly forward or backward. Simultaneously, put your mind on your left laogong point and feel it pressing down to the ground.

11. *Zuo You Fen Shui Long Men Tiao* (左右分水龙门跳) —Swim and Leap over the Dragon Gate

Posture Name Explanation

Zuo you fen shui, or "separate water left and right," refers to swimming. The main movements of this posture involve jumping and turning your sword to the left and right. Named after a well-known natural phenomenon, these movements resemble those of golden carp swimming against the rapids in the Yellow River and leaping to pass over the Dragon Gate. The Dragon Gate, an actual location in the Yellow River where the current is very fast, is a spot where large golden carp can always be seen leaping high out of the water and swimming vigorously against the river's strong current.

In seeking to explain this phenomenon, ancient folktales tell of an imaginary, invisible gate stretched high above the river. It was said that if a fish could leap over the gate, it would instantly be transformed into a dragon. That much sought after transformation was thought to explain the great vaulting leaps made by the fish as they swam upstream. Since the rapids were swift and the legendary gate was thought to be very high, the carp needed to work diligently and tirelessly to complete their journey.

Tales like this express the Chinese ideal that hard work can lead to spectacular achievement and ultimate success. In terms of martial arts, the suggestion is that great accomplishments and high-level mastery can result from long and dedicated practice of even simple and ordinary skills.

11.1. *Shan Bu Heng Lan* (闪步横拦)—Dodge, Step, and Block to the Side

Movements: Look to the west. Turn to the left, leaning slightly back, and turn your left hand outward to the left. Raise your left foot and move it forward while turning it outward as it passes your right foot so that your left toes point to the west. Step toward the west in a baibu. At the same time, drop your right hand to waist level and let the edge of your sword face to the west (fig. 5-11-1).

Application: If your opponent attacks your face or chest with a spear, with-draw your body slightly and stretch your left hand forward to grip the spear (fig. 5-11-2).

Fig. 5-11-1

Fig. 5-11-2

Key Points: It is usually very difficult to grip your opponent's spear directly because spear movements are quick and easily changeable. As a result, it will also be difficult to determine if his or her attack is real or fake, so you must wait until the spear is very close to you before withdrawing your body. At such moments, put your mind on your left laogong point and feel as though your left hand is stretching forward while your body feels as though it is moving back. If you can feel that your hand and body are moving in opposite directions, it will be easier for you to follow the movement of your opponent's spear and to grip it.

11.2. *Shang Bu Zhan Yao* (上步斩腰)
—Step Forward and Chop at Opponent's Waist

Movements: Let your body follow the leftward turn of your left foot so that the toes of your left foot point to the south. Shift your weight onto your left leg and step forward with your right foot, turning your right toes to the south to form a horse-riding stance. Keep turning until your body faces to the south but continue looking to the west.

Simultaneously, let your right hand, holding your sword, follow the turn of your body to the south and put your left hand on top of the ring at the end of your sword's handle. The tip of your sword should point to the west and the edge should face to the south. You will have made a counterclockwise horizontal chop (fig. 5-11-3).

Fig. 5-11-3

Application: Continue the previous movement without interruption. If you can grip your opponent's spear, pull it backward. At the same time, turn to the left and step forward, making a horizontal chop from right to left aimed at your opponent's waist (fig. 5-11-4).

Fig. 5-11-4

Key Points: Keep your mind on your left laogong point. If you can grip your opponent's spear, do not push it sideways. Just follow its motion and pull it backward. Move your body to the right as little as possible so that you can turn and move forward close to your opponent's spear. Do not let your opponent feel that you are gripping his or her spear forcefully. Think about keeping your knees slightly open and letting your body and your left elbow sink down.

11.3. *Ma Bu Fen Zha* (马步分扎)
—Thrust *Dao* and Push Palm in Opposite Direction in Horse-Riding Stance

Movements: Keep looking to the west and let your body sink down slightly. Bring your hands toward each other in front of your body so that your left palm pushes against the end of your sword's handle and your right palm faces up. The tip of your sword should point to the west and the edge should face to the south (fig. 5-11-5). Immediately, extend your right hand, holding your sword, to the right and push your left hand to the left with your left palm facing out. Bend your knees slightly, squat down into a horse-riding stance and keep your head erect (fig. 5-11-6).

Fig. 5-11-5

Fig. 5-11-6

Application: Continue the previous movement without interruption. After you grip your opponent's spear and chop his or her waist, push the spear forward and pull your sword back in front of your body to make a hard cut (fig. 5-11-7). Then, pull your opponent's spear backward and thrust your sword forward toward his or her body (fig. 5-11-8).

Fig. 5-11-7

Fig. 5-11-8

Key Points: In this movement, you need to do both *he,* which means to close in on or get together, and also *kai,* which means to open or to separate. In *he,* your hands should move together as though you want to hold something tightly in your arms and your body should sink down slightly. Imagine that you want to touch your right elbow with your left knee and feel your whole body draw back as though it were a heavy ball.

In kai, your arms should separate and both legs should push slightly outward so that you feel as though your whole body is expanding. Put your mind on your dantian area. Imagine that the force from your left foot can reach directly to the tip of your sword.

11.4. *Zuo Gong Pi Dao* (左弓劈刀)—Left Chop in Left Bow Stance

Movements: Look backward to the east and turn your torso to follow your gaze. Turn your right hand up, holding your sword, so that the edge of your sword faces up. Bend your right elbow and turn your right hand over so that the edge of your sword moves to the left in a vertical chop.

Meanwhile, turn your left hand so that your left palm faces up and then hold the handle of your sword with both hands in *heba,* a two-handed grip. At the same time, turn your body to the east and shift your weight onto your left leg. Both feet should point to the south as you assume a left high side-bow stance. At the end of the chop, the tip of your sword should point to the east, and the edge should face down (fig. 5-11-9).

Application: If your opponent attacks your face or chest with his or her spear, look for a chance to use your left hand to touch or grip the spear. Then, parry it slightly to the right and, at the same time, chop directly at your opponent's head (fig. 5-11-10).

Fig. 5-11-9   Fig. 5-11-10

Key Points: Turn your head back suddenly and look far ahead. Turn your waist to add force to the movement of your sword. Feel as though your sword is chasing your shen when you chop forward and as though your qi can reach to the tip of your sword. Put your mind on your left laogong point to control your sword. The front edge of your sword should carry the force of your chop.

11.5. *Zhuan Shen Qian Tui* (转身前推)
—Turn Body Back and Push Sword Forward

Movements: Look back to the west. Turn your body to the right, relax your right leg and raise your right knee slightly so that only the toes of your right foot touch the ground. You will have assumed a half horse-riding stance. At the same time, drop your right hand, holding your sword, in front of your left hip. Put your left hand on the back of your sword. The tip of your sword should point slightly down with the edge facing down (fig. 5-11-11).

Continue to turn to the right and, at the same time, shift your weight onto your right foot. Step forward to the west with your left foot and shift your weight onto your left leg to assume a left bow stance as you complete the turn. Keep the fingers of your left hand on the back of your sword and use both hands to push the sword forward as you step. The tip of your sword should point to the ground, and the edge should face to the west. Your right hand should be at chest level (fig. 5-11-12).

Application: If your opponent attacks your face or chest with a spear, turn your body to the left and move forward. At the same time, raise your sword vertically

Fig. 5-11-11

Fig. 5-11-12

to parry your opponent's spear to the left (fig. 5-11-13). Maintain contact between your sword and the spear and follow the motion of the spear by dropping your sword in a downward arc behind your body (fig. 5-11-14). Keep sticking your sword on your opponent's spear and step forward while sliding your sword along the spear to cut his or her front hand (fig. 5-11-15).

Fig. 5-11-13

Fig. 5-11-14

Fig. 5-11-15

Key Points: As soon as your sword touches your opponent's spear, stick it with your sword and use quick footwork to follow and chase your opponent. Do not give him or her any chance to evade your approach. Put your mind on your left laogong point to increase the strength of your sword's forward push.

11.6. *Fan Shen Hou Pi* (翻身后劈)—Turn Body Back and Chop Back

Movements: Look back to the east and turn your body to the right. Move your right hand, holding your sword, up and back in a clockwise vertical arc to chop to the east. At the same time, move your left hand in a counterclockwise arc to the left with your left palm facing out. Take a small step back with your right foot and pivot on the ball of your right foot and then pivot on the ball of your left foot. The toes of both feet should point to the north as you assume a horse-riding stance. The tip of your sword should point to the right and slightly up, and the edge should face to the east. Your left palm should face to the west (fig. 5-11-16).

Fig. 5-11-16

Application: If your opponent attacks your face or chest with a spear, look for a chance to use your left hand to touch or grip the spear. Then, pull the spear to your left and at the same time, chop slightly to the right to strike directly at his or her head (fig. 5-11-17).

Fig. 5-11-17

Key Points: Turn your head back suddenly and look far into the distance. Turn your waist so that your sword chases your shen as it chops back toward your opponent. Open your knees slightly and let your body sink down. Put your mind on your left laogong point to increase the feeling that your left hand is pushing in the opposite direction from your chop. Feel that your body is dropping slightly down and that the forces in your hands are moving in opposite directions. At the same time, imagine that your head is suspended from above at your baihui point.

11.7. *Qian Ti Fan Liao* (前踢反撩)
—Kick Forward and Make an Upward Reverse Cut

Movements: Look to the east, slightly shift your weight onto your right leg, and extend your sword slightly to the right (fig. 5-11-18). Pivot on the ball of your left foot and turn the toes of that foot to the west. Shift your weight onto your left foot and turn your body to the left as you bring your right hand, holding your sword, down and forward. Your sword should be held vertically along your right leg with the tip pointing down and the edge facing to the west (fig. 5-11-19).

Continue the previous movement without interruption by swinging your right leg forward in a front kick to the west. At the same time, chop up and for-

ward with your sword keeping it concealed behind your leg during the forward kick. The edge of your sword should face up and the tip should point to the west. Your left arm should move back to touch the handle of your sword (fig. 5-11-20).

Fig. 5-11-18

Fig. 5-11-19

Fig. 5-11-20

Application: If your opponent attacks your abdomen or legs with a spear, aim your front kick at the spear. As you kick, turn your right foot inward and use the sole of your foot to touch the spear so that your kick parries the spear to the left. As you kick forward, swing your sword simultaneously forward to make an upward cut to your opponent's front hand or arm (fig. 5-11-21).

Fig. 5-11-21

Key Points: Turn your head back suddenly and look far ahead. Keep your mind on your left laogong point. Straighten your left leg and turn your waist to bring additional force to your sword and kick. Imagine that your right foot and the front edge of your sword are chasing the same target together.

11.8. Ti Xi Fan Gua (提膝反挂)—Raise Knee and Reverse Hang

Movements: Keep looking forward. Bend your right leg and let your right knee point to the west. At the same time, bend your right wrist and let your right hand relax its grip on your sword so that it moves slightly back. Hold your sword vertically along your right leg with the tip of your sword pointing down. Put your left hand on top of the ring on the handle of your sword (fig. 5-11-22).

Fig. 5-11-22

Application: Your opponent may pull his or her spear back to escape your kick and forward cut from the previous movement and then attack your abdomen or legs with the spear. If this happens, raise your right knee to the left to dodge the thrust of your opponent's spear and immediately drop your sword down to block the spear to the right (fig. 5-11-23).

Fig. 5-11-23

Key Points: Drop your sword along the right side of your body and lift your right knee slightly to the left. Feel as though your body is dodging to the left while your sword parries to the right. Put your mind on your baihui point.

11.9. *Tiao Bu Zhuan Dao* (跳步转刀)—Jump and Swing Sword in a Circle

Movements: Continue the previous movement without interruption by raising your right knee and springing upward with your left leg so that both feet leave the ground (fig. 5-11-24). During the jump, move your right hand back, up, and then forward to swing your sword in a vertical counterclockwise circle on the right side of your body.

Fig. 5-11-24

Let your right foot land first and then put your left foot down a step ahead of your right foot with only the toes of your left foot touching the ground. You will have assumed a high left insubstantial stance. Your right toes should point to the north. As you land, turn your body slightly to the right. When the circular movement of your sword has been completed, the tip of your sword should point up, and the edge should face to the west. At the same time, put your left hand on the back of your sword (fig. 5-11-25).

Fig. 5-11-25

Application: Continuing from the previous movement, if your opponent evades your lower block and turns his or her spear upward to attack your head from the right, raise your right leg and jump toward your opponent. At the same time, swing your sword in a circle, moving it first down, then backward, up, and forward toward your opponent. Because your opponent will be holding his or her spear in front of his or her body, your opponent will naturally attempt to use his or her spear to block your sword (fig. 5-11-26).

Fig. 5-11-26

Key Points: Keep your mind on your baihui point and imagine that your body is suspended from above. Withdraw your abdomen, lift your right knee, and stretch your left leg out to spring upward. When your body is in the air, think about lifting your left knee as high as possible. The closer you can jump toward your opponent, the more effective your attack will be.

11.10. *Ce Shen Pu Pi* (側身扑劈)—Turn Body, Press Sword Down, and Chop

Movements: Continue the previous movement without interruption. Reach slightly forward with your sword and then pull it back and push it down. At the same time, take a half-step forward with your left foot and let the toes of that foot point to the north. Straighten your left leg and bend your right knee to form a right low side-bow stance.

Turn your body slightly to the right as you pull your sword back. Keep your left hand on the back of your sword and push your sword down so that it is parallel to the ground at the level of your right knee. The tip of your sword should point to the west, and the edge should face down (figs. 5-11-27a, b).

Fig. 5-11-27a   Fig. 5-11-27b

Application: Continuing from the previous movement, if your opponent uses his or her spear to block your sword attack, push your sword slightly forward and then immediately press down. If you feel strong resistance from your opponent, keep pushing down and simultaneously shift your weight back and pull your sword backward (fig. 5-11-28). The action of your sword in this move-

Fig. 5-11-28

ment (11.10) brings to completion the swinging motion that began in movement 11.8 and continued through movement 11.9.

Key Points: Withdraw your abdomen to drop your body into a low position. Put your mind on your left laogong point and think about pressing your sword down using the weight of your whole body.

12. *Xia Shi San He Zi You Zhao* (下势三合自由招) —Assume a Low Position with Three Integrations and with Free and Natural Changes

Posture Name Explanation

The important features of this posture include maintaining the integration of external movements and internal components and creatively adding movements according to your feelings. If the integrations are well done, any of the movements can be modified to suit how you feel at the moment. Although the movements of this posture are done from a relatively low position, some height variation does occur in a subtle alternating pattern.

12.1. *Zuo Gong Qian Tui* (左弓前推) —Push Sword Forward and Down in Left Bow Stance

Movements: Continuing without interruption from the last posture, use both hands to push your sword forward and upward. At the same time, raise your body and shift your weight onto your left leg to form a left side-bow stance (fig. 5-12-1).

Fig. 5-12-1

Application: Continue the previous movement. If you feel that your opponent wants to raise his or her spear when you push it down, relax suddenly and follow your opponent's force while raising your body as though to make your sword jump away from the spear. Then, move directly toward your opponent and immediately push your sword forward to cut his or her head (fig. 5-12-2).

Fig. 5-12-2

Key Points: Look forward and straighten your right leg so that your body moves forward to follow your gaze. Feel as though you can spring far forward to attack your opponent. Keep your mind on your left laogong point to strengthen your attack as you push your sword forward.

12.2. *You Pu Chen Cai* (右仆沉采)
—Press Sword Down in Right Side-Bow Stance

Movements: Sink your body and shift your weight back onto your right leg to form a right side-bow stance. At the same time, use both hands to press down on your sword and to pull it back toward your body until the ring of your sword is near your right knee. Keep your sword parallel to the ground with the tip pointing to the west and the edge facing down. When you push down on your sword, raise your head slightly as though it were suspended from your baihui point (figs. 5-12-3a, b).

Fig. 5-12-3a

Fig. 5-12-3b

Application: If, continuing from the previous movement, your opponent raises his or her spear quickly enough to block your sword again, push your sword forward, press it down, and pull it backward, as you did in the last posture (fig. 5-12-4).

Fig. 5-12-4

Key Points: Hollow your chest, withdraw your abdomen and straighten your left leg. Feel as though you are dodging backward. Keep your mind on your left laogong point and press your sword down and slightly back toward your right knee. Then, put your mind on your baihui point to cause your head to rise slightly and make your body more erect.

12.3. *Tui Dao Qian Yong* (推刀前拥)—Push Sword Forward and Up

Movements: Raise your body and shift your weight onto your left leg to form a high side-bow stance. At the same time, turn your body slightly to the northwest. Use both hands to push your sword forward again, but this time raise your right hand to shoulder level and your left hand to stomach level so that the tip of your sword points slightly down as you push your sword to the west. The edge of your sword should face to the west (fig. 5-12-5).

Fig. 5-12-5

Application: If your opponent thrusts his or her spear at your throat, use both arms to raise your sword. Your arms should form a horizontal circle in front of your body. Use your sword, oriented across your opponent's spear, to block the attack from underneath the shaft of the spear. Push your sword slightly forward by expanding your arm circle. Simultaneously, draw your head and upper body back (fig. 5-12-6).

Fig. 5-12-6

Key Points: Put your mind on your tanzhong point, hollow your chest, and push your sword forward with both hands. Feel as though your arms, chest, and sword form a circle and that this circle is expanding. Relax your waist so that the circular power can be moved easily to allow your sword to follow your opponent's spear smoothly.

12.4. *Li Shen Chan Tou* (立身缠头)
—Straighten Body and Raise Right Hand over Head

Movements: Continue raising your right hand, holding your sword, until your right hand is higher than the top of your head. At the same time, turn your right hand over to let the tip of your sword point to the ground and the edge point to the southwest. Bring your left hand in toward your body with your left palm facing to the northeast and the fingers of your left hand pointing upward under your right shoulder. Shift your weight onto your right foot and bring your left foot back slightly to assume a left insubstantial stance (fig. 5-12-7).

Fig. 5-12-7

Application: Continue the previous movement without interruption. As soon as your sword touches your opponent's spear, stick it and expand your arm circle to follow its motion. The handle of your sword should be slightly higher than your head and your left hand should extend forward to grip your opponent's spear (fig. 5-12-8).

Fig. 5-12-8

Key Points: Lift your sword over your head and move it from right to left while simultaneously pushing your left hand to the right so that your body twists. Imagine that your upper body is spiraling upward and that your lower body is spiraling downward. Put your mind on your left laogong point. Feel your body move backward and expand.

12.5. *Ti Xi Guo Nou* (提膝过脑)—Raise Knee and Pass Sword over Head

Movements: Sink your body back on your right foot and, at the same time, raise your left knee slightly. Simultaneously, continue to raise your right arm and then wind it up in a horizontal, counterclockwise circle around your head. When the sword passes over your head, drop it over your right shoulder. Keep the tip of your sword pointing diagonally to the ground until it is behind your right shoulder. The edge of your sword should face up. Raise the toes of your left foot off the ground to assume a left insubstantial stance. Move your left hand diagonally up to the northwest with your left palm facing out (fig. 5-12-9).

Fig. 5-12-9

Application: As soon as you can grip your opponent's spear with your left hand, continue the previous movement without interruption by pushing the spear slightly to the left. Continue to wind your sword around your body to the right (fig. 5-12-10).

Fig. 5-12-10

Key Points: When your sword passes over your head, relax and sink your body slightly down. Feel that power is stored in your right leg and will allow you to jump forward very quickly if the need arises. Put your mind on your mingmen point to relax your waist and make it flexible.

12.6. *Gong Bu Xie Pi* (弓步斜劈)—Chop on Incline in Left Bow Stance

Movements: Continue the previous movement without interruption by looking to the northwest and taking a half-step forward with your left foot. Shift your weight onto your left leg to assume a left bow stance. At the same time, swing your left hand down and then up in front of your face and over your head with your left palm facing out and the fingers of your left hand lined up with the outer edge of your left eyebrow. Move your right hand, holding your sword, up and over your right shoulder and then push it diagonally forward with the tip of your sword pointing diagonally up and the edge slanted to the northwest (fig. 5-12-11). Continue to push your right hand forward in an inclined chop. The tip of your sword should point up and the edge should face to the northwest. At the same time, push your left hand outward (fig. 5-12-12).

Fig. 5-12-11

Fig. 5-12-12

Application: As soon as you move your sword to the right side of your body, continue the previous movement without interruption by pushing your opponent's spear to the left and pulling it backward with your left hand. At the same time, push your sword forward to chop your opponent's left arm or shoulder (fig. 5-12-13).

Fig. 5-12-13

Key Points: Push your left hand to the left and forward and up so that you feel as though you are tracing the circumference of a circle. Put your mind on your right yongquan point to feel *jin,* internal trained power, extending through your body from your right foot directly to the middle edge of your sword. Let this feeling lead you to push your sword straight ahead with your right hand.

13. *Bian He Xie Shi Feng Huan Chao* (卞和携石凤还巢) —Bian He Carries Jade Like a Phoenix Returning to Its Nest

Posture Name Explanation

The combined phrases "Bian He carries jade" and "a phoenix returning to its nest" mean that a task has been completed to perfection.

The events from which the title of this posture derives took place about 2,500 years ago in the Spring and Autumn Period (770 BC to 476 BC) when China was divided into several kingdoms. Bian He, a native of the kingdom of Chu, found what he believed to be an extremely precious piece of jade. He carried the jade to a meeting with King Li of Chu and offered the king his extraordinary gift.

Because jade in its natural state, called *pu,* is often found mixed in or covered by other stones, King Li's experts mistakenly pronounced that Bian He's offering was only an ordinary stone. Bian He was punished for the alleged crime of attempting to deceive the king. Years later, when King Wu succeeded King Li, Bian He tried again to offer the jade, and, once more, it was pronounced unremarkable. Bian He was punished again.

More years passed, and by the time a new king, King Wen, ascended the throne, Bian He was often found crying and clutching the jade to his chest on the mountain where he had made his discovery. When King Wen sent emissaries to investigate, Bian He wailed, "My jade is judged to be a mere stone, and I, a loyal and faithful subject, am persecuted and humiliated. These are the reasons for my lamentations!"

Hearing this, King Wen ordered the stone to be cut open, and what emerged was the largest, most perfect, and exquisite piece of jade the world has ever known. The jade became known as He Shi Bi, the "Jade of Bian He," and Bian He was rewarded with the title of Marquis of Ling Yang.

In general, the phrase "a phoenix returning to its nest" signifies a beautiful and perfect ending. Here, it refers both to the happy outcome of Bian He's efforts, and also to the extraordinary events that later surrounded the beautiful piece of jade.

In the Warring States Period (476 BC to 221 BC), the jade came into the possession of King Huiwen of Zhao. When word of this reached King Shao of Qin, he offered to trade King Huiwen fifteen of Qin's cities for the jade. Because the Kingdom Qin was much stronger than the Kingdom Zhao, King Huiwen had no choice but to acquiesce to the trade.

King Huiwen's emissary, Lin Xiangru, carried the jade to Qin, and offered it to King Shao for close inspection. Quietly observing King Shao's expressions, words, and actions, Lin Xiangru quickly realized that King Shao wanted the jade but had no intention of giving up his cities. Thinking quickly, the emissary said to King Shao, "This jade has but one tiny flaw. If your majesty will allow me, I will show it to you."

Without thinking, King Shao handed the jade back to Lin Xiangru who immediately stepped back, raised it high above his head, and proclaimed, "Unlike your majesty's offer, this jade is pure and flawless. If your majesty should force the issue, then today both the jade and my person shall perish on this spot!" In panic mixed with shame, King Shao allowed Lin Xiangru to return to King Huiwen with the jade intact, thus giving birth to the expression "jade returning to Zhao intact," meaning a mission perfectly accomplished.

Despite this success, the jade was returned to the kingdom of Qin when Qin conquered all the other kingdoms and unified China in 221 BC. He Shi Bi was made into the emperor's seal and, for hundreds of years, served as the official symbol of the state. It was eventually lost in the chaos of the wars that followed the disintegration of the Tang Dynasty.

Just as Bian He and the loyal emissary Lin Xiangru persisted until their tasks were brought to successful conclusions, you must finish the Taiji Dao form and return to the beginning position before your practice can be considered a success. Everything must be done completely and correctly. The movements of this last posture bring the form to a close and return you to your original position.

13.1. *Hui Shen Hou Lan* (回身后拦)—Turn Body Back and Block Down

Movements: Begin to turn your body to the right as you bring your arms together and let your hands cross in front of your body with your left hand over your right elbow. Drop your sword down to the left side of your body. At the same time, pivot on the heel of your left foot and continue turning your body to the right, letting the toes of your left foot point to the north. Lift the heel of your right foot slightly up off the ground and pivot slightly on the ball of that foot (fig. 5-13-1).

Look down and to the right. Swing your right hand, holding your sword, diagonally down and to the right and push your left hand diagonally up to the left and slightly back. The fingers of your left hand should point back. The tip of your sword should point slightly down and the edge should face to the east. Your weight should be on your left leg. Take a small step to the left with your right foot and let only the toes of your right foot touch the ground. Bend your left knee slightly (fig. 5-13-2).

Fig. 5-13-1

Fig. 5-13-2

Application: If your opponent attacks your leg from your right side or from behind, turn your body to the right. Withdraw your leg slightly and extend your right arm with your sword to parry his or her spear to the right (fig. 5-13-3).

Fig. 5-13-3

Key Points: Look and turn to the right, letting your body follow your gaze. Withdraw your abdomen and relax your hips. Put your mind on your right yinlingquan point to cause your right knee to lift slightly up and to the left. Imagine that your arms are expanding in a circle so that your sword moves forward and outward in a parry while your body and legs dodge backward.

13.2. *Ti Xi Fan Ti* (提膝反提)—Raise Knee and Turn Hand Out to Hold Sword

Movements: Look to the east. Turn your right hand clockwise and let the tip of your sword drop down naturally until it points to the ground. At the same time, raise your body, your right foot, and your right knee. Point your right knee to the north and keep pushing your left hand to the left (fig. 5-13-4).

Fig. 5-13-4

Application: If your opponent turns his or her spear upward to attack your head from the right side, continue the previous movement by turning your right hand outward, holding your sword, and raising it to block the spear (fig. 5-13-5). As soon as your sword touches the spear, put your left hand on the handle of your sword to add extra power for pushing the spear up (fig. 5-13-6).

Fig. 5-13-5

Fig. 5-13-6

Key Points: Imagine that your body is twisting. Keep your mind on your right yinlingquan point and lift your right knee. This will cause your lower body to twist to the left. Then, put your mind on your left laogong point and feel it push to the right and back. This will cause your upper body to twist to the right and will move your sword in that direction.

13.3. *Ti Dao Guo Nou* (提刀过脑)—Raise Sword and Pass It over Head

Movements: Step forward with your right foot and shift your weight forward onto your right foot to form a right bow stance. At the same time, raise your right hand holding your sword until it is higher than your head. Your sword should be on the right side of your body, and the tip should point to the ground with the edge facing outward (fig. 5-13-7).

Continue to move your right arm so that it winds your sword in a circle over your head and behind your right shoulder, your back, and finally your left shoulder. At the same time, move your left hand forward and in toward your body while pushing it to the right. Your left arm should cross your right arm. Turn your body slightly to the right (fig. 5-13-8).

Fig. 5-13-7

Fig. 5-13-8

Application: Continue the previous movement without interruption by pushing your sword forward slightly. This will make it easier to keep your sword sticking on your opponent's spear. Follow the movement of his or her spear with your sword by circling your sword around your head to the left side of your body (fig. 5-13-9).

Fig. 5-13-9

Key Points: Coordinate the raising of your right hand and the sinking down of your body. Let your arms and your sword form an expanding circle.

13.4. *Tuo Dao Fan Dai* (拖刀反带)—Pull Sword in Reverse Direction

Movements: When the back of your sword reaches the outer edge of your left arm, move your right hand down and pull your sword horizontally forward with its back touching the outside of your left upper arm. Keep your right forearm oriented horizontally in front of your chest. At the same time, lean forward slightly and shift your weight onto your right foot to assume a right bow stance. Turn on the ball of your left foot until both feet are parallel to each other and point to the east. Turn your head back and look over your left shoulder. The fingers of your left hand should form in an upward hook and extend back to the west (figs. 5-13-10a, b).

Fig. 5-13-10a   Fig. 5-13-10b

Application: Continue the previous movement without interruption by keeping your sword sticking on your opponent's spear. Follow your opponent's movement by stepping forward or backward and to the left or right. Do not mount an attack yet but feel as though you control your opponent and can attack him or her at any time (fig. 5-13-11).

Fig. 5-13-11

Key Points: Put your mind on your left yonquan point and straighten your left leg to generate power that flows directly from your left foot to your right arm and finally to the blade of your sword as you push against it with your left arm. Let your body sink so that you feel as though you can move quickly and lightly to control your opponent. This position is called *lu fu hao xin*—running like a deer and walking like a crane.

13.5. *Jiao Dao Huan Shou* (交刀换手)—Change Sword to Left Hand

Movements: Move your right hand holding your sword forward slightly, and at the same time move your left hand forward and place it under the handle of your sword. Release the handle with your right hand and grip it loosely from underneath with your left hand. Remain in a right bow stance and look forward (fig. 5-13-12).

Fig. 5-13-12

Application: There is no obvious application for changing your grip from your right hand to your left. In traditional martial arts combat, masters change their sword to their left hand and hold it in a fanwo position for a variety of reasons: to show respect; to show off high-level skills; or to free their right hand for another purpose, such as wielding hidden weapons.

Key Points: Look straight ahead. Relax your wrist and stretch your left hand out. Put your mind on your left laogong point.

13.6. *Tui Shen Fen Zhang* (退身分掌)—Shift Weight and Separate Palms

Movements: After transferring your sword from your right hand to your left, open your right hand and stretch both hands forward. Look slightly down and push your hands directly down to hip level. Your left palm should face up and your right palm should face down. Lean slightly forward (fig. 5-13-13).

Continue the previous movement without interruption by moving your right hand down and then back with your right palm turning outward. At the same time, pivot on the ball of your right foot to turn the toes of that foot to the south. Shift your weight back onto your right leg and lightly hit the outer edge of your right leg with the back of your right hand as that hand moves past your right leg.

Continue to move your right hand back until it extends to the west with your right elbow slightly bent and your right palm facing up. Your left hand, holding your sword, should remain extended to the left with the blade resting on your left forearm and the handle pointing diagonally down. At the same time, turn your left arm outward to let your palm face forward (fig. 5-13-14). Keep looking forward and downward to the east.

Continuing without interruption, move your right hand back and up in a curving path. At the same time, turn your right arm so that the palm faces to the west and pushes slightly outward. Raise your body and bring your left foot toward your right foot (fig. 5-13-15).

Fig. 5-13-13

Fig. 5-13-14

Fig. 5-13-15

Application: If your opponent attacks your left leg, withdraw your leg slightly and drop the handle of your sword to block his or her spear. Try to use the guard of your sword to catch the spear (fig. 5-13-16), and, if you succeed, twist your sword outward while simultaneously pushing it down and pulling it slightly back (fig. 5-13-17).

Fig. 5-13-16   Fig. 5-13-17

Key Points: Put your mind on your right laogong point and push it backward and upward. This will cause your body to rise. Imagine that power extends from your right hand to your left hand, holding the sword, and connects your hands and the sword so that they work together as a completely coordinated unit. Feel as though the more your right hand moves up, the more downward power the handle of your sword will acquire.

13.7. *Li Zhang Tuo Tian* (立掌托天)—Raise Palm Up to Push the Sky

Movements: Continue to move your right hand up and to the left until your right arm passes over your face. Then, push it down in a counterclockwise circle until it is in front of your left hip with the palm facing down. Simultaneously, turn your body slightly to the right and move your left hand up, holding your sword, on the left side of your body to head level and then to the right in a clockwise circle until it is in front of your face. Turn your left arm inward slightly so that the palm faces your face. The blade of your sword should rest along your left arm with the tip pointing to the north and diagonally down, the ring pointing to the south and upward, and the edge facing to the east.

At the same time, step forward with your left foot so that it is in front of your right foot. Touch the ground with only the toes of your left foot and bend your left knee to form a left insubstantial stance. Turn your head to look to the south (fig. 5-13-18).

Continue the previous movement without interruption by turning your body to the right and making a circle with your right hand by moving it down, right, and finally toward the back of your body. Simultaneously, make a circle with your left hand by moving it to the right and down in front of your chest. Turn your head to the right as your body turns (fig. 5-13-19).

Fig. 5-13-18   Fig. 5-13-19

Continue without interruption to reverse the turn of your body to the left and to move your hands in their respective circles: your right hand up, right, forward, and finally over your head with the palm facing up and the fingers of your right hand pointing to the east; and your left hand down and left to the left side of your left hip. Hold your sword vertically alongside your left arm with the tip pointing up and the edge facing forward. Bend your left elbow slightly. Turn your head to the left to look to the east and turn your body to follow your gaze (figs. 5-13-20a, b).

Fig. 5-13-20a   Fig. 5-13-20b

Application: The remaining movements are used to adjust your internal feelings as you close your form practice. There are no obvious applications.

Key Points: Keep your mind on your right laogong point to relax your waist and move your arms through their circling paths. Hollow your chest and withdraw your abdomen. Think about pushing your right palm upward and sinking your body slightly downward. Feel very stable.

13.8. *Luo Zhang Huan Yuan* (落掌还原)
—Drop Palm Down and Return to Original Posture

Movements: Raise your body until your right leg is straight and move your left foot back to your right foot to form a feet-together stance. Relax your left shoulder and let your left hand, holding your sword, drop naturally down to the outside of your left leg. Simultaneously, move your right hand to the left with your palm facing east, down, and then to the right in a counterclockwise vertical arc that pushes to the west. Follow the movement of your right hand by turning your head and looking to the west (fig. 5-13-21).

Fig. 5-13-21

Continue without interruption to move your right hand up in a counterclockwise circle over your head with your right palm facing up and pushing upward and the fingers of your right hand pointing to the east. Turn your head and look to the south (fig. 5-13-22).

Fig. 5-13-22

Drop your right hand in a clockwise arc to the west and follow this movement by turning your head to the right as your right hand drops to shoulder level. Let the fingers of your right hand point to the west and your right palm face to the south (fig. 5-13-23). Turn your head again to the south and, simultaneously, drop your right hand down until it rests along the outside of your right leg (fig. 5-13-24).

Fig. 5-13-23

Fig. 5-13-24

Key Points: Keep your mind on your right laogong point to lead the upward movement of your right hand. Imagine that your right palm is pushing very high up and that your feet are being inserted deeply into the ground.

After dropping your right hand down to touch the right side of your right leg, put your mind on your baihui point and imagine that your body is lightly suspended from above. At the same time, think about your whole body relaxing and sinking. Follow these feelings by letting your qi sink down and gather in your dantian area. Relax and maintain this feeling for a while. Feel comfortable as your shen withdraws. Relax your eyelids until your eyes are almost closed.

Tai Ji Shou Shi (太极收式)—**The Ending Form of Taiji Dao**

Posture Name Explanation

There is no movement in this posture. As you end your form practice, you must adjust your internal feeling, completely relax every part of your body, and make yourself comfortable. It is very important for your internal training that you focus on these adjustments and accomplish them fully before turning to other activities. If you do not perform this ending posture correctly, the positive effect of your form practice will be greatly diminished.

Bao Dao Tiao Xi (抱刀调息)—Hold *Dao* and Adjust Breath to Natural Rhythm

Movements: Stand straight and still. Relax your body and adjust your breath until it has returned to its natural rhythm. At this point, your Taiji Dao Thirteen-

Posture Form practice is complete. If you like, you may transfer your sword to your right hand (fig. 5-13-25) and return to the starting posture shown in figure 5-0-1.

Fig. 5-13-25

Key Points: Use your mind to lead your qi down to your huiyin point and then slightly pull this point up. As you breathe in, use your mind to lead your qi up along the dumei on the centerline of your back until it reaches your baihui point. Then, as you breathe out, use your mind to lead your qi down along the renmei on the centerline of the front of your body until it reaches your dantian area.

In this process, your qi moves in a circle called *xiaozhoutian*—the microcosmic orbit throughout your body. You can repeat this qi circle several times, and in each subsequent circle your qi should move more slowly. As your form practice ends, you should feel completely relaxed in both body and mind. You should also have an abiding sense that your body has become intrinsically stronger and imbued with high spirits.

How to Practice the Taiji Dao Form

There are different ways to practice the Taiji Dao form. You can choose first to familiarize yourself with all the physical movements that comprise the form, then to practice each movement separately until you can perform it expertly, and finally to link the separate movements together so that you can correctly perform the whole form without interruption.

Alternatively, you can choose to practice the form from beginning to end without first perfecting the separate movements and then repeat the entire form many times until mastery is reached. Whichever approach you choose, once you have thoroughly learned the form, you should pay attention to the feelings that accompany each movement. To deepen the qualities of your form practice, there are some aspects that merit special attention, regardless of which practice method you choose.

If you have already mastered the Taiji Quan empty-hand form, you will understand that the acquisition of Taiji Quan skills requires that your external movement practice include relaxation, stability, and nimbleness, and smooth, slow, even, and quickly changeable motions performed with a sense of vitality. While these qualities are also important in Taiji Dao form practice, the speed and rhythm of movements in the sword form have special significance.

Because many Taiji Dao sword skills depend on the release of a sudden, explosive force and because your sword gains momentum whenever it is moved, speed and rhythm in the Taiji Dao form will be much more varied than in the empty-hand form, and close attention must be paid to these two attributes. This does not mean that there are differences in principle between Taiji Dao and empty-hand form practice. All the foundational skills mastered through Taiji Quan empty-hand practice apply to Taiji Dao practice, but, in the sword form, you must be concerned with additional details regarding speed and rhythm.

Speed and rhythm are important in Taiji Dao form practice because they contribute to the development of strong internal feelings. In Taiji Dao form practice, unlike empty-hand form practice, the speed of the movements is variable rather than even, and you must remain not only very relaxed but also highly animated throughout. In empty-hand practice, the ideal rhythm is quiet and steady, but in Taiji Dao practice, the rhythm should change often according to your feelings and to the requirements of each skill.

Your sensitivity to rhythm is especially important when fighting. Although it is very difficult to keep your mind clear after executing an uninterrupted sequence of five or more skills, a clear mind remains one of the foremost prerequisites for successful outcome in combat. Finding the right rhythm for each skill can help you adjust your mind and stay alert.

The two conditions that most influence your state of mind are the effectiveness of your physical movements and your degree of nervousness. If your movements are too rushed and disorganized or if you are uneasy, you will have difficulty keeping your mind clear. Taiji Dao form practice can help you learn how to use rhythm to keep your mind clear throughout the continual flow of movement.

Although Taiji Dao form practice is very important for training purposes, it cannot prepare you completely for real fighting. It can help you develop correct feelings, but it does not include all the skills of Taiji Dao. To master real fighting skills, you must focus on your solo practice and understand deeply each individual skill. You must research in detail the many ways each movement, no matter how small, can be used in different situations. You must become familiar with the many variations of each movement and learn how to change smoothly from one to another.

Your training should also include two-person practice, but neither this nor solo practice will sufficiently develop strong internal feeling. Individual skill practice will help you develop a detailed understanding of each skill, but only form practice can accomplish the enhancement of internal feeling. The two kinds of practice are complimentary, and both must be done well and with perseverance.

To develop internal feeling, you must understand at least one application for each movement. When you practice the form, you should imagine that an opponent stands in front of you and that you are fighting with this invisible foe. This will help you incorporate application ideas into every movement. It is said that "when you practice, you should have an opponent although none can be seen."

For application training, it is important to understand that there are some hidden skills in the Taiji Dao form. A hidden skill refers to a skill that does not appear overtly in the form but occurs, instead, in the practitioner's mind or internal feeling. Skills that require gripping your sword with both hands provide an example. Although you never actually grip the sword handle with your empty hand in the Taiji Dao form, you should imagine gripping it with both hands as though you were using the two-handed skill in real combat.

Internal feeling is one of the most important aspects of internal martial arts practice, and great attention must be paid to it. As an internal martial art, Taiji Dao requires deep consideration and thorough mastery of this internal element. Internal feeling has multiple aspects. It includes the feeling that your spirit is aroused and focused, that your mind is excited and alert, and that your body is not only capable and powerful but also deeply relaxed. It includes also the sense that you can move nimbly while still maintaining stability and deep root. Finally, your sword must function as if it were a part of your body, allowing you to control its movements freely, naturally, and completely.

When your internal feeling is strong, you will be brave but not rash, quick but not careless, excited but not rushed, and able to focus on any target while still remaining aware of everything going on around you. With strong internal feeling, you will be determined and tough on the inside but calm and dispassionate in your external demeanor. All of these qualities can be increased through conscientious and correct Taiji Dao form practice.

Chapter Six

Two-Handed Taiji Dao Skills

Taiji Dao is classified under *dan dao,* the sword category in which only one sword is used at a time. Although most Taiji Dao skills are executed with one hand, the long handle of *dao* lends itself to two-handed grips. Chapter Five introduced the traditional thirteen-posture form, in which only a few hidden skills are practiced with two hands. This chapter focuses on these two-handed Taiji Dao skills.

The two-handed grips used for these skills can increase the power of the skills, and because power is closely and inversely related to changeability, the first section of this chapter presents a brief discussion of these two variables. After a brief introduction to the relationship between power and changeability and its relevance to *dao* skills, the differences between one-handed and two-handed grips will be discussed and then a short form for two-handed practice will be described.

Balance of Power and Changeability

The two important aspects of sword skills are power and maneuverability. Ideally, both would be maximized, but this happy circumstance can never be realized because whenever either of these aspects increases, the other inevitably decreases. Given this inverse relationship, it is important to understand and balance both of these qualities in your practice.

Power

The power of a weapon is a function of its momentum, and momentum varies directly with the weight of the weapon and the speed of its motion. The heavier your sword and the faster you move it, the greater its momentum will be and the more powerful your sword skills will become.

Obviously, one way to increase momentum, and thereby power, is to use a heavier sword. (See Chapter Two for a more detailed discussion.) Usually, however, you will have selected your sword based on your body size and condition, and you will use that same sword whenever you practice or fight. For these reasons and because most skills do not require an increase in momentum, it is not likely that you will choose a sword that is heavier than the one suitable for your size, condition, and the majority of sword skills.

A second alternative for increasing momentum is to increase the speed of your sword's motion. This can be accomplished in several ways, the first of which is to increase the amount of physical force you exert on your sword. Unlike the weight of your sword, force can be varied quite easily, but this choice requires that your muscles work harder, and this, in turn, will make it more difficult for you to relax. Increasing the size of your muscles is another way to make your movements more forceful. Finally, you can increase the forcefulness of your sword's movements by using two-handed grips.

A third option for adding momentum is to increase the size or duration of your sword's movements. This choice, however, will make your overall body posture more open and therefore more vulnerable to attack from your opponent. Clearly, each option for increasing speed has both advantages and disadvantages.

However achieved, increased momentum has both advantages and disadvantages. The greater your weapon's power or momentum, the harder it will be for your opponent to defend directly against your attack by blocking it or changing its path. However, it will be more difficult for you to stop or change the path of your attack, making you more vulnerable if your opponent's reaction demands an immediate adjustment on your part. In short, increasing the power of your sword can make a situation more dangerous for both you and your opponent.

Changeability

Changeability or maneuverability refers to the ability to change a particular skill quickly and smoothly to a different skill. It requires excellent sword control, and the timing and direction of the changes are critical factors.

Timing refers to changes made while your sword is in motion. In general, it is easier to make changes at the beginning and end of a sword movement because the momentum of your sword is relatively low at these two points. Changing a movement midway, when its momentum is high, requires increasing the already strong force that generated the initial momentum.

Although your sword's movements should always involve every part of your body, consider for a moment the control offered your sword by only your hands and arms. When your sword is swung, the control for directional changes comes from your shoulders, elbows, and wrists. The biggest changes are those that use your shoulder, and the most refined are those that use your wrists. In all cases, relaxation is important so that your arms remain flexible. Do not grip your sword with any more force than is necessary to maintain good control, and remember that increases in changeability usually involve decreases in power.

Balancing Power and Changeability

Because power and changeability are desirable qualities but cannot be maximized simultaneously, learning how to achieve the ideal balance between them is a very important part of martial arts practice. Each skill must be thoroughly understood so that you can determine the points at which power can effectively be increased and the points at which changes can be made most easily. Pay close attention to these points as you practice.

Even with a detailed understanding of the power and changeability requirements for each sword skill, it is usually possible to maximize only one of these characteristics at a time. Combining the two is always very difficult.

Comparison of One-Handed and Two-Handed Sword Grips

Most single-sword skills are executed with just one hand. Changeability is higher when you use only one hand to hold your sword, and, as a result, the most subtle sword skills are one-handed skills. There are circumstances, however, when additional power is needed, and this is most commonly accomplished by using a two-handed grip.

In many groups, when practitioners use two-handed grips, they must place both hands close together on the handle of the sword because the handle length of most regular single swords is eight inches or less. Although power is increased when two hands are used, much flexibility is lost if the two hands must be placed close together. In Taiji Dao, there are special two-handed grips that can add power without unnecessarily sacrificing maneuverability.

A Taiji *dao* is usually held in a one-handed *zhengwo,* or standard grip, in which the blade points forward (fig. 6-1). In the first of the two most commonly used two-handed grips, your second hand should be placed on the handle of your sword very close to the ring (fig. 6-2), whereas, in the second grip, that hand should be placed on the ring itself (fig. 6-3). The hand closer to the guard of the sword is usually called *qianshou* (前手), or front hand. In figures 6-2 and

6-3, the right hand is qianshou. The hand farther away from the sword guard or closer to the ring of the sword, which in figures 6-2 and 6-3 is the left hand on the lower part of the handle or on the ring, is called *houshou* (后手), or rear

Fig. 6-1

Fig. 6-2

Fig. 6-3

hand. In either case, your second hand should grip your sword loosely to ensure that your grip is flexible enough to balance power with maneuverability.

In the frequently used two-handed Taiji *dao* grips, your hands supplement each other: one hand usually controls your sword while the other adds power. For most small-movement skills, your right or front hand will be used to control all changes in timing, direction, and skill choice, and your left or rear hand will be used to increase power. For most large-movement skills, the relationship is reversed so that your left or rear hand controls changes while your front or right hand adds power. Either way, the controlling hand must remain relaxed so that quick changes can be made whenever needed, and the power hand must stay relaxed to enable precise adjustments when additional strength is required. Compared to one-handed grips, two-handed grips allow for great flexibility because your hands can exchange roles at any time. Maneuverability and power adjustments can be achieved by either hand, even within the same skill.

To summarize, the advantages of one-handed sword grips are quickness, agility, and changeability. One-handed grips also allow your reach to be longer because you can turn your body more than is possible with two-handed grips. Finally, one-handed grips incorporate Taiji principles more fully than two-handed grips do. The disadvantage of one-handed grips is that they do not always provide all the power needed for the successful execution of a skill.

With two-handed grips, more power is generated, but there is a corresponding loss of quickness, agility, and changeability. The two kinds of grip can be combined for optimal results if you hold your sword with one hand when executing a main skill and add your second hand when extra power is needed. You have very flexible options about which grip to use, and your choice always depends on the circumstances you face at a given moment.

Description and Illustrations of the Two-Handed Sword Form

In the traditional Taiji Dao thirteen-posture form, most skills are one-handed skills, and many of the two-handed applications are "hidden," which means that you should keep them in mind when you are doing the form but should not show them outwardly in your movements. This kind of mental practice will make it possible for two-handed applications to emerge naturally if you engage in a real fight. To practice two-handed skills directly, the short combination form called *Tai Ji Shuang Shou Dao Lian Huan Dao Fa* (太极双手刀连环刀法)—Taiji Two-Handed Sword Linking Skills—will help you focus on the basics of these skills.

This short combination form contains ten postures: the beginning and ending postures and eight combination skills called "methods." The form is sometimes referred to as *Shuang Shou Dao Ba Fa* (双手刀八法)—the Eight Methods of Two-Handed Sword Skills. The posture name list is presented here.

1. *Qi Shi* (起势)—The Beginning Form
2. *Feng Lun Fei Xun* (风轮飞旋)—Wind Wheel Spinning at High Speed
3. *Feng Huang Xun Wo* (凤凰旋窝)—Phoenix Circling Its Nest
4. *Zhui Feng Gan Yue* (追风赶月)
    —Chasing the Wind, Catching the Moon
5. *Shi Zi Rou Qiu* (狮子揉球)—Lion Playing with a Ball
6. *Qing Long Jiao Wei* (青龙搅尾)—Black Dragon Stirring with Its Tail
7. *Fan Jiang Jiao Hai* (翻江搅海)
    —Churning Up the River and Stirring the Sea
8. *Li Pi Hua Shan* (力劈华山)—Chopping Hua Mountain

9. *Chan Jiao Zhi Ci* (缠搅直刺)
   —Winding, Agitating, and Straight-Thrusting Skills
10. *Shou Shi* (收势)—The Ending Form

To practice this combination form, begin your training by thoroughly practicing each posture separately and repeatedly until you get the right feeling. Then, practice the entire form from beginning to end. Pay attention to the timing, direction, angle, force, application, and internal feeling for each movement.

When you practice this form by yourself, imagine that an opponent is attacking you with a spear. It is said that, "when practicing alone with no one in front of you, you must feel as though someone is there. When fighting with an opponent in front of you, you must feel as though you are alone."

When you practice applications, your shen should be very concentrated so that you can anticipate and clearly see every movement your opponent makes. Your mind should be quiet, clear, and focused so that you can accurately assess exactly what your best options are. Your qi must be stable and flow smoothly throughout not only your body but also your sword. It is said that your qi should fill your sword and lead your jin to reach every part of your sword. Your physical movements should follow all these internal feelings to move quickly, nimbly, stably, accurately, and harmoniously. From internal components to external movements, your whole body should be coordinated and fully integrated with the parts and movements of your sword. All these elements must function together as a single unit.

In this short combination form, your left hand must be very flexible so that it can be used in different ways. Specifically, the form can be practiced either with *heba*—both hands gripping the handle of your sword—or with one hand gripping the handle of your sword and the other hand gripping the ring. These grips can be exchanged during your form practice.

1. *Qi Shi* (起势)—The Beginning Form

Posture Name Explanation

The beginning posture includes several movements designed to prepare you for fighting. As stated in the oldest known treatise on swordsmanship, your mind should remain calm and focused, and your body should be relaxed and alert. While outwardly you should be soft, serene, and composed like a fair maiden, your internal state should be like that of a fierce tiger fully imbued with energy and spirit. When motionless, you should be stable, and when moving, your movements should be quick, continuous, and integrated.

1.1. *Ti Dao Yu Bei Shi* (提刀预备势)—Carry Sword in Preparatory Posture

Movements: Stand straight and look forward. Drop your hands down naturally and hold your sword in your right hand in *zhengwo*—standard grip. Stay focused and alert, quiet your mind, breathe smoothly, and let your body relax deeply. Feel ready to fight (fig. 6-1-1).

Fig. 6-1-1

Key Points: The beginning posture in this form is different from the thirteen-posture form in that it is designed specifically to prepare you for fighting. It is important that you look straight ahead to concentrate your shen and sink your qi down to create a feeling of great stability. You should be alert and ready to move immediately in any direction.

1.2. *Che Zuo Bu Fu Hu Shi* (撤左步伏虎势) —Step Back with Left Foot in Subduing Tiger Posture

Movements: Move your right hand forward until your sword is at chest level. Put your left hand on the handle of your sword and grip it lightly. Step back with your left foot and shift most of your weight onto it. Drag your right foot back slightly and let only the toes of your right foot touch the ground. You will be in a right insubstantial stance. At the same time, turn your body slightly to the left and pull both hands back so that the handle of your sword is in front of your abdomen. The tip of your sword should be at shoulder level with the edge facing down (fig. 6-1-2).

Fig. 6-1-2

Key Points: As you pull your sword back, your right hand should push slightly forward so that the main pullback force comes from your left hand. Simultaneously, sink your body slightly to gain a feeling of stability.

You should feel that your sword is strong and powerful and that you can defend against any force from any direction. Because the internal trained force is related to qi, it is called "to fill your sword with your qi." Imagine an opponent coming toward you. Look forward and concentrate.

1.3. *Che You Bu Cang Dao Shi* (撤右步藏刀势)
—Step Back with Right Foot in Hiding Sword Posture

Movements: Step back with your right foot and shift most of your weight onto it. Drag your left foot back slightly and let only the toes of your left foot touch the ground. This forms a left insubstantial stance. At the same time, turn your body to the right and move both hands so that the handle of your sword is in front of your right ribs. The blade of your sword should be vertical with the tip pointing up and the edge facing to the right. Keep looking forward (fig. 6-1-3).

Fig. 6-1-3

Key Points: When you move your sword back, your arms should form a circle, and you should feel as though the circle is expanding. Feel qi flowing strongly through your sword, making it powerful. Simultaneously, sink your body slightly to increase a feeling of stability. Imagine an opponent coming toward you but not yet mounting a real attack, and feel ready to move back at any moment to maintain a safe distance from him or her. Although the physical movement in this posture is not quick, you must remain fully concentrated.

Application: The most popular and powerful infantry weapon is a spear, and it is both faster and more maneuverable than a sword, so defending against it is very difficult. If you swing your sword at every sign of attack, you may not be able to defend yourself when a real attack comes. If your opponent comes toward you, step just far enough back to keep a safe distance. Maintain your concentration and observe his or her movements carefully and patiently while you wait for an opportunity to attack. As you step back, keep your sword in front of your body for protection (fig. 6-1-4). Alternatively, move your sword to the side of your body. This will create the impression that your body is open and vulnerable and will encourage your opponent to attack. Although dangerous, this tactic is your most realistic and practical option when you are fighting an opponent armed with a longer, superior weapon (fig. 6-1-5).

Fig. 6-1-4   Fig. 6-1-5

2. *Feng Lun Fei Xun* (风轮飞旋)
—Wind Wheel Spinning at High Speed

Posture Name Explanation

In ancient mythology, the wind wheel, also called the wind-and-fire wheel, was a magic weapon. When thrown, it was said to fly at a high speed, creating wind and fire as it spun through the air destroying everything that collided with it.

In this posture, your sword is moved in vertical circles quickly and powerfully like a wind wheel. The movement is a *yang*—hard attribute—skill, and if you are close to your opponent you can use it for attack or defense as you move straight ahead or as you retreat. It can be used whether your opponent's attack is real or fake.

2.1. *Che Zuo Bu Ce Shen Fan Liao* (撤左步侧身反撩)
—Step Back with Left Foot and Turn Body Sideways to Make Upward Cut

Movements: Step back with your left foot and shift your weight onto it. As you step, use the force in your legs to make your body turn to the left and use the turn to cause your arms and hands to drop back, down, and finally forward. Your sword should move in a clockwise vertical circle on the right side of your body (fig. 6-2-1).

Continue without interruption to swing your sword up until it is at head level. The tip of your sword should point forward and the edge should face up as you deliver this upward cut skill (fig. 6-2-2).

Fig. 6-2-1   Fig. 6-2-2

Key Points: Look straight ahead. Feel as though your sword is chasing your gaze. As you execute the upward cut, the force from your legs should reach to the tip of your sword, and the movements of your sword and your body should be integrated so that they form one continuous motion. Although your body turns to the left, you should keep facing forward and direct your shen straight ahead.

When you swing your sword up, focus your mind on your mingmen point. Control the movement of your sword with your right hand and add extra force by using your left hand to pull on the sword's handle. Imagine that you are swinging a big, long-handled sword. You should feel that your sword is so powerful when it is swung that nothing can block it.

2.2. *Che You Bu Ce Shen Fan Liao* (撤右步側身反撩)
—Step Back with Right Foot and Turn Body Sideways to Make Upward Cut

Movements: Move your sword up without interruption until it is in front of your left shoulder with the tip pointing up and the edge facing back. Sink your body slightly to make yourself more stable (fig. 6-2-3). Continue to move your sword back in a vertical circle and simultaneously step back with your right foot (fig. 6-2-4). Turn to the right as you continue the circle and let the turn of your body bring your sword forward (fig. 6-2-5). Continue moving your sword in the vertical circle until it is at head level, with the tip pointing forward and the edge facing up (fig. 6-2-6).

Fig. 6-2-3

Fig. 6-3-4

Fig. 6-2-5

Fig. 6-2-6

Key Points: Keep looking forward and imagine that your sword is chasing your gaze. Turn to the right as you swing your sword. Focus your mind on your mingmen point and feel as though only your waist is turning. Keep your hips stable and remain facing forward. Concentrate your shen straight ahead.

As you swing your sword through its circular path, use your right hand to provide most of the control of your weapon. Your left hand should provide additional force by pulling on the sword's handle. Imagine that you are swinging a big sword with a long handle to perform this upward cut skill.

This movement should be connected very smoothly with the previous movement, as though one big wheel were rolling endlessly. There should be a strong feeling of qi in your body and sword.

2.3. Che Zuo Bu Ce Shen Xie Kan (撤左步侧身斜砍)
—Step Back with Left Foot and Turn Body Sideways to Make Diagonal Chop

Movements: Step back with your right foot. At the same time, push your right hand slightly outward and turn your wrists to raise your sword until your right hand is at shoulder level (fig. 6-2-7) and your sword is in front of your body with the tip pointing forward and up and the edge facing forward. Shift your weight slightly back (fig. 6-2-8). Chop down and slightly to the left and at the same time, let your body sink down (fig. 6-2-9).

Fig. 6-2-7

Fig. 6-2-8

Fig. 6-2-9

Key Points: In this movement, the turning of your wrists and the chop should be small and quickly and smoothly done. Continue to use your right hand to provide most of the sword control and the pull of your left hand to add extra force to the swing of your sword. As you chop, feel your qi sink down. Make sure that your whole body is integrated. Look forward and concentrate your shen straight ahead.

Application: At the beginning of a fight, your opponent will often try to confuse you by making many fake or shallow attacks. If you lose concentration, he or she will mount a real and deep attack. In this case, step back to maintain a safe distance and swing your sword in circles to cut your opponent's spear. It is not critical that your timing be exactly right, but you must pay careful attention to the angle of your swing.

In this combination skill, there are left and right upward cuts and one chop to your opponent's spear. Make sure that the edge of your sword crosses your opponent's spear, and shift your body slightly to the left or right to make the appropriate adjustment.

If your opponent thrusts his or her spear at your chest or head, step back with your left foot, turn your body to the left, and make a left upward cut. Pull your sword slightly to the left to ensure that it crosses his or her spear. Also, when you step back with your right foot, push your sword slightly forward to increase the chance that your sword will cut your opponent's spear from underneath (fig. 6-2-10). You can follow up with an immediate right upward cut (fig. 6-2-11).

This combination can be repeated as many times as required to cut your opponent's spear, and any upward cut can be immediately followed by a downward chop. If your upward cut misses, turn your hand back when your sword is at head level and chop directly and obliquely down on your opponent's spear (fig. 6-2-12). If your sword is good enough and your force sufficiently strong, you will achieve the ultimate goal of breaking your opponent's spear. If you are able to cut only halfway into the spear or if your sword gets stuck in the spear, stay close to your opponent and follow his or her movements.

Fig. 6-2-10

Fig. 6-2-11

Fig. 6-2-12

3. *Feng Huang Xun Wo* (凤凰旋窝)—Phoenix Circling Its Nest

Posture Name Explanation

"Phoenix circling its nest" means to swing your sword in horizontal circles with the grace and smoothness of a phoenix soaring above its nest with its wings spread. Your sword should swing smoothly, lightly, and accurately to the left and right like the wings of a phoenix. The qualities of this posture are the opposite of those in the previous skill. Here, the skill is a soft attribute or *yin* skill. Although not hard or powerful, it must be done with great agility and mastery. All the elements of distance, timing, angle, and force must be correct and executed with refined control.

3.1. *Shang Zuo Bu Zuo Shang Ge Jia* (上左步左上格架)
—Step Forward with Left Foot and Block Up to the Left

Movements: Step forward with your left foot and turn your body slightly to the left. At the same time, turn your right hand inward and raise it to head level. The edge of your sword should face up. Your left hand should follow, and then pull your sword to the left (fig. 6-3-1).

Fig. 6-3-1

Key Points: When you step forward, feel as though your body were sinking as you dodge slightly to the left. Focus your mind on your mingmen point to push your body forward along a zigzag path. Look forward and slightly to the right from underneath your sword. The force from your right hand should push your sword up, while the force from your left hand should pull your sword to the left.

3.2. *You Ning Shen Zuo Qian Xuan Dao* (右拧身左前旋刀) —Turn Right with Left Forward Spinning Slice

Movements: Continuing without interruption, turn your hands in a circle from left to right so that your sword moves in a counterclockwise horizontal circle in front of your body in a left spinning slice at shoulder level. The edge of your sword should face outward (fig. 6-3-2).

Fig. 6-3-2

Key Points: Look straight ahead. Turn your hands so that your sword smoothly moves through a small circle. When you make the left spinning slice, put your mind on your mingmen point to think of turning your waist to the right. At the same time, pull your left hand slightly to the left and push your right hand to the right.

3.3. *Shang You Bu Gua Lan Fan Ya* (上右步挂拦翻压) —Step Forward with Right Foot to Parry and Press Down

Movements: Shift your weight forward onto your left leg and turn your body slightly to the right. At the same time, turn your right hand outward and raise it to head level. The edge of your sword should face up. Your left hand should follow, and then pull your sword to the right (fig. 6-3-3).

Continue without interruption by stepping forward with your right foot and turning your body slightly to the left. At the same time, turn your right hand so that your right palm faces up. Your sword should be on the left side of your body with the tip pointing to the right and the edge facing forward. The blade should be parallel to the ground. Let your body sink slightly with most of your weight on your left leg. Use your left hand to press down lightly on your sword (fig. 6-3-4).

Fig. 6-3-3

Fig. 6-3-4

Key Points: Look forward and slightly to the left. The raising of your sword and the turn of your right hand should be smoothly done. When your sword is parallel to the ground, push your right hand forward and press your left hand down on your sword. Feel as though the whole weight of your body were on your sword, causing it to become heavy and move downward. Relax your waist and hips to make your footwork very nimble. You should feel as though the more nimble your step, the heavier your sword becomes.

3.4. *Zuo Ning Shen You Qian Pian Xiao* (左拧身右前片削) —Turn Left and Make Right Forward Scooping Chop

Movements: Continue without interruption to sink down and press on your sword. When you feel your left leg push upward against the weight of your body, follow this feeling by taking a half-step forward with your right foot and moving your sword forward in a circling path to make a right scooping chop (fig. 6-3-5).

Fig. 6-3-5

Key Points: Keep looking forward. Relax your waist and feel your body sink down and compress your left leg. Then, feel a bounce in your left leg causing your body to spring immediately up. Follow this feeling by suddenly chopping up and forward with your sword. Put your mind on your mingmen point to control your force. Use your right hand to offer more chopping force and use your left hand to control the direction and angle of your chop. Slightly stretch your arms out to feel as though your qi can be moved to the front edge of your sword.

Application: With this skill, your sword moves in horizontal circles to cut forward from the left and right. The movement of the left scooping slice is smaller but faster than the movement of the right scooping chop. Each forward cut should be preceded by either an upward block or a side parry, but neither of these movements should be hard. The purpose of the block or parry is to make contact with your opponent's spear, and the key point when executing the subsequent chop or scooping slice is to control the spear by keeping your sword sticking on it. You must maintain this contact until your opponent loses balance. When he or she does, you can break the contact between your sword and his or her spear and deliver your forward cut.

If your opponent thrusts at your chest or face with his or her spear, turn your hands up and move your sword up to make an upward block. Your block should be quick but not hard. Move your body slightly forward to ensure that you can maintain contact with your opponent's spear when he or she pulls it back (fig. 6-3-6).

Fig. 6-3-6

As soon as your sword touches your opponent's spear, make a small circle to push the spear to the left side of your sword (fig. 6-3-7). Drop your sword and sink your body slightly. Press your sword on your opponent's spear so that the spear is underneath your sword. Maintain contact with and control of the spear and turn your body to the right to deliver a scooping slice to the right side of your opponent's neck (fig. 6-3-8).

Fig. 6-3-7

Fig. 6-3-8

If your opponent thrusts at your chest or face with his or her spear, move your sword up in a quick, soft, upward parry to the right (fig. 6-3-9). Move your body slightly forward to make sure your sword maintains contact with the spear before your opponent pulls it back it. Drop your sword on the right side of your body and step forward. Press your sword down and sink your body as though to bear down with your entire weight on your sword and on your opponent's spear (fig. 6-3-10). If the timing, distance, and direction of your movement are correct, your opponent will become unbalanced and will lean forward. At this moment, quickly lift your sword up and away from the spear in a right scooping chop to the left side of his or her neck (fig. 6-3-11). Because he or she is off balance, your opponent will find it difficult to follow the upward springing movement of your sword.

Fig. 6-3-9

Fig. 6-3-10

Fig. 6-3-11

4. *Zhui Feng Gan Yue* (追风赶月) —Chasing the Wind, Catching the Moon

Posture Name Explanation

The wind is invisible to us; the moon is visible but lies outside our grasp. To chase the wind and catch the moon means to pursue a goal passionately, believing it can be achieved despite all evidence to the contrary. The feeling in this posture is a yearning to do a task well, even if it is thought to be impossible.

With this skill, your sword is used to chase your opponent, not just his or her spear and body, but also his or her internal components of jin, qi, yi, and shen. You must fervently believe that you can catch your opponent and dominate him or her and, at the same time, remain calm, focused, and relaxed. The basic Taiji Quan skills of zhan, nian, lian, and sui are applied in this forward-chasing skill.

4.1. *Tui Zuo Bu Ti Xi Xia Lan* (退左步提膝下拦) —Step Back with Left Foot and Raise Knee to Make Downward Parry

Movements: Shift your weight back onto your left leg and turn your body slightly to the left. At the same time, follow the motion of your right scooping chop by moving your sword back and to the left (fig. 6-4-1). Withdraw your abdomen slightly and continue to shift your weight. Raise your right knee and point it to the left. At the same time, move your sword down and then to the right in a curving path to create a low right parry. The tip of your sword should point down and the edge should face to the right. (fig. 6-4-2).

Fig. 6-4-1   Fig. 6-4-2

Key Points: Look forward and slightly down. As you withdraw your abdomen and raise your right knee, you should feel as though your body is moving quickly and lightly. It should seem ready to jump up in a lively way. Put your mind on your baihui point to keep your body stable. Feel the turn of your body originating in your supple and relaxed waist. Your right hand should turn smoothly while your left hand follows.

4.2. *Shang You Bu Gun Dao Qian Tui* (上右步滚刀前推) —Step Forward with Right Foot and Roll Sword to Push Forward

Movements: Turn your hands over to roll your sword so that the tip points to the right and the edge faces forward. At the same time, as you put your right foot down on the ground, immediately take a long step forward to form a right bow stance and push your sword forward and down (fig. 6-4-3). The handle of your sword should be at stomach level. Turn your hands so that your right palm faces up and your left palm faces down (fig. 6-4-4).

Fig. 6-4-3   Fig. 6-4-4

Key Points: Look forward and down. As you push your sword, feel your qi sinking down. Most of the force for the forward push should come from your right hand, while most of the force for the downward push should come from your left hand. Put your mind on your yongquan point. Feel the force for your forward push come from your left foot and the force for your downward push come from the weight of your body. Your right knee should feel springy.

4.3. *Shang Zuo Bu Zhan Gan Heng Tui* (上左步粘杆横推)
—Step Forward with Left Foot, Stick Sword on Shaft of Spear, and Push

Movements: Step forward with your left foot to form a left bow stance. At the same time, raise your sword slightly up and immediately push it forward with both hands (fig. 6-4-5).

Fig. 6-4-5

Key Points: Look forward and down. Use your right hand mainly to push your sword forward and your left hand mainly to push it down. Do not directly raise your sword but relax your arms so that your sword will naturally rise. Put your mind on your jiaji point to feel as though your back is rounded. Feel that you can continuously step quickly forward to chase, contact, and control your opponent's spear.

4.4. *Shang You Bu Zhan Gan Shang Tui* (上右步粘杆上推)—Step Forward with Right Foot, Stick Sword on Shaft of Spear, and Push Upward

Movements: Step forward with your right foot to form a right bow stance. At the same time, raise your sword to chest level and push it forward and up. Your right hand, with the right palm facing up, should provide more of the force for the upward push, and your left hand, with the left palm facing down, should offer more of the force for the forward push (fig. 6-4-6).

Fig. 6-4-6

Key Points: Look forward and slightly up. While your right hand provides most of the force for your forward push, you should feel as though your body were dropping or sinking down. This feeling will create in your opponent a sense that your sword is very heavy.

Relax your waist and let your left hand follow this feeling with a small push upward. When your hands are slightly raised, keep your arms relaxed and feel your elbows drop down. Put your mind on your tanzhong point to create a hollow feeling in your chest and make your arm circle expand slightly.

Application: This skill consists of four techniques: one low parry and three forward pushes. All four should be done smoothly and continuously while you maintain contact with your opponent's spear and chase it without interruption. Your hands and arms should remain relaxed so that you can easily follow any change your opponent makes and prevent him or her from pulling back and moving away from you. Sink your body to improve your stability and step quickly and nimbly not only so that you can chase your opponent's spear but also so that your pushes will be more powerful.

If your right leg is forward and your opponent thrusts his or her spear at it, move back and raise your right knee to dodge the attack. At the same time, move your sword down in a curving path from left to right in a low right parry (fig. 6-4-7). As soon as your sword touches your opponent's spear, roll your sword until the edge faces forward. At the same time, step forward with your right foot and let your sword cross underneath your opponent's spear. Ignore the force of the spear pressing down on your sword and use the edge of your sword to chase first his or her front hand and then front leg (fig. 6-4-8). Step quickly and unhesitatingly toward your opponent (fig. 6-4-9) and keep your sword in contact with his or her spear.

Fig. 6-4-7

Fig. 6-4-8

Fig. 6-4-9

Because the spear is a long weapon and the sword is a short one, you must get as close as possible to your opponent in order to mount an effective attack (fig. 6-4-10). As you approach, however, your opponent is likely to step back or sideways to maintain a safe distance. The sensitivity developed through Taiji push-hands training can help you maintain your pursuit of your opponent, regard-less of how far back he or she moves and how many directional changes he or she makes. You can alternate hands to change the angle of your force as you continue to push on your opponent's spear. If your opponent pushes down with his or her spear, move forward to chase his or her rear hand; if your opponent pushes the end of the spear forward to block you, push upward to chase his or her front hand. Keep pressuring your opponent so that he or she does not have an opportunity to repeat the attack.

Fig. 6-4-10

5. *Shi Zi Rou Qiu* (狮子揉球)—**Lion Playing with a Ball**

Posture Name Explanation

A lion is big and powerful; a ball, small, light, and easily manipulated. The name of this posture advises that, like a lion, you should think of yourself as much bigger than your opponent and able to control him or her totally, not by fighting but rather by toying with him or her as though he or she were a ball. You should use a very soft, smooth force, reserving your great strength only if a situation arises that requires it. Stay relaxed and apply the basic Taiji Quan skills of zhan, nian, lian, and sui in this side-to-side power skill.

5.1. *Shang Zuo Bu Fan Dao Ce Ya* (上左步翻刀侧压) —Step Forward with Left Foot and Turn Sword to Press Down

Movements: Step forward with your left foot and turn your hands to move your sword up in a counterclockwise circle in front of your body. The tip of your sword should point up, and the edge should face forward (fig. 6-5-1). Move your body back slightly and drag your left foot slightly back. At the same time, bring your hands close to your stomach. Continue to move your sword by pushing it to the left (fig. 6-5-2).

Key Points: Look forward. Focus your mind on your mingmen point to feel

Fig. 6-5-1   Fig. 6-5-2

your body turning and rolling smoothly and softly. Turn your sword over so that it follows the turn and roll of your body movement. Feel your upper body and your sword rolling from right to left like a single, smooth, soft, and heavy ball.

5.2. *You Ce Shen Tui Dao Ping Mo* (右侧身推刀平抹)
—Turn Right and Push Sword to Make a Horizontal Wipe

Movements: Immediately after dragging your left foot back in the previous movement, step forward again with your left foot to form a left bow stance. Continue to move your sword down to the left until the tip points to the left and the edge faces forward. Let the back of your sword rest against your left arm. Turn your body to the right and, following this turn, use your left arm to push your sword forward to make a cut (fig. 6-5-3). As soon as the tip of your sword points forward, lean your body forward to increase the power in your left arm for the push forward. Simultaneously, pull your hands back and shift your weight slightly back so that your sword moves back and then sideways in a horizontal wipe (fig. 6-5-4).

Fig. 6-5-3

Fig. 6-5-4

Key Points: Keep looking forward when your body turns to the right. Keep your mind on your mingmen point to maintain the feeling in your upper body and your sword of a ball that is rolling and turning slightly forward in a horizontal clockwise circle. Push your left arm down on the back of your sword and apply continuous pressure. Use your right hand to augment the downward force and use your left hand to pull your sword slightly back.

5.3. *Qian Yi Shen Ce Shen Ping Zha* (前倚身侧身平扎)
—Lean Forward and Turn to Side to Thrust

Movements: Shift your weight forward to form a left bow stance. At the same time, push your hands forward to thrust your sword forward with the tip pointing forward and the edge facing to the right (fig. 6-5-5).

Fig. 6-5-5

Key Points: Keep applying pressure on the back of your sword with your left arm and imagine that your sword is affixed to your body. Push your right foot forward to feel as though your body is fully integrated and the power from your right foot is flowing directly to the tip of your sword. Look straight ahead and let the tip of your sword chase your gaze as it is thrust forward. Use your right hand to keep your sword stable and your left hand to control the direction of your thrust.

Application: The basic Taiji Quan skills of zhan, nian, lian, and sui are applied in this posture. Keep your sword sticking your opponent's spear so that you can follow his or her movements and make changes softly and smoothly. The most common change used in this skill is called a wipe cut and involves circling your sword around your opponent's spear.

In a wipe cut skill, you must maintain pressure on your sword as it makes contact with your opponent's weapon and is pulled against the weapon to cut it. This skill is typically used when you are very close to your opponent and do not have enough space to swing your sword. Instead, you should push on the back of your sword with your left arm to increase the pressure on your opponent's spear.

Coordination and integration are very important in this skill, the second part of which involves a straight thrust with the blade of your sword held parallel to the ground. You should be close to your opponent when you thrust forward.

If your opponent tries to push his or her spear down while your sword is sticking it and positioned across and below it, do not push directly against the downward force. Instead, relax your hands and drop your elbows so that your sword rolls to the right side of the spear softly and smoothly (fig. 6-5-6) and then continues rolling until it is on top of the spear (fig. 6-5-7).

Fig. 6-5-6

Fig. 6-5-7

Turn your body to the right and move your sword forward to cut your opponent's front hand, left arm, chest, or neck (fig. 6-5-8). As soon as your sword makes contact with your opponent's body, push your sword with your left arm to maintain pressure on his or her spear and pull your sword back to make a wipe cut (fig. 6-5-9). Then, immediately lean forward and thrust toward your opponent, as you drive forward with your right leg to increase the power of your thrust. Follow this force by turning your body slightly to the left and pushing with both hands (fig. 6-5-10).

Fig. 6-5-8

Fig. 6-5-9

Fig. 6-5-10

If your movements are correct, the full force of your body will be focused on the tip of your sword, making your thrust very powerful. It is usually to your advantage to keep your sword in contact with your opponent's spear when you make this thrust because such contact allows you to maintain control during the entire sequence of movements.

6. *Qing Long Jiao Wei* (青龙搅尾)
—Black Dragon Stirring with Its Tail

Posture Name Explanation

Black dragons are considered to be especially fierce and powerful, capable of creating enormous waves whenever they stir up the sea with their tails. When executing this skill, imagine that you are a black dragon and that your sword is your tail. Use the force of your whole body to move your sword in a circling chop that moves up and forward as though it were the waving tail of a dragon.

This is a very powerful skill in which the chop is followed by a quick, powerful, straight-ahead thrust. The chop and thrust should be linked smoothly together. Stay relaxed and apply the basic Taiji Quan skills of zhan, nian, lian, and sui in this *gong zhong rou*—soft-within-hard skill.

6.1. *Zuo Ce Shen Xi Shen Xuan Dao* (左侧身吸身旋刀)
—Turn to the Left and Withdraw Body for Whirling Chop

Movements: Move both hands down in front of your stomach and let the tip of your sword point up and the edge face forward. At the same time, turn your body to the left until you are facing forward. Sink your body slightly down (fig. 6-6-1).

Follow the sinking feeling by shifting your weight back onto your right leg. Drag your left foot back slightly and raise your left heel to form a left insubstantial stance. At the same time, continue to turn your body to the left and turn your right wrist so that your sword moves in a clockwise circle in front of your face until the tip points forward at face level and the edge faces to the left (fig. 6-6-2).

Fig. 6-6-1

Fig. 6-6-2

Key Points: The act of withdrawing your body is commonly referred to as *xishen*. *Xi* means to suck, inhale, or draw into, and this *shen* means body. The goal of xishen is not to move your whole body back but rather to feel as though you are withdrawing your upper body, especially your chest or stomach area. When you experience the feeling of withdrawal in your upper body, let your body sink slightly and, at the same time, imagine that your arms are expanding so that your sword is pushed slightly forward. Look forward. Focus your mind on your tanzhong point. While your right hand controls the turn of your sword, your left hand should pull lightly on your sword to provide extra force.

6.2. *Che Zuo Bu Ce Shen Hui Gou* (撤左步侧身回勾) —Step Back with Left Foot and Turn to the Right for Back Hook Parry

Movements: Turn your right hand outward to the right and push your left hand up. This will cause the tip of your sword to turn down and the edge to face forward (fig. 6-6-3). Continue to move your sword backward and turn your body to the right. Your sword should be on the right side of your body with the handle at chest level and the tip pointing to the ground. Let your right leg bear all your weight and sink your body down slightly to make your right leg very stable. At the same time, step back with your left foot to form a right bow stance (fig. 6-6-4).

Fig. 6-6-3   Fig. 6-6-4

Key Points: Look down and then backward. When you step back and parry back with your sword, feel your baihui point pushing forward to lead your body as it moves forward. Use your right hand to offer more force to the wave of your sword and your left hand to control its direction.

6.3. *Che You Bu Ning Shen Jiao Pi* (撤右步拧身搅劈)—Step Back with Right Foot and Turn to the Left to Swing Sword Up and Chop

Movements: Push off with your right foot to take a quick step back and form a left bow stance. Be careful not to shift your weight back before stepping. At the same time, look forward and swing your sword from behind. The technical term for the swing of your sword is "stir up," so it is here that the movement of your sword is likened to the action of a black dragon's tail. As your sword swings, it should circle up and then forward in preparation for a powerful forward chop (fig. 6-6-5).

Fig. 6-6-5

Key Points: Make sure that the force of your step back and the force of your forward chop are integrated so that they merge into one fluid movement. Feel that these movements start from the turn of your mingmen point. Turn your head to look straight ahead and use your shen (internal component) to lead your forward chop. Imagine that your sword quickly chases your gaze.

As you chop, use both hands to offer a powerful forward force to the wave of your sword, as though you were throwing something far forward. At the end of the chop, use your right hand to push your sword chop forward continuously and use your left hand to pull your sword slightly back and, at the same time, sink your body slightly down.

6.4. *Zuo Xu Bu Xi Shen Ya Dao* (左虚步吸身压刀)—Assume Left Insubstantial Stance, Withdraw Abdomen, and Press Sword Down

Movements: Shift your weight back onto your right leg and drag your left foot back slightly, letting only the toes of your left foot touch the ground to form a left insubstantial stance. At the same time, withdraw your abdomen, pull both hands back, and raise your left knee. The tip of your sword should point forward, and the edge should face down (fig. 6-6-6).

Fig. 6-6-6

Key Points: Look forward and down. Put your mind on your shenque point. The withdrawal of your abdomen and the pull of your sword backward must be integrated. Both elbows should tightly touch your ribs to prevent your pushing directly down on your sword. You should feel, instead, that the weight and stability of your sword have created the downward power.

6.5. *Jin Zuo Bu Qian Zhi Tu Ci* (进左步前直突刺)—Step Forward with Left Foot and Thrust Straight Ahead Quickly and Powerfully

Movements: Take a large, quick step forward with your left foot to form a left bow stance. At the same time, push your sword forward with both hands in a powerful straight-ahead thrust (fig. 6-6-7).

Fig. 6-6-7

Key Points: Look straight ahead and use your shen to lead your thrust. Feel as though the thrust is quick and powerful and can extend very far. The power of the thrust should start from your right foot, go through your right leg, waist, back, shoulders, arms, and hands, and then reach to the tip of your sword. All parts of your body should be coordinated and integrated to function as one unit so that you feel power flowing directly from your right foot to the tip of your sword. At the same time, let your body sink down on your left leg to make you more stable.

Application: This skill includes two power moves, a chop and a thrust, both of which require the use of full-body force made possible only when all your movements and the internal components of jin, qi, yi, and shen are integrated. When you swing, or stir up, your sword, your movements should be quick and powerful as though you want to churn up your opponent's spear and hurl it away. Although the forces generated by your body's movement backward and your sword's chop forward are in opposite directions, the two movements supplement and balance each other.

As you thrust your sword forward quickly and powerfully, you should lunge toward your opponent with a long, strong stride that draws on force starting in your right foot and flowing through your right leg, waist, back, arms, hands, and finally to the tip of your sword. This sequence should be expressed as one smooth movement. Your left hand should push forward to provide the force for your thrust, and your right hand should push forward and slightly down.

If your opponent attacks your head with a spear, drop your body slightly and use your sword to parry the spear to the left (fig. 6-6-8). If your opponent pulls the spear back and attacks your leg again, drop your sword down to parry the spear to the right (fig. 6-6-9). If your right low parry is well executed, you can stick your sword to the spear and then step forward or back to maintain contact between the weapons (fig. 6-6-10).

Fig. 6-6-8

Fig. 6-6-9

Fig. 6-6-10

At the same time, try to move closer to your opponent and quickly swing your sword toward him or her so that his or her spear is hurled upward (fig. 6-6-11). Continue to move your sword forward smoothly in a powerful chop to your opponent's head. You should feel as though you are throwing your opponent and his or her spear far away (fig. 6-6-12).

Fig. 6-6-11

Fig. 6-6-12

The whole process of stirring up and chopping forward must be done in one quick and powerful movement that moves and unbalances your opponent. If he or she is able to move back quickly enough to escape your chop, you should lunge toward your opponent and thrust your sword directly at his or her chest. If your opponent thrusts at your chest, use your sword to parry the spear slightly to the left (fig. 6-6-13), and then immediately thrust forward (fig. 6-6-14).

Fig. 6-6-13

Fig. 6-6-14

7. *Fan Jiang Jiao Hai* (翻江搅海)
—Churning Up the River and Stirring the Sea

Posture Name Explanation

The name of this skill is meant to suggest forceful motion. Imagine that you are a giant standing in a river or in the sea using a large sword to churn up the water. All the movements of your sword and body, whether side-to-side or up-and-down, must be fluid and powerful. When you move your sword to one side, your body should move slightly to the other side in an undulating pattern similar to that of a swimmer. Stay relaxed and apply the basic Taiji Quan skills of zhan, nian, lian, and sui in this *rou zhong gong*—hard-within-soft skill.

7.1. *Zuo Dian Bu Xi Shen Xia Lan* (左点步吸身下拦)—Assume Left Insubstantial Stance and Withdraw Body with Low Parry

Movements: Shift your weight back and sink your body onto your right leg. Drag your left foot back and let only the toes of that foot touch the ground to form a left insubstantial stance. At the same time, withdraw your abdomen and raise your left hand slightly so that the tip of your sword drops down. Turn your right hand up and push it lightly to the left. The edge of your sword should face to the left as you execute a left low parry (fig. 6-7-1).

Fig. 6-7-1

Key Points: Look forward and down. When you make the low parry, your footwork should be very nimble. Alternate your focus between your left and right huantiao points and imagine that they are pulling upward alternately as you focus on them. Feel as though you can step forward quickly. When your right hand pushes your sword to the left, use your left hand to pull your sword slightly up.

7.2. *Shang You Bu Xi Shen Xia Lan* (上右步吸身下拦)
—Step Forward with Right Foot and Withdraw Body with Low Parry

Movements: Step forward with your right foot and let only the toes of that foot touch the ground to form a right insubstantial stance. Keep your abdomen withdrawn and, at the same time, turn your right hand to the right causing the edge of your sword to face to the right. The tip of your sword should continue to point down. Simultaneously, pull your left hand slightly to the left so that the tip of your sword moves slightly to the right in a right low parry (fig. 6-7-2).

Fig. 6-7-2

Key Points: Keep looking forward and down. Make sure your footwork is very nimble when you execute the low parry and keep alternating your focus between your left and right huantiao points as you imagine that each point is being pulled upward in turn. Follow this feeling by raising your knees. Feel as though you can step forward quickly. When your right hand pushes your sword to the right, use your left hand to pull your sword slightly up.

7.3. *Shang Zuo Bu Ce Shen Zuo Ke* (上左步侧身左磕)
—Step Forward with Left Foot, Turn Body, and Jab to the Left

Movements: Step forward with your left foot and let only the toes of that foot touch the ground to form a left insubstantial stance. Keep your abdomen withdrawn. At the same time, push your left hand down so that the tip of your sword rises and turn your right hand inward to make a small circle. Turn your body slightly to the left. Quickly push your right hand slightly to the left. The edge of your sword should face back and to the left and the blade should be in front of your left shoulder as you deliver a left *ke*—jab or parry (fig. 6-7-3).

Fig. 6-7-3

Key Points: Look forward and slightly to the left. When you jab to the left, move your sword slightly forward and move your body slightly backward. Feel as though your left hand is sinking down as it pulls your sword slightly downward. You should feel as though your body is extending and sinking slightly.

7.4. *Shang You Bu Ce Shen You Shan* (上右步侧身右扇)
—Step Forward with Right Foot, Turn Body, and Knock Away to the Right

Movements: Step forward with your right foot and let only the toes of that foot touch the ground to form a right insubstantial stance. Keep your abdomen withdrawn. At the same time, push your left hand down to bring the tip of your sword up and turn your right hand outward to make a small circle. Turn your body slightly to the right. Quickly pull your right hand back slightly. The edge of your sword should face forward and the blade should be in front of your right shoulder as you execute a right *shan*—knock away or parry (fig. 6-7-4).

Fig. 6-7-4

Key Points: Look forward and slightly to the right. When you make the right knock-away block, move your sword slightly forward and feel your body sink and move slightly back. Feel very stable.

7.5. *Jin You Bu Fei Shen Dian Pi* (进右步飞身点劈)
—Step Forward with Right Foot and Lunge Forward to Peck Down and Chop

Movements: Keep your abdomen withdrawn and raise your right knee. At the same time, move both hands in front of your chest. Slightly hollow your chest (fig. 6-7-5).

Step forward and stomp lightly with your right foot as you form a right bow stance. Drag your left foot slightly forward. At the same time, push both hands forward and chop straight ahead with a *dian pi*—peck down and chop (fig. 6-7-6).

Fig. 6-7-5   Fig. 6-7-6

Key Points: Look straight ahead. Feel as though all parts of your whole body are gathering together, first to store power and then suddenly to explode and launch that power forward. Feel as though your power can reach directly to the tip of your sword.

7.6. *Dian Zuo Bu Fei Shen Zai Pi* (垫左步飞身再劈)
—Take Preparatory and Replacement Step with Left Foot
and Lunge Forward to Chop Again

Movements: Maintain the feeling that your abdomen is withdrawn. Step forward with your left foot and place it just to the left of your right foot. As soon as your left foot lands on the ground, push up with your right foot to raise your right knee in a *dianbu*—a preparatory or replacement step. At the same time, move both hands, holding your sword, back in front of your chest. Hollow your chest slightly (fig. 6-7-7).

Step forward and stomp lightly with your right foot to form a right bow stance. Drag your left foot slightly forward. At the same time, push both hands forward and chop straight ahead with your sword in another dian pi (fig. 6-7-8).

Fig. 6-7-7   Fig. 6-7-8

Key Points: Look straight ahead and focus your mind and your gaze on the same point. Take an unbroken series of quick steps forward and deliver a powerful chop. This chop and the previous chop should form one continuous movement directed at the same target.

Application: This skill includes four defenses and two attacks. The defenses cover the left lower quadrant, right lower quadrant, left upper quadrant, and right upper quadrant. As though clearing a path, your sword moves left and right and up and down to parry or block. You should feel as though your body is withdrawing when you are parrying and moving forward when your sword changes direction. Although your parries and blocks must be very powerful, it is important that you remain thoroughly relaxed and nimble as you deliver them. When you parry or block to the left, imagine that your body is moving forward from the right and vice versa.

As soon as you clear a path using your defense skills, step forward quickly and repeatedly, if necessary, to mount a powerful attack using dian pi. In this combination skill, the peck-down component is very quick, while the chop is powerful. Stomping your front foot fosters a quick and powerful expression of internal components and helps to increase the integration of your body, sword, and the sequence of internal components.

If your left leg is in front of your right leg and your opponent attacks your left leg with a spear, withdraw your abdomen, drag your left leg back, and make a left low parry with your sword. As soon as your sword touches your opponent's spear on the left side, you should feel as though you can move forward immediately from the right (fig. 6-7-9). If your opponent pulls the spear back and attacks your right leg, step forward with your right foot, withdraw your abdomen, and again make a low right parry with your sword. As soon as your sword touches your opponent's spear on the right, you should feel as though you can move forward immediately from the left (fig. 6-7-10).

Fig. 6-7-9

Fig. 6-7-10

If your opponent pulls his or her spear back and attacks your chest, step forward with your left foot, hollow your chest, and raise your sword to make a left jab or parry. As soon as your sword touches your opponent's spear on the left, you should feel as though you can immediately move forward from the right (fig. 6-7-11). If your opponent pulls the spear back and attacks your chest again, step forward with your right foot, hollow your chest, and, at the same time, use the back of your sword to parry or knock away the spear. As soon as your sword touches the spear on the right, you should feel as though you can immediately move forward from the left (fig. 6-7-12).

Fig. 6-7-11

Fig. 6-7-12

Maintain the sword-to-spear contact, and rise up slightly to bring your opponent's force slightly forward. At the same time, raise your right knee in preparation for a long stride forward (fig. 6-7-13). Take a quick, long step forward with your right foot and, at the same time, push your sword forward along your opponent's spear until it is close to his or her head. Then, stomp your right foot and push your forearms forward quickly and suddenly as though you were chopping forward and shaking your wrists as if to peck down. Feel force gathering in your body and being released from the front edge of your sword (fig. 6-7-14). This sequence of parrying (fig. 6-7-15), chopping, and pecking down (fig. 6-7-16) can be repeated several times.

Fig. 6-7-13

Fig. 6-7-14

Fig. 6-7-15

Fig. 6-7-16

8. *Li Pi Hua Shan* (力劈华山)—**Chopping Hua Mountain**

Posture Name Explanation

The name of this posture comes from an ancient myth about the daughter of the supreme god, the Jade Emperor. The Emperor became infuriated when his daughter fell in love with a human being and left heaven to marry her beloved. To punish her for descending to earth, he imprisoned her underneath a great mountain called *Hua Shan* or Hua Mountain. Many years later, her son Chen Xiang became a hero when he rescued his mother by chopping Hua Mountain in half with an enormous magical axe.

The central skill used in this posture is *pi*, a powerful chop and a cardinal sword skill. When executing pi, you should imagine that you have enough power to split anything. Not often used in Taiji Dao, this *gang*—hard and straight skill—should be applied only when you are sure that the circumstances are right and that you can perform it very well.

8.1. *Zuo Gai Bu Xi Shen Ya Dao* (左盖步吸身压刀) —Take Left Cover Step, Withdraw Body, and Press Sword Down

Movements: Step forward with your left foot and turn the toes of your left foot outward to form a covering stance. At the same time, turn your body to the left and push your right hand slightly forward. As your body turns, turn your right hand up and pull your left hand back until it is in front of your stomach. The tip of your sword should point forward, and the edge should face to the left. Let your body lean slightly forward to increase the pressure on the blade of your sword (fig. 6-8-1).

Fig. 6-8-1

Key Points: Look forward and slightly down. When you turn your body to the left, feel your qi sinking down and also feel as though you are holding a heavy object in your right hand. This should simultaneously generate a feeling that your body is sinking and a feeling that your right hand is pushing up. At the same time, you should pull your sword back with your left hand and lean forward. These feelings and movements will create a sense of great stability.

8.2. *Shang You Bu Ju Dao Shan Lan* (上右步举刀扇拦) —Step Forward with Right Foot, Raise Sword to Knock Away or Parry

Movements: Step forward with your right foot to form a right bow stance. At the same time, relax your hands and turn your body slightly to the left (fig. 6-8-2).

Shift your weight onto your left leg and simultaneously raise your body until your left leg is almost straight. At the same time, drag your right foot back, letting just the toes of your right foot touch the ground, and raise both hands until your right hand is over your head. The tip of your sword should point up, and the edge should face forward. Hollow your chest slightly (fig. 6-8-3).

Fig. 6-8-2   Fig. 6-8-3

Key Points: Look forward. When you step forward with your right foot, continue to drop your body and pull your sword back to create downward pressure. Then, when you drag your right foot back and raise your sword, you should feel as though your body is sinking down on your left leg to store energy for a long lunge step whenever it might be needed. When raising your sword, push up with both hands and pull back slightly and quickly with your right hand.

8.3. *You Jian Bu Fei Shen Qian Pi* (右箭步飞身前劈)
—Right Lunge Step with Quick Forward Chop

Movements: Lunge forward with your right foot and drag your left foot forward to form a right bow stance. At the same time, swing your sword in a forward chop at head level. Push your sword forward with your right hand and let your left hand initially follow, and then pull your sword slightly back (fig. 6-8-4).

Fig. 6-8-4

Key Points: Look straight ahead and chop your sword forward to chase your shen, expressed in your gaze. Feel as though your sword can immediately and directly reach the spot marked by your gaze.

Initially, the power for your chop should come from both arms. When the chop is almost complete, continue to chop powerfully forward with your right hand, but pull your sword slightly back with your left hand. At the same time, sink your weight onto your right leg so that the pull of your left hand and the sinking of your body combine to increase your stability and balance. Your chop must be hard, quick, and accurate.

Application: The chopping skill in this posture is a primary *dao* skill. For best results, your *dao* should have a curved shape and a thick back. As a whole, the chopping movement should be big and fast although the first half of the movement is relatively slow and leaves much of your body open to attack. The second half of the movement is very fast but does not easily allow for changes of direction.

These attributes of a hard chop are not generally compatible with Taiji principles, and, as a result, this type of committed action is usually avoided in Taiji Dao, especially when you are defending against a much quicker and more maneuverable weapon like a spear. Instead, Taiji Dao is typified by quick, lively, changeable, and subtle skills. In the occasional circumstance when a hard chop is appropriate, you must have your opponent firmly under control.

If your opponent attacks your chest or head with his or her spear, withdraw your body slightly, raise your sword, and use the flat, right surface of your blade to parry the spear lightly to the right (fig. 6-8-5). As soon as your sword touches the spear, slide it down along the shaft of the spear to cut your opponent's front hand or to thrust toward his or her chest. Lean forward at the same time to close the distance between you and your opponent and to increase the pressure of your sword on the spear.

Fig. 6-8-5

If your opponent moves the spear away, his or her body will be completely exposed, so the only logical choice for him or her will be to push the spear to his or her right (fig. 6-8-6). When you feel this sideways force, immediately step forward with your right foot. Maintain contact with the spear and maintain pressure on the contact point. At the same time, raise your sword straight up. Now, your opponent's only choice will be to step back (fig. 6-8-7).

Fig. 6-8-6

Fig. 6-8-7

Keep contact between the weapons and follow the movement of your opponent's spear so that it cannot be pulled away to initiate another attack. At this point, your opponent will be firmly under your control, and conditions will be ideal for a hard chop. Lunge forward as far as possible and move your sword along the spear. Just before chopping at your opponent's head, use your right hand to push the spear slightly to the right. Your sword and the spear should remain very close to each other but should not actually touch. This small gap makes it possible for you to deliver your chop more quickly (fig. 6-8-8).You must maintain control over your opponent's spear at all times.

Fig. 6-8-8

9. *Chan Jiao Zhi Ci* (缠搅直刺)
—Winding, Agitating, and Straight-Thrusting Skills

Posture Name Explanation

Normally, the winding, agitating, and straight-thrusting skills resemble those of a spear or a straight double-edged sword more than those of a regular *dao*. Because, however, a Taiji *dao*, unlike a regular *dao*, is thin and long with a double-edge in the front portion of the blade, these skills are quite commonly applied in Taiji Dao practice.

The winding and agitating skills in Taiji Dao should be done softly and smoothly in order both to control your opponent's weapon and to close the distance between you and your opponent so that you can reach him or her with your thrust. The skill described in this posture is a *yuan rou*—circling and soft skill.

9.1. *Shang Zuo Bu Xi Shen Chan Rao* (上左步吸身缠绕)
—Step Forward with Left Foot, Withdraw Body, and Wind and Circle Sword

Movements: Step forward with your left foot and let only the toes of that foot touch the ground to form a left insubstantial stance. At the same time, withdraw your abdomen slightly and pull your sword back until the ring is close to your body. The tip of your sword should point forward, and the edge should face down. When you pull your sword back, relax your wrists and use the tip of your sword to draw clockwise circles (fig. 6-9-1).

Fig. 6-9-1

Key Points: Look forward and slightly downward. Generate power from your right leg to the back of your waist. Put your mind on your mingmen point to turn your waist in a circular motion. Your sword should follow the motion of your waist and move in a spiral. Power should travel from your leg to the tip of your sword.

9.2. *Shang You Bu Fei Shen Tu Ci* (上右步飞身突刺)—Step Forward with Right Foot, Launch Body Forward, and Make Quick Hard Thrust

Lean forward slightly and shift your weight onto your left leg so that your right leg becomes relaxed and empty. Move your right leg to the right side of your left foot. This will create downward pressure on your sword and will similarly cause downward pressure to be stored in your left leg in preparation for a powerful push forward (fig. 6-9-2). Without interruption, follow the feeling from the previous movement to lunge forward with your right foot quickly and suddenly to form a right bow stance. At the same time, push your sword forward with both hands in a straight, hard thrust (fig. 6-9-3).

Fig. 6-9-2

Fig. 6-9-3

Key Points: Look straight ahead into the far distance. Chase your gaze with the tip of your sword in a quick thrust and imagine your whole body moving forward quickly as well to chase your sword. Feel the power of the thrust originate in your left foot and flow directly through your leg, waist, back, arms, and hands.

Application: This skill is commonly used to defend against a straight thrust from a spear or straight sword. The goal is to control your opponent by using your sword to wind around or agitate his or her weapon and by blending together the skills of sticking, following, parrying, and blocking. Do not let your opponent separate his or her weapon from yours.

You can circle your sword in any direction in order to follow your opponent's weapon, but make sure that you are always moving his or her weapon to the outside of the drawn circles. Because you will be moving slightly forward or back as you circle your sword, the circles will take the form of inward or outward spirals. Withdraw your body slightly so that your arms gain suppleness. You should be prepared to step forward for a quick, hard straight thrust as soon as an opportunity presents itself.

If your opponent attacks your chest or face with his or her spear, raise your sword to touch the underside of the spear (fig. 6-9-4). As soon as your sword makes contact with the spear, turn your right wrist outward to move your sword in a clockwise circle, first up and to the right (fig. 6-9-5) and then down (fig. 6-9-6). This circle will move the tip of the spear away from the front of your body. Maintain some downward pressure on your opponent's spear and immediately lunge forward and thrust straight ahead (fig. 6-9-7).

Fig. 6-9-4

Fig. 6-9-5

Fig. 6-9-6

Fig. 6-9-7

10. *Shou Shi* (收势)—The Ending Form

Posture Name Explanation

This movement is used to finish your form practice with a turn of your body. You can conclude your practice at this point or repeat the entire sequence described above in the opposite direction. Because the form is short, it is common to repeat the sequence several times without interruption.

10.1. *Hou Zhuan Shen Cang Dao Shi* (后转身藏刀势)
—Turn Body Back in Hiding Sword Posture

Movements: Turn your head to look back and follow this head movement with a turn to the left and a pivot on your right heel that turns your right foot inward. At the same time, pull your hands back and drop your left elbow so that the tip of your sword points straight up on the right side of your body. Raise your left knee to form a left insubstantial stance. In this posture, it should seem as though you are hiding your sword behind your body (fig. 6-10-1).

Key Points: Imagine an opponent approaching from behind. Feel alert and wary as you turn quickly around. Be ready to dodge back to defend against a possible attack.

Fig. 6-10-1

10.2. *Che Zuo Bu Fei Hu Shi* (撤左步飞虎势)
—Step Back with Left Foot in Flying Tiger Posture

Movements: Step back with your left foot and raise your right knee to form a right insubstantial stance. At the same time, turn your body to the left. Drop your sword down in front of your abdomen and then swing it to the left and up until the handle is beside the left front part of your head. The tip of your sword should point forward, and the edge should face up (fig. 6-10-2).

Key Points: Look straight ahead. Step back and feel as though you need to keep a safe distance from which to observe your opponent more clearly. Keep your body relaxed and your mind quiet and focused.

Fig. 6-10-2

10.3. *Bing Bu Huan Yuan Shi* (并步还原势)
—Feet Together Stance with Return to Original Posture

Movements: Raise your body and straighten your left leg. Put your right foot next to the right side of your left foot and simultaneously turn your body to the right. At the same time, open your left hand and let your right hand, holding your sword, drop down to the right side of your right leg. Put your left hand on the left side of your left leg and keep looking forward (fig. 6-10-3).

Fig. 6-10-3

You have now completed the physical movements of the form. Relax your body and adjust your breath. When your breathing becomes deep and smooth, your form practice has ended.

Key Points: Look straight ahead but withdraw your shen. Quiet your mind and relax your body. Let your breath return naturally to a slow, deep, regular rhythm.

Application: The two major movements of the ending posture concern how to prepare for fighting. When your sword is in the lower right quadrant, as though hiding behind you, you are presenting the appearance of weakness, but internally you are preparing for a fight. This state is described as "soft outside and hard inside."

When your sword is in the left upper quadrant, as if to show off, you are making a display of strength and signaling a readiness to fight. Internally, however, you should be soft and relaxed. This state is described as "hard outside and soft inside." Your main goal is to maintain focus and readiness for combat.

If your opponent attacks you from behind, turn your head to look at him or her. At the same time, sink your weight onto your right leg to create the feeling that your whole body is withdrawing. Hold your sword behind you as if to hide it and give an outward impression of softness while inwardly you prepare to fight vigorously. Do not focus on the tip of your opponent's spear but rather concentrate on his or her body (fig. 6-10-4).

If you feel you cannot adjust well to your opponent's attack, simply step back, turn to the left and raise your sword. Be very patient and careful and wait for another opportunity. Your posture should reflect a show of hard power, but inside you should be softly relaxed. Continue to concentrate on your opponent, not on the tip of his or her spear (fig. 6-10-5).

Fig. 6-10-4

Fig. 6-10-5

Chapter Seven

Fighting Skill Training

Taiji Dao fighting principles and training methods are the focus of this chapter. A variety of concepts will be introduced to explain how to defend against different kinds of weapons, and fighting principles will be illustrated using practice examples based on the skills and techniques discussed in previous chapters. Information about how to apply fighting skills and techniques will be presented in detail. The issues of timing and range will be given special attention.

Fighting Principles

As in Taiji Dao training, Taiji Quan principles and methods must be observed in your Taiji Dao practice. Using the fundamental Taiji Quan techniques of zhan, nian, lian, and sui, you should avoid direct force against your opponent's force and, instead, borrow force from your opponent and use it to beat him or her. According to Taiji Quan tenets, you should use a small amount of force to control your opponent's larger force and attempt to lure your opponent into "emptiness." Your overall goal is to achieve maximal efficiency with minimal force. This requires that you find the best time and angle for your attack and defense.

Because the Taiji *dao* is a short weapon, you must fight bravely and with great perseverance, but, because it is also a Taiji weapon, your skills must be soft, relaxed, and smoothly applied. You should avoid using the edge of your sword to strike your opponent's weapon. Your footwork is a key element when defending against long and/or heavy weapons and must be quick, nimble, changeable, stable, and balanced.

In the discussion that follows, it is assumed that two martial artists with weapons confront each other in a large space. In this simple situation, the fundamental Taiji principles upon which all the Taiji Dao skills and techniques are based can be clearly identified and described. Under more complicated conditions, specialized principles would apply.

Basic Skills Used to Defend against the Spear

Basic Principles

You are already in a difficult situation if you are using a short weapon to fight an opponent with a long weapon. It is said that skill grows stronger with every inch of a weapon's length, so the question of how to use a short weapon to defend against a long weapon is a critical issue in every martial arts group. Theoretically, it is not possible to use a short weapon to defend against a long weapon except in special cases, for example, if the fight occurs in a small area. It is said that when a fighter with a short weapon prevails against a fighter with a long weapon, it does not mean that the skill of the former fighter is good but rather that the skill of the latter is poor.

In traditional martial arts weapons practice, the spear is the most powerful and effective weapon. A well-known adage characterizes the spear as a thief, meaning that it is changeable and quick and its easily faked movements are tricky and very difficult to predict, identify, and defend against. If your opponent holds a long weapon like a spear and you have a short weapon like a *dao,* he or she will be able to reach you long before you can reach him or her. In addition, your opponent can easily and quickly create large changes in the movements of his or her spearhead with only small movements of the hands. Rapid changes created by such small and subtle manipulations will be very difficult for you to detect in time to mount a successful defense.

The most common spear attack skill is a straight thrust, which, if done correctly, will appear to you only as one small, rapidly approaching point, like an arrow speeding toward you. You will have great difficulty making contact with the incoming spear, and because a spear is long and its movements are changeable, quick, and deceptive, you will have trouble making correct adjustments during a spear attack. The situation is somewhat analogous to using a pistol against a distant machine gun.

You will have a chance to win only if your opponent's spear skills are not good. Although spear is a powerful weapon and difficult to defend against, high-level spear skills are difficult to practice and master. It is said that even ten years of dedicated spear practice may still not be sufficient, but if you research spear skills in detail and practice your *dao* skills with dedicated effort, you may have the opportunity to succeed against spear masters. Learning to defend against spear attacks is the most important aspect of Taiji Dao practice.

Three precepts based on the characteristics of long weapons describe how swords can be used to defend against spears. These three concepts, if applied well, will increase your chance for victory. Unfortunately, spear masters are also aware of these tactical ideas and are skillful at preventing their use.

Using a Short Weapon as a Long One

Because spears are much longer than swords, a spear master can easily injure a sword master before the sword master is able to get close to his or her attacker. The ability to avoid the spear's tip and move close enough to the spear master to mount a counterattack is among the sword master's most important skills. This skill is called *duan bing chang yong* (短兵长用), or "using a short weapon as if it were a long weapon," and the key points for its proper execution are sticking or controlling the shaft of the spear and possessing quick and agile footwork.

Avoiding insubstantial and attacking substantial

The tip of the spear, considered the insubstantial part, is quick and changeable in its movements. This makes it difficult to judge if an incoming attack is real or fake. The substantial part of the spear, considered the part of the shaft nearest the front hand and the front hand itself, is relatively slow and unchangeable in its movement. The second sword precept for defending against a spear is *bi xu ji shi* (避虚击实), or "avoiding insubstantial and attacking substantial." This principle advises you to direct your attack to the substantial part of your opponent's spear while avoiding the insubstantial part.

Give-Up-Life Sword

The most difficult requirement in defending against a spear is assessing whether an attack is real or fake. Typically, a spear master will mount a real attack only after he or she has made many fake attacks to confuse and trap his or her opponent. The spear master will wait patiently until he or she feels his or her attack can be successful.

Once a spear master has initiated a real attack, however, the direction and speed of his or her spear cannot easily be changed. The *dao* master should wait until the spear master makes the mistake of mounting a real attack at the wrong place or time and then immediately defend against the attack and advance toward the spear master in a counterattack. This strategy is dangerous, somewhat counterintuitive and not easy to accomplish. In essence, it requires that the sword master defend himself or herself against a spear attack by inviting that attack, for example, by springing quickly and nimbly toward the tip of the long weapon. This third option for defending against a spear is called *she ming dao* (舍命刀), or "give-up-life sword."

Practice Examples

In this section, several skills will be discussed as training examples for use in your fighting practice. In each case, you should imagine that your opponent faces you and holds a spear at the shortest safe distance from you. This is the point at which your opponent can almost reach you with his or her spear but would have to step forward with his or her front foot to make actual contact.

If your opponent just wants to test you, he or she will move his or her spear only slightly toward you and then pull it quickly back. If the tip of the spear moves two feet or more away from you each time, the spear is said to come "shallowly"; if the tip moves less than two feet away from you each time, it is said to come "deeply." Usually, a shallow approach indicates a fake skill, and a deep approach indicates a true and dangerous attack. A shallow attack is more difficult to adjust to and deflect, while a deep attack is easier to anticipate and manage but more dangerous if it succeeds. In the examples below, both the timing of your opponent's attack and the distance between the two of you when his or her attack is initiated are of crucial importance and will determine the adjustments you should make to defend yourself and find your best opportunity for a counterattack.

Chopping Skills

A chop or cut to the shaft of your opponent's spear is the principal sword skill. Given that most spear shafts are made of wood or bamboo, chopping or cutting the shaft can cause serious damage. Even if no damage is caused, contact with the shaft of your opponent's spear will allow you to stick and follow the spear's movements.

When using chopping skills, try to direct your chop to the middle or lower part of your opponent's shaft. Because he or she can change the movements of the head of the spear very quickly, it will be difficult for you to make contact with this part of the weapon. The more closely you direct your chop to your opponent's front hand, the easier it will be to strike his or her spear. This is referred to as an attack to the substantial part.

Zheng fan pi kan (正反劈砍)—chop from both sides: Both *pi* and *kan* are chopping skills. Usually, the movement of pi is bigger and more linear than the movement of kan. These two skills can be accomplished separately or together. If your sword chops diagonally down from right to left, the skill is called *zheng*. If the chop moves diagonally down from left to right, the skill is called *fan*. Zheng and fan chops can be alternated in smooth succession as many times as needed.

When your opponent approaches, step back to maintain a safe distance from which to observe the attack. Wait until he or she launches a deep attack. If your opponent is overly cautious, you can move closer to him or her to invite the attack.

Consider a situation in which you turn your body slightly to the right and hold your sword on your right side with the tip pointing up (fig. 7-1-1). When your opponent launches a deep attack, turn your body to the left to dodge the attack. Do not move your body away from the path of the spear any more than is absolutely necessary, even if the spear is very close. At the same time, chop down with your sword from right to left. Try to make the angle between the blade of your sword and your opponent's spear twenty to sixty degrees. If the angle is smaller than twenty degrees, your chop will probably not make contact with the spear.

Fig. 6-7-1

If your chop strikes the middle of your opponent's spear correctly, it will cut into the shaft. In the execution of this skill, called *zheng pi kan* (fig. 7-1-2), and in the similar skill of *fan pi kan* (figs. 7-1-3 and 7-1-4), you must remain relaxed and follow your opponent's force to avoid having the edge of your sword damaged by his or her spear.

Fig. 7-1-2

Fig. 7-1-3

Fig. 7-1-4

Zheng fan liao (正反撩)—upward cut from both sides: The *liao* skill is an upward cut. When your sword cuts diagonally up from right to left, the skill is called *zheng;* when the cut is diagonally upward from left to right, the skill is called *fan.* Zheng and fan can be alternated to produce a continual sequence of cuts.

Imagine a situation in which you turn your body slightly to the right and hold your sword on your right side. As in the preceding situation, wait for an incoming deep attack (fig. 7-2-1). As soon as it is launched, turn your body to the left and, at the same time, cut upward with your sword from right to left in a *zheng liao* (fig. 7-2-2). Pull your sword slightly to the left so that the angle between the blade of your sword and the underside of your opponent's spear is between twenty and sixty degrees. Aim your cut at the middle of the shaft of your opponent's spear. Relax and follow your opponent's force to avoid damage to the edge of your sword. *Fan liao* (figs. 7-2-3 and 7-2-4) is similar to zheng liao, differing only in the direction of the upward cut.

Fig. 7-2-1

Fig. 7-2-2

Fig. 7-2-3

Fig. 7-2-4

Zheng fan xiao (正反削)—scooping slice from both sides: Xiao is a light cut or chop done with a scooping motion. When your sword cuts or chops forward from right to left, the skill is called zheng. When the cut or chop extends from left to right, it is called *fan*. Zheng and fan can be alternated as many times as needed.

Stand straight and hold your sword naturally with the tip pointing down as you wait for a deep attack (fig. 7-3-1). When it occurs, turn your body slightly to the right and, at the same time, move your sword up and slightly to the right. Use the flat side of your sword to touch and follow your opponent's spear. Drop the tip of your sword down to the right so that your sword is horizontal to the ground and positioned over and across your opponent's spear. Ideally, your sword should make contact with his or her spear in the middle of the shaft. Move your sword to follow the incoming force.

Fig. 7-3-1

Sink your body so that your weight is added to your opponent's spear and keep sticking the spear with your sword (fig. 7-3-2). At the same time, move forward toward your opponent and continue to exert pressure on the spear so that he or she cannot pull it back (fig. 7-3-3). If your movement is correct, you will gain control of your opponent.

Fig. 7-3-2

Fig. 7-3-3

Stay relaxed, follow your opponent's force, and do not let him or her move away from you. Then, suddenly push your sword down slightly in a move called "jump your sword" and deliver a scooping chop or forward slice to your opponent's neck using a *zheng xiao* (fig. 7-3-4) or a *fan xiao* (figs. 7-3-5 through 7-3-8).

Fig. 7-3-4

Fig. 7-3-5

Fig. 7-3-6

Fig. 7-3-7

Fig. 7-3-8

Zheng fan jiao pi (正反搅劈)—stir-up chop from both sides: *Jiao* means to stir up or to flip. It is designed to move your opponent's spear in an upward circle as you prepare to deliver a chop. If you move your sword upward from the right side of your body, the skill is called *zheng jiao;* if from the left side, it is called *fan jiao.* Zheng jiao and fan jiao can be alternated in an uninterrupted sequence.

Stand straight and hold your sword naturally with the tip pointing diagonally down. As above, wait until your opponent launches a deep attack (fig. 7-4-1). Then, turn your body slightly to the right, and at the same time turn your hand outward and let your sword drop down to parry your opponent's spear slightly to the right. Use the flat side of your sword to touch the spear in the middle of the shaft (fig. 7-4-2).

Fig. 7-4-1

Fig. 7-4-2

Follow the incoming force by moving your sword back. Simultaneously step forward with your left foot so that your opponent's spear is on the right side of your body and your sword is positioned obliquely underneath the spear and maintains contact with it (fig. 7-4-3).

Fig. 7-4-3

Continuing without interruption, move your sword backward, up, and then forward in a circle to fling your opponent's spear up and back toward him or her. The force used for this movement should originate in your feet and flow through your legs, waist, back, shoulders, arm, hands, and finally to the tip of your sword. Your movements must be very smoothly coordinated and integrated so that your opponent feels as though the spear is being flipped out of his or her hands.

Shift your weight forward onto your left foot and lean forward toward your opponent. When your opponent's spear is thrown backward, chop directly at his or her head (fig. 7-4-4). If your movement is correct, your opponent will be under your control. Remain relaxed and follow your oppo-

Fig. 7-4-4

nent's force so that his or her spear cannot be moved away before being flipped backward by your jiao skill.

When your sword moves over your head, you can push it suddenly forward with added force as though you were throwing it forward. This will cause your opponent's spear to move away from the centerline of his or her body, opening a path for you to strike his or her head using a *zheng jiao pi* or a *fan jiao pi* (figs. 7-4-5 through 7-4-9).

Fig. 7-4-5

Fig. 7-4-6

Fig. 7-4-7

Fig. 7-4-8

Fig. 7-4-9

Shan kan (扇砍)—knock away and chop: *Shan,* the most common block-and-parry sword skill, involves using the back of your sword to knock away your opponent's spear. When a regular sword is used, this skill can be delivered with a lot of force because the back of such a sword is strong. When the sword is a Taiji *dao,* however, less force should be used, and more emphasis should be placed on sticking and following.

To begin shan, stand straight and hold your sword naturally with the tip pointing down. Wait until your opponent launches a deep attack to your stomach or higher (fig. 7-5-1), and, as soon as it occurs, turn your body slightly to the right. At the same time, move your sword up and slightly to the right. Aim at the middle of the shaft of your opponent's spear and use the back of your sword to knock his or her spear up and away. The less force you use to accomplish this skill, the easier it will be to stick and follow your opponent's spear (fig. 7-5-2).

Fig. 7-5-1

Fig. 7-5-2

While sticking your opponent's spear, move your sword up, back, and slightly to the right. This will cause your opponent to lean forward in an attempt to maintain balance and regain control. As your opponent leans, the pressure he or she exerts on the spear will increase. Be careful not to move your sword back too far or too quickly as you will break the contact between your weapon and your opponent's weapon (fig. 7-5-3).

Fig. 7-5-3

Finally, swing your sword suddenly forward along your opponent's spear and chop down at his or her head. Make sure that your sword is in front of the centerline of your body and that it points to the centerline of your opponent's body. Keep your sword sticking on his or her spear throughout your downward chop so that your force always controls your opponent's force. At the same time, step forward with your front foot to get closer to him or her (fig. 7-5-4).

Fig. 7-5-4

Sticking and Following Skills

The sticking and following principles of Taiji Quan are of central and special importance in Taiji Dao. The sticking and following skills that derive from these principles are often more efficient than direct block or strike skills.

If the handle of your opponent's spear is made of iron or some other hard material, the use of chopping skills will not only be ineffective but will also damage your sword. If you are fighting an opponent armed with this kind of spear, Taiji Dao sticking and following skills are always a better choice than chopping skills.

The Taiji *dao* skills described next can increase your ability to stick your sword on your opponent's spear and follow it. This ability will allow you to get closer to your opponent and control his or her spear, thereby rendering the long weapon less useful and your own weapon more effective.

Zuo you shang xia ge zhan (左右上下格粘)—left and right, up and down soft parrying and sticking: In the *ge* skill, the flat side of your sword is used to touch and parry your opponent's spear softly to the side. It is the most commonly applied defense skill in Taiji Dao. If done with the tip of your sword pointing up, the skill is called high soft parrying; if done with the tip pointing down, it is called low soft parrying. Both high and low soft parrying can be done on either side of your body.

Usually, when your opponent aims an attack at or above your chest, you should respond with a high soft parry. If the attack point is lower than your stomach, you should use a low soft parry. If the attack point is around your stomach, you can use either a high or low soft parry. Although ge is presented here as a separate skill, it can be very usefully combined with a wide variety of attack skills.

Stand straight, hold your sword naturally and wait for a deep incoming attack (fig. 7-6-1). If the attack is to your stomach or higher, move your sword forward and up and slightly withdraw your body. Let the tip point up and use the flat side of your sword to make soft contact with the left side of your opponent's spear as close to the middle of the shaft of the spear as possible. As soon as your sword touches your opponent's spear, move it slightly to your left in a high soft parry (fig. 7-6-2). Keep sticking and following your opponent's spear so that you can maintain control through the contact point.

Fig. 7-6-1

Fig. 7-6-2

This parry can also be done to the right as shown in figures 7-6-3 and 7-6-4. Like high soft parries, low soft parries can be done to the left (figs. 7-6-5 and 7-6-6) and to the right (figs. 7-6-7 and 7-6-8).

Fig. 7-6-3

Fig. 7-6-4

Fig. 7-6-5

Fig. 7-6-6

Fig. 7-6-7

Fig. 7-6-8

Once your sword touches your opponent's spear in any ge skill, you should immediately move forward to get closer to him or her and continue to stick and follow his or her spear. Your footwork must be quick and nimble. If your soft parries have been done correctly, your opponent will be unable to defend himself or herself, and it will be safe for you to mount an attack.

The key point of ge is to keep your arm relaxed. Acute sensitivity is also fundamental to the effective application of this skill. You must be able to arrive at a correct understanding of your opponent's movements and motives from what you feel happening at the touch point between the two weapons.

Stepping Skills

Quick and nimble footwork is the most important skill in Taiji Dao practice. When an opportunity presents itself, you must be able to step in quickly to take advantage of the situation, and, when you are in danger, you must be able to step back just as quickly to escape the situation. *Jianbu* (lunge step), *dianbu* (preparatory and replacement step), and *diantiaobu* (toe-hop step) are common steps that can be used in most situations.

Qian pu ge lan (前扑格拦)—spring forward and parry softly: The skill known as "give up your life and spring toward the tip of your opponent's spear" is one of the most decisive sword skills used to defend against a spear attack. Since it is often very difficult to determine whether your opponent's incoming attack is real or fake and to adjust accordingly, it may occasionally be necessary to invite an attack by appearing to give your opponent a tempting opportunity. You can force him or her to launch a true attack by springing directly toward the tip of his or her spear.

The key to the success of this skill is the timing of your footwork. You must know when and how far to step forward and when you should stop. Because this is a very dangerous skill, it requires great courage, and you must be ready to sacrifice your life, although your intention, of course, is not really to die but rather to create an opportunity to win.

Stand straight and hold your sword naturally while you wait for a deep attack (fig. 7-7-1). If your opponent fakes shallow attacks to confuse you, step forward directly toward him or her so that your chest moves closer to the tip of his or her spear. At the same time, raise your sword to make your opponent feel that if he or she does not attack you, you will be able immediately to strike with your sword (fig. 7-7-2).

Fig. 7-7-1   Fig. 7-7-2

If your spirit ignites and you are able to capture your opponent's full attention, and if the timing of your forward movement is correct, your opponent will become nervous and launch a genuine thrust attack to your chest. Take advantage of this opportunity by continuing to move forward and parrying your sword to the left (fig. 7-7-3).

Fig. 7-7-3

As soon as your sword touches your opponent's spear, stop moving forward. At the same time, hollow your chest and push your sword slightly forward so that your sword, your right arm, and your chest form a circle in front of your body. Parry your sword to the left along this circle so that the tip of your opponent's spear just misses making contact with your chest. Because the attack is real, your opponent will not be able to stop the movement of his or her spear as it passes harmlessly along the left side of your body (fig. 7-7-4).

Fig. 7-7-4

Take a lunge step or a preparatory and replacement step to move quickly toward your opponent with your sword sticking to his or her weapon. As you get closer to your opponent, your control will increase. With your sword in front of his or her body, your opponent will not be able to pull his or her spear back, and you will be able to attack him or her in any way you choose.

A common and easily applied attack skill in this situation involves cutting your opponent's front hand with your sword as it slides ahead of you along the shaft of his or her spear. If your opponent moves his or her hand away to avoid your cut, his or her whole body will be open to attack (fig. 7-7-5). You can also use a similar skill to parry your opponent's spear to the right (figs. 7-7-6 through 7-7-9).

Fig. 7-7-5

Fig. 7-7-6

Fig. 7-7-7

Fig. 7-7-8

Fig. 7-7-9

Gun dao jin bu (滚刀进步)—roll sword and step forward: This skill is similar to the skill just described, but it includes the addition of a rolling sword feature that makes the skill even more efficient. When your sword makes contact with your opponent's spear, and you begin to move toward him or her along the spear, your opponent will be able to push the spear to the side in an attempt to block the approach of your sword. If you continue to slide your sword directly forward, it will be difficult for you to advance against your opponent's force because your weapon is much lighter than your opponent's weapon. If you roll your sword as it moves along the spear, however, you can generate a powerful sideways force to counter and overcome your opponent's force. When rolling your sword, your footwork must be quick and nimble so that you can enter immediately into the open space cleared by the rolling skill.

Stand straight and hold your sword naturally while you wait for a deep attack (fig. 7-8-1). If your opponent attacks your knee, raise your right hand and stretch it forward so that the back of your sword touches the shaft of your opponent's spear from the side. At the same time, take a quick, small step slightly back (fig. 7-8-2). As soon as your sword touches your opponent's spear, push your sword slightly to the left and simultaneously turn your wrist outward to roll your sword on the spear. At the same time, use toe-hop steps to move quickly and nimbly toward your opponent (fig. 7-8-3). Keep your sword sticking on your opponent's spear and slide it toward his or her front hand and body with quickening steps. Do not give him or her a chance to escape back (fig. 7-8-4). You can also use a similar skill to parry your opponent's spear to the right (figs.7-8-5 through 7-8-8).

Fig. 7-8-1

Fig. 7-8-2

Fig. 7-8-3

Fig. 7-8-4

Fig. 7-8-5

Fig. 7-8-6

Fig. 7-8-7

Fig. 7-8-8

Spear fighters very commonly use quick, continuous combinations of real and fake thrusts to attack the knees and feet of their opponents. Toe-hop steps are very useful in this circumstance. If faced with such a situation, you should dodge the spear thrusts with a series of toe-hops and use a continuous sequence of soft parries to thwart the attack. As soon as your sword makes contact with your opponent's spear, keep sticking and rolling your sword on the weapon and move quickly toward him or her from whichever side your parrying allows. (figs. 7-8-9 through 7-8-14).

Fig. 7-8-9

Fig. 7-8-10

Fig. 7-8-11

Fig. 7-8-12

Fig. 7-8-13

Fig. 7-8-14

Empty-Hand Skills

Only the head of the spear is dangerous in spear thrusts, which are the most common spear attack skills. If you can avoid contact with the head, you may be directly able to grip the shaft of your opponent's spear. In principle, grabbing your opponent's spear with your empty hand is considered the ideal skill. The proper execution of this skill allows you to control your opponent completely and makes it exceedingly difficult for him or her to defend himself or herself in any way.

As with push-hands practice, your study of Taiji Quan empty-hand skills, which are fundamental to Taiji Dao, will make it possible for you to sense the intentions and anticipate the movements of your opponent. Empty-hand skills will help you understand how to change jin and how to control your opponent and upset his balance. In Taiji Dao, empty-hand skills are highly efficient and can be even more effective than sword skills.

In order to grip your opponent's spear, you must get close to him or her. Obviously, you should not grip the head of the spear because it is sharp. You will also have difficulty grabbing the first two feet of the shaft behind the head of the spear because this part of the spear can be easily and rapidly maneuvered by small hand movements of your opponent. Your best option is to move close to your opponent, establish some control, and then use your empty hand to grip the middle part of the spear.

Two common skills, included in the practice routine that was described in Chapter Four, will be discussed here to illustrate methods for gripping your opponent's spear.

Chan tou guo nao (缠头裹脑)—wind-up block and wrap-around head: This skill includes two parts. The first is a block-and-parry skill in which your sword moves around your head and body from the left. The second requires that you grip your opponent's spear with your empty hand and chop him or her from the right.

Stand straight and hold your sword naturally as you wait for your opponent's deep attack (fig. 7-9-1). When the attack is to your chest, turn your body to the left slightly and simultaneously move your sword forward and slightly to the left. Placing your sword as close as possible to your opponent's front hand, use the flat or edge of your sword to block your opponent's spear lightly and then parry it to the left. Stick and follow the spear continuously (fig. 7-9-2).

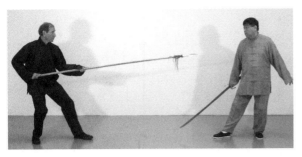

Fig. 7-9-1

Fig. 7-9-2

As soon as your sword parries your opponent's spear to the left, circle your sword around your head and body from the left with the tip pointing down. At the same time, move your body back and then forward to approach your opponent. When your sword starts to move backward, stretch your left hand forward to grip the shaft of your opponent's spear. Contact between your sword and your opponent's spear will make it easier for you to grip his or her weapon because you will be able to feel the movements of the spear more clearly (fig. 7-9-3).

Fig. 7-9-3

When you grip your opponent's spear, push it to the left and pull it back slightly. At the same time, chop your sword toward him or her from the right. Move your arms together in a large horizontal circle. Adjust the jin in your left hand so that it can be used to control and unbalance your opponent (fig. 7-9-4).

Fig. 7-9-4

Guo nao chan tou (过脑缠头)—passing overhead block and wind-down: Like the previous skill, this skill includes two parts. The first part is a block-and-parry skill in which your sword moves around your head and body from the right side of your body. The second part involves gripping your opponent's spear with your empty hand and chopping him or her from the left.

Wait for a deep attack from your opponent while standing straight and holding your sword naturally (fig. 7-10-1). If the attack is aimed at your chest, turn your body slightly to the right and simultaneously move your sword forward and slightly to the right. Place your sword as close as possible to your opponent's front hand and use the flat or edge of your sword to block your opponent's spear lightly and then to parry it to the right. Your sword should stick and follow your opponent's spear (fig. 7-10-2).

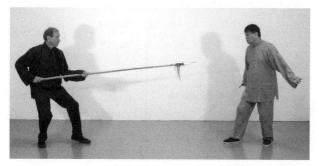
Fig. 7-10-1

Fig. 7-10-2

As soon as your sword parries your opponent's spear to the right, move your sword around your head and body from the right. Simultaneously, move your body back and then forward to approach your opponent. When your sword starts to move backward, stretch your left hand forward to grip the shaft of your opponent's spear. If you can maintain contact between your sword and your opponent's spear, it will be easier to grip his or her weapon because you will be able to feel its movements at the touch point (fig. 7-10-3).

Fig. 7-10-3

After gripping your opponent's spear, push it to the right and pull it back slightly. Move your sword around your head and body with the tip pointing down and chop your opponent from the left. Move your arms together in a large horizontal circle as you make your chop and adjust the jin in your left hand so that you can control and unbalance your opponent (fig. 7-10-4).

Fig. 7-10-3

Contact and Control Skills

Whenever contact occurs between your sword and your opponent's spear, you should follow and control him or her from the contact point as you would in push hands. From this contact point, you will be able to feel your opponent's movements and use them to unbalance him or her. You will be in a position to attack your opponent as soon as an opportunity arises. Taiji Dao contains several special skills for making contact with and controlling your opponent.

Shuang shou zhan nian jia tui kong (双手粘黏架推控)—stick on, block, bush, and control with both hands: To gain better control of your opponent, you must be able to maintain contact between your weapon and your opponent's weapon. The skill that allows you to accomplish this goal is called sticking. After sticking your opponent's spear, for example, you can use pushing or blocking skills to control his or her movements. Control of your opponent requires that you always aim your sword at his or her hands with the goal of cutting them. Your efforts will make it difficult for your opponent to concentrate, to change the flow of his or her internal force, and to maintain balance. Several sticking skills are described in this section.

Stand straight and hold your sword naturally as you wait for a deep attack (fig. 7-11-1). If your opponent launches a deep attack to your chest, turn your body slightly to the left and, at the same time, move your sword forward to parry the spear to the left (fig. 7-11-2). As soon as your sword makes contact with your opponent's spear, keep your sword sticking on the spear and take a step forward.

Fig. 7-11-1

Fig. 7-11-2

Put your left hand on the back of your sword at the contact point so that you can feel the movements of your opponent's spear and body. Continue to stick and follow the spear with your sword and use your internal feeling and strength to control him or her (fig. 7-11-3). As soon as you gain some control of your opponent as well as of the spear, slide your sword along the shaft of the spear to cut his or her front hand (fig. 7-11-4).

Fig. 7-11-3

Fig. 7-11-4

Similar skills allow you to parry your opponent's spear to the right and then stick the spear and push your sword forward (figs. 7-11-5 through 7-11-8). With other skills, you can block your opponent's spear upward and then push your sword forward (figs. 7-11-9 through 7-11-12)

Fig. 7-11-5

Fig. 7-11-6

Fig. 7-11-7

Fig. 7-11-8

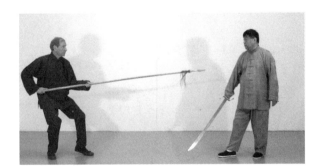

Fig. 7-11-9

Fig. 7-11-10

Fig. 7-11-11

Fig. 7-11-12

Zhan nian qiang gan zuo you fan (粘黏枪杆左右翻)—stick on spear and turn over left and right: A basic Taiji Quan principle holds that your opponent's force should never be directly resisted. Instead, you should follow his or her force in order to change and control it. You must be relaxed in order to follow your opponent's movements naturally and ensure that the incoming force does not fully land on your body. You must also sense and follow the direction of your opponent's force so that you can modify it so smoothly, naturally, and subtly that he or she cannot clearly feel the change. Finally, you should gain control of your opponent by leading him or her into a state of imbalance and instability.

Stand straight and hold your sword naturally while you wait for an incoming deep attack (fig. 7-12-1). If your opponent attacks your chest, turn your body slightly to the left and, at the same time, move your sword forward to parry your opponent's spear to the left from underneath (fig. 7-12-2). Stick your sword on the spear as soon as contact is made.

Fig. 7-12-1

Fig. 7-12-2

If your opponent sweeps the spear to the left to strike powerfully at your head, it will be difficult for you to defend against the force of this heavier weapon by blocking or pushing the spear directly to the left. Instead, relax and stick and follow the spear while slightly raising your sword. Then, turn your sword over and around the spear so that the blade of your sword moves from the left side of the spear to the right. Your sword and your opponent's spear should be moving in the same direction (fig. 7-12-3). As soon as your sword turns over your opponent's spear, continue to stick on the spear and keep turning your sword very smoothly until it is on top of your opponent's spear. Then, slide your sword along the shaft of the spear to cut your opponent's front hand (fig. 7-12-4).

Fig. 7-12-3

Fig. 7-12-4

If, after you cut him or her, your opponent lifts the spear and tries to hit you from your right side, do not resist the attack. Stay relaxed and follow your opponent's force by lifting your sword (fig. 7-12-5). Keep your sword sticking on the spear and raise your hands until the tip of your sword turns down and your sword is underneath the spear. This change must be made very smoothly (fig. 7-12-6). Finally, slide your sword along the bottom of the shaft of the spear to cut your opponent's front hand (fig. 7-12-7).

Fig. 7-12-5

Fig. 7-12-6

Fig. 7-12-7

There are similar skills for turning your sword from right to left (figs. 7-12-8 through 7-12-11) and then following your opponent's force to turn your sword again to the right (figs. 7-12-12 and 7-12-13). If your opponent tries to press his or her spear down, you should not use direct force to push your sword up. Instead, slide your sword forward along the spear while lifting your sword slightly up. If your opponent continues to press the spear down, his or her front hand will become tight, relatively immobile, and correspondingly easy for you to cut. If your opponent does succeed in moving his or her hand away, the downward pressure on the spear will be immediately reduced, and you will be able to lift it up easily and render it useless (fig. 7-12-14).

Fig. 7-12-8

Fig. 7-12-9

Fig. 7-12-10

Fig. 7-12-11

Fig. 7-12-12

Fig. 7-12-13

Fig. 7-12-14

Basic Skills Used to Defend against Heavy Weapons

Basic Principles

A weapon is referred to as heavy if it weighs noticeably more than your sword and if a direct sword attack against it will not be successful. Your Taiji *dao,* for example, is not strong enough to prevail in a direct upward block against an axe or a large chopping sword with a thick back. There are two basic skills that can be used to defend against a heavy weapon. The first is to follow the movement of the heavy weapon from behind rather than trying to block it from the front. The second is to take advantage of the time lapse that occurs when the movement of a heavy weapon is changed from one skill to another.

Although a heavy weapon can generate a very quick and powerful attack that is almost impossible to defend against directly, the movement of the weapon will be initially slow but subsequently difficult to change once the weapon has gathered momentum. As a result, a heavy weapon cannot be used effectively to fake an attack because its movements are hard to hold back or change. There is, of necessity, always a delay when your opponent changes from one heavy-weapon skill to another, and this delay provides an opportunity for you to mount an attack with your sword. Several commonly applied principles for defending against heavy weapons are discussed in the next section.

Avoiding Substantial and Attacking Insubstantial

As previously defined, the substantial part of a heavy weapon refers to the part that is most powerful; the insubstantial part to the section that is least powerful. The substantial part of a heavy weapon is usually the part closest to the tip, and the insubstantial and more maneuverable part is the section near the hand holding the weapon. The guiding principle for defense against a heavy weapon is *bi shi ji xu* (避实击虚), or avoiding the substantial part and attacking the insubstantial part. This means to avoid direct force and instead create an open space through which to attack your opponent's hands or the weakest part of his or her weapon.

Following Skills

The skill called following is commonly used to avoid applying direct force against a heavy weapon and is a special skill in Taiji Quan practice. For defending against a heavy weapon, following skills are always applied from behind. If, for example, your opponent attacks you with a large chopping sword, you should stick your sword on the back of his or her weapon and follow it. Then, you will be able subtly to redirect the motion of his or her sword with very little force.

Practice Examples

Several practice examples are provided next to illustrate how a variety of *dao* skills can be effectively used to defend against a heavy weapon. The assumption in each example is that your opponent is using a large, heavy sword against your *dao*.

When both weapons are short, a distance of about three steps between you and your opponent is considered safe. As you move toward each other from this distance, you must pay very close attention to your opponent's footwork. At a distance of two steps, you will be in great danger because your opponent will be able to reach you with his or her weapon. In this situation, you should concentrate on your opponent's shen and body movements.

Ce shan fan liao (侧闪反撩)—side dodge and upward cut: Two points are important for the proper execution of this skill. The first is that you must move close to your opponent as soon as he or she begins to move his or her weapon because this is the point at which your opponent's weapon will move most slowly and give you your best chance to attack. The second point is that you must elude the powerful force of his or her weapon and attack its weakest or most insubstantial part.

Stand straight and hold your sword naturally. Keep your mind calm and focused on your opponent's footwork while you wait for him or her to attack (fig. 7-13-1).

Fig. 7-13-1

If your opponent steps toward you and lifts his or her sword to chop you, step forward to approach him or her (fig. 7-13-2), and when you are close enough for your opponent's sword to chop directly at you, step and dodge to the left in as small a movement as possible. You can create a feeling of safety by leaning back and to the left. At the same time, lift your sword up underneath your opponent's wrist (fig. 7-13-3) and, as soon as your sword touches his or her wrist or forearm, pull your sword to the left and make an upward cut (fig. 7-13-4). This skill can also be done with a step and dodge to the right (fig. 7-13-5).

Fig. 7-13-2

Fig. 7-13-3

Fig. 7-13-4

Fig. 7-13-5

Fan gua (反挂)—hang back: In a parry skill, you should stick your sword on the back of your opponent's sword and then move backward along a curving path as though you were hanging your sword up on his or her sword. Your sword should move in the same direction as your opponent's sword. As his or her sword moves forward, yours should move back to follow. You should not resist your opponent's force directly.

Stand straight and hold your sword naturally. Keep your mind calm and concentrate on your opponent's footwork. Wait until your opponent attacks (fig. 7-14-1).

Fig. 7-14-1

If your opponent steps toward you and lifts his or her sword to prepare a chop, step forward to approach your opponent. Lift your sword and use the back of it to touch the back of his or her weapon as though you were hanging your sword on it (fig. 7-14-2). Keep sticking and following your opponent's sword and, simultaneously, parry it to the right with as small, light, and smooth a movement as possible. This parry allows you to push from behind to make a slight change in the direction of your opponent's force without resisting his or her force directly (fig. 7-14-3).

Fig. 7-14-2

Fig. 7-14-3

When your opponent's chop misses its mark and his or her sword is on the right side of your body, push your sword suddenly down and quickly up to chop at your opponent from right to left. The forward momentum of your opponent's heavy weapon will make it difficult for him or her to move his or her sword back quickly enough to defend against your attack (fig. 7-14-4).

Fig. 7-14-4

Ce ya qian xiao (侧压前削)—side passing and forward scooping chop: This is a parry and chopping skill. If your opponent attacks you with a powerful chop, it will be too dangerous for you to block his or her weapon directly from the front. You can, instead, parry your opponent's sword from side-to-side with the flat of your blade or the back of your sword. This move does not require much force, and you can then make a circle with your sword to press your opponent's sword down and attack him or her.

Stand straight and hold your sword naturally. Keep your mind calm and concentrate on your opponent's footwork. Wait until your opponent attacks you (fig. 7-15-1).

Fig. 7-15-1

If your opponent steps toward you and lifts his or her sword to chop you, step forward to get closer to him or her. Lift your sword and use the flat of the blade to touch the left side of the flat of your opponent's sword (fig. 7-15-2). Keep your sword sticking on and following his or her sword as you parry it to the left in a circular path. Rather than exerting force against force, this circling parry allows you to push from the side to change the direction of your opponent's sword. Press down on his or her sword as it reaches the left side of your body at the level of your stomach or hip (fig. 7-15-3).

Fig. 7-15-2

Fig. 7-15-3

When your opponent's chop misses its target, move your sword upward in a continuation of its circular path to attack your opponent with a fast scooping chop. The momentum of your opponent's heavy weapon will prevent him or her from moving his or her sword back in time to defend himself or herself (fig. 7-15-4). This skill can also be done from your right side with the back of your sword (figs. 7-15-5 through 7-15-8)

Fig. 7-15-4

Fig. 7-15-5

Fig. 7-15-6

Fig. 7-15-7

Fig. 7-15-8

Basic Skills Used to Defend against Short Weapons

Basic Principles

Most short weapons are light but very maneuverable, so large and powerful skills are not usually needed to defend against them. More commonly, all that is required is to stick on the light weapon and follow its movement. If you observe Taiji Quan principles and use Taiji push-hands skills to control and unbalance your opponent, you will be able to develop many refined and detailed short-weapon defense skills. These will include small, quick, and hard skills, like strikes or hits that can easily knock a light weapon away without damaging your sword.

Practice Examples

In the following training examples, imagine that your partner or opponent is standing in front of you armed with a *jian,* a straight double-edged sword. The first three examples are two-person practice routines that can be repeated many times, and the remaining examples are descriptions of fighting skills. In all the examples, your body should be relaxed, and the movements of your sword should be smooth. You should pay close attention to how your partner moves and feel his or her sword skills so that you can respond as correctly as possible.

Ping quan (平圈)—horizontal circles: This routine requires that you stick your sword on your partner's jian and follow it as it moves in a horizontal circle. In the first half of the circle, when your sword is moving toward you under your partner's sword, your task is to follow and slightly redirect the movement of his or her sword. In the second half, when your sword moves toward your partner and is on the top of his or her sword, your task is mainly to control your partner and prepare your attack.

When your partner lifts his or her sword up, stretch your arm forward until your sword touches your partner's sword from underneath (fig. 7-16-1). Imagine that your partner moves his or her sword forward to attack your face, and keep your sword sticking on and following his or her sword as it moves back in a circular path. At the same time, shift your weight back (fig. 7-16-2).

Fig. 7-16-1

Fig. 7-16-2

Keep circling your sword so that it moves from the left side of your body to the right. At the same time, turn your sword slightly down as it passes in front of your body and continue turning it so that it pushes your partner's sword outward and presses it down until you are in a good position to control his or her weapon (fig. 7-16-3).

Fig. 7-16-3

Continue without interruption to circle your sword forward to attack your partner from his or her left with a cut to his or her head. Your partner's sword should follow yours through its circular path (fig. 7-16-4) and then pass across your partner's face. He or she should get ready to move forward and begin the routine again (fig. 7-16-5). You and your partner should repeat this circle and other similar exercises many times (figs. 7-16-6 through 7-16-9).

Fig. 7-16-4

Fig. 7-16-5

Fig. 7-16-6

Fig. 7-16-7

Fig. 7-16-8

Fig. 7-16-9

Li quan (立圈)—vertical circles: In this routine, you should stick your sword on your partner's jian and follow it in a vertical circle. In the first half of the circle, your sword moves toward you as you follow and lightly parry your partner's sword; in the second half, your sword moves toward your partner as you seek to control and attack him or her.

When your partner lifts his or her sword up, stretch your arm forward so that the flat of your sword touches his or her sword from the left (fig. 7-17-1). Imagine that your partner moves his or her sword forward to attack your face. Stick your sword on your partner's sword and follow it back in a vertical circle and, at the same time, shift your weight back (fig. 7-17-2). Keep your sword vertical and lightly parry your partner's sword to the right as it moves through the circle. At the same time, push your partner's sword slightly outward and press it down so that your sword is in a good position to control it (fig. 7-17-3).

Fig. 7-17-1

Fig. 7-17-2

Fig. 7-17-3

Without interruption, move your sword forward in a continuation of the circle to cut your partner from the front. Your partner's sword should follow your sword as it moves through the circle (fig. 7-17-4). Then, your partner should lift his or her sword up over his or her head while you keep your sword sticking on your partner's sword and following it (fig. 7-17-5). Imagining that he or she might try to chop your head again, begin the vertical circle again (fig. 7-17-6). You and your partner should practice this skill and other circling movements hundreds of times (figs. 7-17-7 through 7-17-11).

Fig. 7-17-4

Fig. 7-17-5

Fig. 7-17-6

Fig. 7-17-7

Fig. 7-17-8

Fig. 7-17-9

Fig. 7-17-10

Fig. 7-17-11

Ying mian quan (迎面圈)—front circles: This routine differs from the two just described only in that your sword spirals forward as the circling proceeds. In the first half of the circle, your partner's sword moves toward you underneath your sword, and your task is to control his or her weapon. In the second half, as your sword moves toward your partner, your task is to follow and parry his or her weapon.

When your partner moves his or her sword toward you, stretch your arm forward to touch the sword from the left side with the flat of your sword (fig. 7-18-1). Imagine that your partner moves his or her sword forward to attack your face and keep your sword sticking on your partner's sword and following it through the circular path. At the same time, shift your weight back (fig. 7-18-2) and continue to move your sword in the circle as though stirring your partner's sword. Then, parry it to the right and down so that your sword is on top of his or her sword in a good position to control his or her weapon (fig. 7-18-3).

Fig. 7-18-1

Fig. 7-18-2

Fig. 7-18-3

At this point, your partner should move his or her sword up from the left, and you should follow without interruption (fig. 7-18-4). Then, your partner should lift his or her sword up while you keep your sword sticking on his or her sword and following it (fig. 7-18-5). Imagine that your partner can again attack your head, and continue to move your sword through the circle (fig. 7-18-6). This partnered exercise and others like it should be practiced many times (figs. 7-18-7 through 7-18-9).

Fig. 7-18-4

Fig. 7-18-5

Fig. 7-18-6

Fig. 7-18-7

Fig. 7-18-8

Fig. 7-18-9

Because the next examples illustrate fighting skills rather than practice routines, the person referred to as your partner in the previous examples will be referred to as your opponent in the discussion that follows.

Quan lan zhi ci (圈拦直刺)—circling parry and straight thrust: This quick and sudden skill is similar to the others already described but includes the addition of a thrust. In it, you first make a circling parry with your sword and then spiral your sword forward so that it stirs your opponent's sword out of the way. Finally, you attack your opponent with a thrust skill.

When your opponent attacks you from the front, hold your sword in a low position and concentrate on his or her footwork (fig. 7-19-1). If your opponent thrusts directly at your body, lift your sword and move it in a front circular parry. As soon as your sword makes contact with his or her sword, add extra power and speed to your movement in order to stir your opponent's sword away (fig. 7-19-2). Make sure you can control your force so that you do not add too much power to the movement of your sword. As soon as your opponent's sword is moved away, step forward and thrust straight toward his or her body (fig. 7-19-3).

Fig. 7-19-1

Fig. 7-19-2

Fig. 7-19-3

Lan pi (拦劈)—parry and chop: Although rare in Taiji Dao, hard blocks are sometimes used to defend against light weapons. This skill involves first a quick block that knocks your opponent's sword away and then a parry to the left in preparation for your attack. When using a hard block, be sure to use the minimum amount of force necessary and avoid using the edge of your sword to block the edge of your opponent's sword directly. Try instead to block his or her sword from the side. This will reduce the likelihood that your hard block will damage the edge of your sword.

If your opponent chops at your head, block the attack by lifting your sword up from the left side of his or her weapon (fig. 7-20-1) and add a small amount of power to your sword just as the two weapons are about to make contact. Because your opponent's weapon is light, this sudden addition of force will quickly knock his or her sword sideways (fig. 7-20-2). Make sure that your movement is not too big and that you use just enough force to provide a short, hard blow to your opponent's sword. In knocking your opponent's sword aside, do not let your own sword move far from your centerline. As soon as your sword hits your opponent's sword, you will feel as though you are bouncing slightly back. At this moment, turn your wrist and chop forward toward your opponent's head (fig. 7-20-3).

Fig. 7-20-1

Fig. 7-20-2

Fig. 7-20-3

Gua pi (挂劈)—hang back and chop: This skill involves adding extra power to your sword as you follow your opponent's light weapon back during an incoming attack. The sudden application of additional force will knock his or her weapon away to the right and make it difficult for your opponent to reestablish his or her initial momentum. At this moment, you should launch an attack by suddenly changing the direction of your sword from backward to forward.

When your opponent holds his or her sword in a high position, stand straight, remain stable, and hold your sword in a low position (fig. 7-21-1). If your opponent uses his or her sword to chop at your head, lift your sword and follow his or her sword back. Chase your opponent's sword from behind and, when the back of your sword is about to make contact with your opponent's, suddenly create a push against his or her weapon by adding a small amount of power to your sword. This hard push will quickly knock your opponent's sword aside because of its light weight and because both swords are moving in the same direction (fig. 7-21-2).

Control your force carefully so that your push is not too hard and keep the movements of your body and sword as small as possible. As soon as you knock aside your opponent's sword, turn your wrist and chop forward toward his or her head (fig. 7-21-3).

Fig. 7-21-1

Fig. 7-21-2

Fig. 7-21-3

Shang jia xie kan (上架斜砍)—upward block and diagonal chop: In real fighting, anything can happen. If you are defending against a short, light weapon, you will occasionally have no choice but to use a hard block, perhaps even to strike the edge of your opponent's sword with the edge of your own. In this situation, you should use as little force as possible and finish your block as quickly as possible to avoid damaging your sword any more than absolutely necessary. The *shang jia xie kan* skill exemplifies this point. In this skill, you should suddenly add power to an upward block to knock aside your opponent's weapon and make it difficult for him or her to regain his or her initial movement. While your opponent's attack is interrupted, you should change the motion of your sword from back to forward and strike toward him or her. When applying this skill, it is important that you control yourself well and not let your opponent confuse you with a fake attack.

When your opponent holds his or her sword in a high position, stand stably and hold your sword in a lower position (fig. 7-22-1). If your opponent uses his or her sword to chop at your head, raise your sword to block directly upward. Try to use the strongest part of your sword, the root, to execute this hard block and add a small amount of sudden power to your sword just before it makes contact with your opponent's weapon. Your strike will quickly and definitively knock your opponent's light sword away to the left (fig. 7-22-2).

Fig. 7-22-1

Fig. 7-22-2

Use as little force as possible and do not move your body or your sword more than necessary as you knock your opponent's sword aside. As soon as your sword hits his or her sword, turn your wrist so that your sword moves forward in a diagonal chop to his or her head from the upper left to the right and down (fig. 7-22-3). The same skill can be used to knock your opponent's sword away to the right in which case your diagonal chop will extend from the upper right to the lower left (figs. 7-22-4, 7-22-5, and 7-22-6).

Fig. 7-22-3

Fig. 7-22-4

Fig. 7-22-5

Fig. 7-22-6

Ke (磕)—jab: *Ke* is a small but quick and sudden block that is often used to knock light weapons away. If your opponent has a light weapon, it will be very easy for him or her to fake an attack because his or her weapon allows for movements that can be quickly changed. If you try to block a fake attack with a hard block, and your block misses, you will be in a dangerous position. Small, fast jabs will be far more effective than hard blocks in this situation.

When your opponent holds his or her sword in a high position, stand stably, hold your sword in a middle position, and try to move closer to your opponent (fig. 7-23-1). Although you risk being attacked whenever the distance between you and your opponent is small, you also have a potential advantage because the closer you are to your opponent, the more difficult it will be for him or her to make changes in his or her movements. Be especially careful in such circumstances to maintain your focus and to protect the centerline of your body with your sword.

Fig. 7-23-1

If your opponent lunges forward and thrusts toward your chest, evade this attack by turning your body slightly to the left and simultaneously stepping forward with your right foot to get closer to your opponent. At the same time, use the root of your sword to jab his or her sword to the left (fig. 7-23-2). Your movement must be quick and sudden but not too forceful. It is usually sufficient to move your sword only half a foot. Bring your sword back to the centerline of your body as soon as possible after your jab.

Fig. 7-23-2

Za (砸)—reverse hammer block: *Za,* like ke, is a small, quick, and sudden skill used to block an attack by knocking away your opponent's light weapon. This skill involves turning your sword over so that you can use the back like a hammer to strike down on the opposing weapon. Using the back of your sword will prevent damage to the edge.

When your opponent holds his or her sword in a high position, stand stably, hold your sword in a low position, and try to move closer to your opponent (fig. 7-24-1). Be very vigilant and guard your centerline whenever the distance between you and your opponent is small. If your opponent thrusts toward your chest, withdraw your body slightly and simultaneously move your sword over your opponent's weapon from the left (fig. 7-24-2).

Fig. 7-24-1

Fig. 7-24-2

Then, suddenly turn your sword over so that the back faces the ground and strike down quickly on your opponent's sword. There must be a spring to your movement, and you should remain relaxed. Keep your movement as small as possible (fig. 7-24-3) and bring your sword back to the centerline of your body immediately after your downward block.

Fig. 7-24-3

Mental Practice for Fighting

Fighting with weapons is much more dangerous than empty-hand fighting. In the latter case, you can receive multiple punches or kicks and still have many chances to win. In combat with weapons, however, if you receive even a few attacks before you reach your opponent with your weapon, you will lose not only your chance to win but possibly also your chance to survive the confrontation. It is traditionally said that, in theory, when opponents are armed, only one attack is needed to decide the victor.

In martial arts fighting, two factors determine which combatant has the advantage. The first is physical condition and the second is skill level, with the more muscular and highly trained fighter having the better chance for victory. Of the two factors, physical condition, which includes size, strength, speed, flexibility, coordination, and reaction time, has more influence than skill in empty-hand fighting, but the reverse is true in combat with weapons. A traditional view is that if you want to know a martial artist's overall skill level, find out how well he or she does when fighting with weapons.

As humans, we cannot perform perfectly according to design. Unlike machines, we have sensations, emotions, sensitivity, spirit, intentions, and thoughts, all of which influence our behavior.

No matter how physically able and highly skilled you may be, your psychological state will significantly affect your behavior in a fight. If you are very nervous, your body will be tight, your reactions will be slow, and your movements will be stiff and disorganized. It is unlikely that you will be able to execute skills correctly under such conditions. It will also be difficult for you to keep your mind clear and accurately assess your opponent's behavior in order to make correct decisions. Success in fighting depends on how well you can maintain balance among a variety of psychological factors. For this reason, advanced Taiji Dao practice must include careful attention to mental training. Some of the most important characteristics of mental training are discussed in this section.

Courage: This characteristic is of paramount importance in a fight. Being brave, however, is not easy when you are faced with a brightly shining and extremely sharp weapon. If you are afraid of fighting, you will have little chance to win, but your bravery must be tempered with prudence so that it is not expressed rudely or rashly. Fortunately, everyday conflicts are not typically settled by armed confrontation, so most people rarely, if ever, have the need to marshal the kind of courage needed for martial arts weapons combat.

Confidence: The foundation of courage is confidence in your skills. It is said that high-level skills will always make people brave. To build up this confidence, you must practice hard every day.

Composure: Your mind must always be settled and calm during a fight, despite quickly and constantly changing conditions and the many diversionary tricks that your adversary will try. If you lose your focus, you will make many mistakes. You must learn to adjust immediately to changing circumstances so that you do not become dazed and confused. You must also be able to control the rhythm of your movements while disturbing your opponent's rhythm.

Patience: Patience is especially important when you are in trouble in a fight. This quality can help you conserve energy and keep your mind clear. When you find yourself in a precarious position, do not rush to resolve the situation. Your haste will make it hard for you to think clearly, and it is likely that you will waste your energy using skills that are inappropriate to the circumstances. Patience will help you solve your problems most efficiently.

You must also be patient even when you are not in trouble but only frustrated by not yet having found a way to win. In this situation, patience will help you stay calm while waiting for your opponent to make a mistake that gives you an opportunity to defeat him or her.

Perseverance: Never give up in a fight. In Taiji Quan, you want your opponent to use his or her true force directly so that you can borrow it easily and use it against him or her. If you understand this principle, you will often choose to release your real force only in the last moments of a fight when your opponent thinks he or she can beat you and so reveals his or her true intention and skill. As a result, these moments also present you with your best chance to assess your opponent's attack clearly and to use this knowledge to beat him or her. When you are in a dangerous situation, persist one more second and your best opportunity may come.

Alertness: One of the most common and dangerous mistakes in fighting is to underestimate your enemy. It is said that underestimating your opponent will lead you to defeat. If you think your opponent is not good, you will lose your focus, and your mind and movements will slow down. You must remain alert, relaxed but not nonchalant, and always fiery in spirit. A traditional adage advises that "when you see a cat, treat it like a tiger."

Mental training is not easy, but it can bring about meaningful change in your character and personality. In Taiji Dao practice, where some of the training methods are dangerous, careful attention to psychological factors is critical.

Protection during Practice

To master fighting skills, solo practice is not enough. If you really want to understand these skills, you must practice with a partner. Compared to empty-hand skill practice, weapons skill practice with a partner is much more dangerous, so it is very important that you understand how to protect yourself and your partner. There are two ways to avoid or reduce harm: use protective equipment and thoroughly understand the method of practice. With these two conditions met, you will be able to exercise good control throughout the training process.

Regarding equipment, you should use a wooden sword to learn skills and wear protective armor to avoid injury. The bamboo swords that are sometimes used in training are too light, have too much spring, and are too dissimilar from real swords to provide you with correct feelings. Swords made from heavier woods are more useful for developing your skills because their heft and feel make them more similar to real swords.

The protective armor used in martial arts training is not the same as armor used in real warfare. Historically, different groups made their own armor, most commonly from cloth into which bamboo slips were inserted. Modern practice armor can be simple or complex, and, if you are practicing special skills, it may be necessary only for some parts of your body. Unfortunately, protective armor for sword practice is difficult to find in today's market.

Never engage in training without sufficient protection, and, without appropriate armor, do not practice dangerous partnered skills at full-speed. Safety concerns must always be paramount. Even when wooden swords and protective gear are used, weapons training remains dangerous, and great care must always be taken.

A correct set of practice methods can prevent or reduce training injuries. Each student should practice only those skills exactly appropriate to his or her ability level, and the first step in practicing any skill is always to do the correct movement in slow motion. Only advanced students should try full-speed fighting practice.

In exercise drills, usually no more than three techniques should be practiced in an uninterrupted sequence. Including more than three techniques in a series can easily cause a loss of rhythm and concentration, and this loss, in turn, can lead to increased mistakes and risk of injury. Beginners should focus on only one technique at a time in order to maximize the usefulness and safety of their practice.

Most of the responsibility for proper and safe training rests with masters. They must first explain every skill in detail to their students and then demonstrate the correct execution of these skills. They should anticipate and explain every point of danger and every dangerous situation that can possibly arise. They should be acutely watchful and able to maintain control of every aspect of their students' actions, especially timing and rhythm. Finally, they should have a thorough understanding of each student's skill level and personality.

No matter how much care is taken and protection provided, injuries may still occur. You must be constantly mindful and meticulous in each step of your training to reduce the chances for harm to the minimum.

Partnered Training of Fighting Skills

Partnered practice is the key component of your fighting training. However good your form and solo skill practice may be, your feelings and responses will be very different and probably considerably less relaxed when you are confronted with an armed opponent.

Mental training and technical training are the two focal aspects of partnered practice. In mental training, your goal is to learn how to remain quiet, relaxed, alert, and brave. In technical training, you should work to improve your timing and your ability to sense and accurately assess distances, degrees of danger, and qualities at the touch point such as pressure and angle of attack. Through partnered practice, you will learn to keep your mind clear and make appropriate adjustments to your own movements as well as to those of your partner. Your skills will undergo and benefit from continual revision as your two-person training proceeds.

Partnered training can be separated into two categories, each of which includes several steps. In the category called feed training or fixed-skill fighting training, your partner should tell you in advance which skill he or she will use to attack you and should agree not to change this plan. In the second category, called free-skill fighting training, which mimics real combat, both you and your partner can use any skill you want without giving the other advance notice. Unlike actual combat, however, you and your partner should avoid causing injury to each other and should focus on perfecting your skills rather than on winning or losing.

In feed training, the first step is single-skill practice in which your partner, no matter what kind of weapon he or she uses, should attack you with a single skill announced in advance. You should defend against the attack and possibly launch a counterattack. Focusing on only one skill at a time and practicing it repeatedly will provide you with an excellent opportunity to develop correct feelings and master each skill. Initially, you should relax and execute every tiny movement of each skill slowly and correctly. Then, you can gradually quicken the pace of your movements until full speed is achieved.

In the second stage of feed training, you and your partner should use skills in combination with each other to mount attacks and defenses in a smooth, continuous flow of motion. This kind of practice will improve your ability to move nimbly and change skills without pausing.

In free-skill fighting training, the first step is for you and your partner to control your own forces so that your weapons make only light contact, as you would in Taiji push-hands practice. Taiji Quan principles and skills should be properly applied as you practice gaining control of each other. You and your partner should keep your weapons in constant contact so that the touch point is maintained as it would be in Taiji push hands.

The second step in free-skill fighting training is called *dian dao wei zhi* (点 到为止), or "touch then stop," which means to stop as soon as contact is made. While you and your partner should attack each other using real skills, each of you must stop your attacks as soon as your weapons touch your partner's body. You can strike each other's weapon as hard as needed for a successful attack, but you must avoid striking each other's bodies. This requirement demands careful practice. It is not easy to shift momentum and withdraw your force in time to avoid injury to your partner.

A possible disadvantage of learning to stop an attack just as contact is made is that this ability can become a habit and make it difficult for you to carry through a complete attack in a real fight. The third step in free-skill fighting training is designed to mitigate against this possibility. If you and your partner have reasonable protection and use wooden swords and take care not to hurt each other, you should practice competition fighting at full power and speed. This final stage of your free-skill fighting training allows you to experience many of the mental and physical challenges of real combat.

Final Words

Taiji Dao from Beginning to End

Before you learn Taiji Dao, you should have a thorough knowledge of the Taiji Quan empty-hand form, the foundation of all Taiji Dao skills. You should be able to execute the basic stances, steps, and body movements, and you should understand the fundamental qualities of relaxation, stability, nimbleness, and smoothness. You should also have mastered push-hands skills so that you can remain relaxed when touched and can develop the sensitivity and ability to change that are required for successful Taiji Dao practice. You should also understand the basic Taiji Quan techniques of zhan, nian, lian, and sui. The greater your understanding and mastery of these techniques and abilities, the easier it will be for you to learn Taiji Dao. Typically, three years of form and push-hands training are required before students in many groups are even permitted to touch swords.

To learn Taiji Dao, the first step, as discussed in Chapter Two, is to find a sword that suits you well in its balance, weight, length, and shape. If you have to use a regular broadsword to practice Taiji Dao, you should understand and pay attention to the differences between the two kinds of sword.

The second step is to become thoroughly familiar with your sword by first practicing simple movements, like circling, until your hands remain relaxed and can adeptly control your sword. You should be able to manipulate your sword quickly and smoothly through a wide variety of changes in speed, direction, angle, and degree of power. Your sword should come to feel like an extension of your body, whether gripped by one hand or two.

The third step is to practice each basic skill many times, or as said in traditional terms, "a thousand times," until you can understand and perform each skill well. Keep your feet in a fixed position so that you can focus only on the feeling in your hands and body as you direct your sword through the basic movements of each skill. In learning how to control your sword, pay careful attention to grips, blade angles, changes in the amount of force applied to your sword, and the applications of each skill.

When you have acquired excellent sword control and mastery of the basic skills with your feet in a fixed position, you should begin moving your feet as you practice each skill. Pay particular attention to your footwork and the coordination and integration of your body.

The fourth step in weapons training is to learn forms. Form practice can help you increase a variety of important feelings. These include a feeling for the flow of the internal components, a feeling for the rhythm of different movements, and a feeling for sustained, uninterrupted motion. All these feelings will enhance your internal and external integrations and will coordinate the movements of all parts of your body with each other and with your sword. Your shen, yi, qi, jin, physical movements, and sword will function smoothly and harmoniously together.

Form practice can help you learn the correct rhythm for your movements, and maintaining correct rhythm will help you control the psychological factors that affect your chance for success in combat or competitive situations. Without this ability, you can easily become anxious and quickly develop tightening muscles, a pounding heartbeat, and irregular breathing. In a state of anxiety, your movements will slow down, your attention will blur, and your mind will become confused. Correct rhythm, on the other hand, allows your body to relax and your mind to remain clear even when you are in danger.

Your ability to sustain continuous movement is measured by the number of movements you can do well without interruption. In individual sword practice, most people can smoothly execute three to five movements in one uninterrupted sequence. Form practice can greatly enhance this ability.

After completing these steps, your basic sword abilities should be good enough for you to begin solo and partnered application training. Start your solo practice by focusing on your favorite skills. These will be determined mainly by your physical characteristics and conditioning and by your internal feelings. There will be some skills that you always do very well and others that you find more difficult. The more thoroughly you have practiced the basic sword skills, the more skills you will be able to apply comfortably at this beginning stage of your application training.

Once you have chosen your favorite skills, research them deeply so that you understand them in detail and in all their possible variations. Then, find ways to combine them in routines and practice these routines with a partner until you can perform them smoothly and effectively. Diligent partnered practice of such combinations in feed training will markedly advance your application practice, and free-skill training with a partner will complete your applications practice.

It is extremely important always to keep in mind the Taiji principle that correct applications never depend on pre-designed skills or routines. Instead, you must follow your partner or opponent and adapt your responses to his or her ever-changing movements. The purpose of practicing the combination routines is not to rehearse the routines for direct application in fights, but rather to gain a better understanding of the component skills themselves. Once you have mastered the skills, you will have no further need for the routines.

Although there are few, if any, occasions to engage in real sword fights today, we are fortunate to have inherited the excellent skills of traditional Taiji Dao. Despite the fact that the original purpose to harm and defeat one's adversaries is no longer the primary goal of Taiji Dao practice, the fighting skills and mental focus that can be achieved through Taiji Dao training continue to have value. Taiji Dao practice, founded on the principles of Taiji Quan, can provide improvements in health and a greater enjoyment of the beautiful movements, skills, and feelings that physical training offers. Modern-day practitioners who pursue the art of Taiji Dao also seek to add interest and meaning to their lives. Contemporary study of Taiji Dao will deepen your knowledge of Taiji philosophy, and these principles will promote a fuller understanding of many aspects of daily life and a more complete appreciation for Chinese culture.

This book will have served its purpose if it provides the guidance and encouragement that make it possible for you to achieve and enjoy the many benefits that sincere and thoughtful Taiji Dao practice offers.

ABOUT THE AUTHOR

Devoted master of martial arts Zhang Yun began his studies of Shaolin Quan, Tongbei Quan, and Chinese wrestling at a young age. At sixteen, he started his internal martial arts training with Master Luo Shuhuan and Grandmaster Wang Peisheng, from whom he received instruction in many disciplines. Since the 1990s, Zhang Yun has taught martial arts classes throughout the United States and has conducted more than fifty seminars in the United States, Europe, and China. He is the author of *The Art of Chinese Swordsmanship: A Manual of Taiji Jian* and is the translator of Lu Shengli's *Combat Techniques of Taiji, Xingyi, and Bagua.* Born and raised in Beijing, China, he now resides with his wife and son in Pittsburgh, Pennsylvania.

About North Atlantic Books

North Atlantic Books (NAB) is a 501(c)(3) nonprofit publisher committed to a bold exploration of the relationships between mind, body, spirit, culture, and nature. Founded in 1974, NAB aims to nurture a holistic view of the arts, sciences, humanities, and healing. To make a donation or to learn more about our books, authors, events, and newsletter, please visit www.northatlanticbooks.com.